National Affects

National Affects

The Everyday Atmospheres of Being Political

Angharad Closs Stephens

BLOOMSBURY ACADEMIC
LONDON • NEW YORK • OXFORD • NEW DELHI • SYDNEY

BLOOMSBURY ACADEMIC
Bloomsbury Publishing Plc
50 Bedford Square, London, WC1B 3DP, UK
1385 Broadway, New York, NY 10018, USA
29 Earlsfort Terrace, Dublin 2, Ireland

BLOOMSBURY, BLOOMSBURY ACADEMIC and the Diana logo are
trademarks of Bloomsbury Publishing Plc

First published in Great Britain 2022
Paperback edition published 2024

Copyright © Angharad Closs Stephens, 2022

Angharad Closs Stephens has asserted her right under the Copyright, Designs and
Patents Act, 1988, to be identified as Author of this work.

For legal purposes the Acknowledgements on pp. xiv–xv constitute an
extension of this copyright page.

Series design by Adriana Brioso
Cover image: *Pigeons taking flight at Swansea Bay*, 2017, by Math Roberts
(http://mathroberts.com)

Bloomsbury Publishing Plc does not have any control over, or responsibility for, any
third-party websites referred to or in this book. All internet addresses given in this
book were correct at the time of going to press. The author and publisher regret any
inconvenience caused if addresses have changed or sites have ceased to exist, but
can accept no responsibility for any such changes.

A catalogue record for this book is available from the British Library.

A catalog record for this book is available from the Library of Congress.

ISBN: HB: 978-0-7556-4143-7
PB: 978-0-7556-4147-5
ePDF: 978-0-7556-4145-1
eBook: 978-0-7556-4144-4

Typeset by Newgen KnowledgeWorks Pvt. Ltd., Chennai, India

To find out more about our authors and books visit www.bloomsbury.com
and sign up for our newsletters.

Diolch Elliw a Brychan. Chi'n werth y byd!

I Rhodri. Diolch cariad.

'What then of my stories? What then of criticism? The important thing is to stay within the compass of their force and imagination.'

-- Michael Taussig, Walter Benjamin's Grave, Chicago and London: The University of Chicago Press, 2006: 89.

Contents

Figures

Preface

Moved by the world

In January 2016, I moved to Swansea (Abertawe) in South West Wales. During that winter, it rained non-stop for two months. I drove from Gateshead in North East England, where I had been living since 2007, and made the journey with my partner and young children in a borrowed car, as I had crashed my car in a road accident nine months earlier. The children were four and one years old at the time: too young to object to being moved around. We arrived and parked outside Joe's Ice Cream Parlour in the Mumbles – a café that is iconic for its ice cream recipe. We looked at the café's neon blue lights glowing in the dark as we decided which one of us would go out to get milk and something to eat.

We arrived at our temporary house and it continued to rain. I went out to buy a new pair of shoes, appreciating that my old shoes would not work in this city. How did people live with so much rain? Did it rain like this *every day*? In the North East, it was cold almost all year round, but rarely wet. I had got used to the dry weather: its effects on how I styled my hair and what I would wear.

We began the work of establishing new habits. It was strange and comforting being able to play Welsh language radio in the car, and hear this language spoken in work. But beyond that, England and Wales (Cymru) did not seem *that* different. I had not lived here for fifteen years and I was not sure what I expected from this move. When people asked big questions, such as *why did you move then*? I found myself ill prepared to answer. I was looking for light, landscape, creativity and a different pace, but these were not explanations that I could easily give a new colleague in the corridor. I shrugged, and probably looked a little lost.

My move to Swansea, Wales, and back to the small country where I grew up, was six months prior to the Brexit vote. I had left Wales because of my desire to see the world and to escape ideas about home, belonging and identity. But at this point, I found myself surrounded by them, louder and more certain than I'd ever known them. I walked the streets wondering what I had moved into.

This marginal country remains young in terms of its history as a legitimate political unit, with its own democratic structures. The *Senedd* (the Welsh Parliament) was only established in 1999, and it represents the people of

Wales as part of a devolved government within the British state. Prior to this achievement, culture was pretty much all Wales had to define itself – music, poetry, stories and a language that some wanted to save and others wanted to leave behind, on account of its unmodern sounds and cadences. There is now a consensus around the claim that there is a 'people of Wales', and a citizenry, where previously there were movements, organizations, desires and experiences but no official political subject.

When I was growing up in the 1980s, there were two powerful political narratives available for articulating what it meant to be Welsh. The first was romantic nationalism, and the idea that a way of life could be preserved through a state of one's own. In this version, identity formed the resources for imagining a contrasting experience to Britishness, placing Welshness alongside other experiences of marginalization. The second was modern socialism, which said that Wales needed to organize by class rather than identity. For some in this camp, the Welsh language signalled the dangerous politics of ethnicity and threatened to divide the British class movement,[1] seen as the only route towards resisting domination. These two traditions – of green and red politics – represented two equally self-certain positions that made it difficult to consider a political standpoint that situated itself in between, and which had doubts about either position.

Moving back to Wales in 2016, I found that much had changed. With the establishment of a Welsh Parliament, the political parties had become conversant with working together and found on many occasions that they had common ground. They could direct their ire against a new other: the Westminster Parliament and England. There were strange new realities, such as the way the Welsh language was no longer an issue that led activists to climb up television masts and block bridges.[2] Since 2011, it is an official language of Wales, and therefore subject to government-set targets for the numbers that speak it and legally binding standards for public-facing institutions and organizations. Wales has become a framework for governing. Wales now also has a value: it is something to be marketed, ranked and entrepreneurialized. But whether as value, governance unit or identity, what remains marginal is a sense of Wales as a puzzle, and as an experience that none of the dominant narratives, now or back then, are quite able to capture. This is the puzzle of being in between nation and state, identity and difference, inside and outside. It is an experience that informs a critique of domination, while often remaining blind to its own patterns of exclusion. It is a shared history produced by feeling constricted, even as it also informs alternative, capacious ideas about being-with-others. What motivates this book is the desire to develop other ways of understanding being political, formed from this in-between experience, and which bypass the language and concepts of the nation-state. *National Affects* names both the dominant ideas about identity and belonging that circulate around us, and the affective connections to place, people and culture that remind us of other experiences of being together.

* * *

Starting in Swansea, Wales, this book travels to London, Paris, New York, to ideas about Europe as well as global politics. While parts of Swansea are among the most deprived in Wales, in the eighteenth century, it formed Wales's first industrial town, and a global centre for copper and brass production. This means it has connections to colonialism, empire and the slave trade.[3] In the twentieth century, it suffered from the heavy bombing of the German Luftwaffe, which in 1941 destroyed many parts of the city and killed 230 people. It has also been subjected to the modernization dreams of urban planners. This city has known great achievements and great destruction. While Wales (Cymru) has become more established and confident in its role as a devolved nation, this city remains without a clear sense of where it fits in. It lies in between Wales and Britain, Europe and the world, the sea and the mountains. But this is also its strength: its sense of self is uncertain, marginal and multiple. The people's sense of identity often comes from no more than a shared love of how the light warms the streets and flickers on the sea. At different points in this book, I turn to this city's 'affective atmospheres' – its gathering spaces, collective memories and creative acts – to explore how forms of togetherness exceed ideas about 'us and them'.

Overall, this book presents a way in to studying the global politics of nations and nationalism that sidesteps efforts at measuring and comparing the attitudes and perceptions of identities presumed to pre-exist politics and analysis. Instead, I follow the role of moods, ambiance, affects and feelings in political life to generate starting points that allow for hesitation. While my aim is to consider what can be done to resist intensified nationalism, I refuse to explain this as a set of ideas that some set of people subscribe to and define the political task as that of changing their minds. For me, such an approach risks allowing theory to become a tool of domination. I am more interested in theories that begin from the streets, and from listening to what is going on in all its inconsistency and tension. This allows us to see how – even when the atmospheres around us appear so stifling and heavy – they can also be loosened, shifted and retuned. The critique, of course, is that I am too patient in my pursuit of change. This may be so, but it comes in part from a refusal to adopt the master's tools to dismantle the master's house. The chapters that follow are led by a desire to develop new forms of theorizing the contemporary world. They are focused on the possibilities for intervening in the present and opening possibilities for living otherwise.

Acknowledgements

A special thanks to all the people who have supported me in writing this book: Pete Adey, Ash Amin, Louise Amoore, Ben Anderson, Catherine Bennett, David Bissell, Dan Bulley, Dave Clarke, Beckie Coleman, Rachel Colls, Claudine Conway, Mike Crang, Paul Davies, Siwan Davies, Marcus Doel, Leila Dawney, Tim Edensor, Jenny Edkins, Madeleine Fagan, Jo Fong, Branwen Gruffydd Jones, Sonia Hughes, Jef Huysmans, Caroline Lane, Eugene McCann, Derek McCormack, Joe Painter, Anna Pigott, Sarah Pink, João Pontes Nogueira, Dorota Poreba, Michal Poreba, Ben Rogaly, Mike Shapiro, Wil Stephens, Rob Walker, Ben Wellings and Maja Zehfuss. I am very grateful to them.

Parts of this work have been presented at the following universities: the Association for the Studies of Ethnicities and Nationalism seminar series, London School of Economics (2016), seminar on 'The Emotional Life of the City', at LSE Cities (2018), seminar on 'Public Sentiments' at École des Hautes Etudes en Sciences Sociales, Paris, France (2018), seminar at the Geography Department, Sussex University, UK (2018), Geography Department, Melbourne University, Australia (2019), Geography Department, Plymouth University, UK (2020), and Centre for Global Politics, Economy and Society, Oxford Brookes University, UK (2020).

My sincere thanks to all the people at these events for their great comments and to those that organized them. This book also benefited enormously from teaching fantastic students at the International Political Sociology Winter School, International Relations Institute, Pontificia Universidad Católica, Rio de Janeiro (2018) and at the Gregynog Ideas Lab IX, Gregynog Hall, Drenewydd/ Newtown, Cymru/Wales (2019).

Thank you to Martin Coward, Debbie Lisle, Amanda Rogers, Nisha Shah, Shanti Sumartojo and Martina Tazzioli for playing a significant part in ensuring I completed the book, for their hospitality and encouragement. Thanks to Carolyn Pedwell for her love and friendship and sending regular WhatsApp messages that kept me going, and to Naeem Inayatullah and Vicki Squire for their brilliant editorial comments which improved the work in the final stages. I am grateful to my mum, Elan Closs Stephens, for supporting me always.

I could not have managed without the excellent editorial assistance of Franz Bernhardt. Thanks also to all the PhD and postgraduate students that have worked with me in Swansea during this period. Many of the ideas in this book have developed through conversations with them.

My thanks to the Leverhulme Trust for supporting this book with a research fellowship that funded fieldwork and valuable time to complete several chapters, and to Swansea University Geography Department for funding research support. A Coleg Cymraeg Cenedlaethol small grant supported an early pilot project, and many of the ideas in this book began with the intellectual communities at Durham University Geography Department and Durham's Institute of Advanced Studies. Finally, my sincere thanks to Nayiri Kendir, and all the team at Bloomsbury, for guiding this project.

Chapters 1 and 5 and the interlude 'A Hot Afternoon' form revised versions of articles previously published: 'The Affective Atmospheres of Nationalism', *Cultural Geographies*, 23(2) 2016: 181–98; 'Feeling 'Brexit': Nationalism and the Affective Politics of Movement', *GeoHumanities*, 5(2), 2019: 405–23; and part of a forum on 'The Spaces and Politics of Affective Nationalism' convened by Marco Antonsich and Michael Skey, *Environment and Planning C: Politics and Space*, 38(4), 2020: 586–9.

Introduction

How do ideas about 'us and them' take form in ordinary spaces, in ways that are both deeply felt and hardly noticeable? This book engages affect to examine how the nation 'flickers into presence' and travels alongside a jumble of ideas, postures, gestures, emotions, histories and attachments in everyday life.[1] It asks how ideas about a common nation often emerge subtly, sometimes unexpectedly, as a feeling in a room or on a timeline, and in shared ideas that suddenly strengthen. Since the 2007–8 global financial crisis, we have seen a resurgence in talk about 'the people', a rise in overt racisms and policies explicitly designed to keep migrants and racialized citizens out of the nation, as well as increased resentment towards women, trans people and people of colour.[2] What I argue in this book is that understanding the nation through its affective force is central to addressing how nationalism endures and returns in global politics. The task of addressing how the nation persists as the principal form of articulating belonging requires that we examine how it becomes anchored in cultural practices, and what Raymond Williams once described as 'structures of feeling'.[3]

The principal approaches in studies of nations and nationalism have situated the nation in relation to the waning of religious authority in Europe, the shift to modern, industrialized societies, and as part of the history of decolonization.[4] But ideas about the nation also unfold in everyday ways, a point articulated in Michael Billig's *Banal Nationalism*, Tim Edensor's *National Identity, Popular Culture and Everyday Life*, Paul Gilroy's *After Empire* and Ghassan Hage's *White Nation*.[5] I want to follow Sara Ahmed in making feeling and affects *central* to understanding how ideas about 'us and them' gain their force and maintain their authority. As Ahmed puts it, emotions and affects are 'precisely about the intimacy' of being-with-others.[6] They connect us to other bodies, 'through being moved by the proximity of others'.[7] Rather than think that emotions and feelings follow from the condition of being part of a social group however, Ahmed turns this assumption around. She argues that it is *through* affects and emotions that the very ideas of inside and outside take form. I want to bring this affective approach together with the focus on the everydayness of nationalism to examine how ideas about the nation are mobile and lively, able to emerge and retreat. I want to show that national affects appear as sometimes noisy and at other times subtle, how they make some spaces feel more compressed than they might otherwise be, affecting what bodies feel able to do. In contrast to an approach that begins with territory, the history of modernity or memory, this book addresses the nation affectively to better understand its enduring force in world politics.

The turn to affect in the social sciences presents an opportunity for engaging the study of nations and nationalism anew. It points to 'the grounding and ungrounding of emotional life in relationships', in ways that travel between humans and touch non-human materials.[8] These visceral forces are something distinct from conscious knowledge or personal emotions. Put another way, affect is about more than our own emotional responses.[9] It features the transmissions between humans as well as non-human bodies, and how these enable 'bindings and unbindings, jarring disorientations and rhythmic attunements'.[10] Understood in this way, affect emerges as central to politics. As the recent rise in populist and nationalist governments have demonstrated, objects, bodily movements, gestures and refrains are integral to the assembling of global politics – be that the role of a baseball cap worn by a US president, or a phrase such as 'Making Britain Great Again'. These aesthetic materials and narrative tunes move us to different degrees and in various ways. And they invite us to ask, what do affects do?[11] The study of affect suggests that politics involves more than 'an idea, decision or choice taken at a moment'. As the sociologist of dance Randy Martin puts it, politics is also 'a transfigurative process that makes and occupies space'.[12] Attuning to how bodies move, feel and are affected in space is central to addressing the political.

While this book takes nationalism to be a very current problem, I avoid treating this subject as an all-encompassing structure or an ideology that particular groups subscribe to. Instead, I address how ideas about the nation crop up or press upon us, as part of an atmosphere and through the 'convergence of bodies, sensations and relations'.[13] As the postcolonial theorist Homi Bhabha writes, the nation remains both 'an obscure and ubiquitous form of living the locality of culture'.[14] Getting to know these moments calls for an approach that is attuned to experience, felt perceptions and what sometimes remains unspoken. It encourages us to examine the role of architecture, design, materials and environment in political life, as well as objects, light, buildings and mood in everyday spaces.[15] To that end, I draw on novels and performance works, conversations with dancers, theatre directors and artists, and place these alongside theoretical ideas from the academic discipline of Human Geography. I also draw on academic literatures from Politics, International Relations and Cultural Studies, and include autobiographical stories about my own encounters with politicized moments, as part of an effort to grasp the microdynamics through which world politics takes shape. I try to acknowledge my own place in these structures of feeling, following Jenny Edkins's point that academics should not consider themselves above that which they are studying, but 'part and parcel of the ecosystem'.[16] Altogether, I pursue a style of writing that writes against the fantasies of certainty and purity that are currently circulating.[17] As Deborah Dixon puts it, this requires eschewing 'the sharp-edged sureties of frames and taxonomies, subjects and their others and surfaces and borders'.[18] Studying national affects has led me to experiment with another style of academic writing.

What makes an affect specifically national in form? As Ben Anderson and Helen Wilson explain, affects cannot be straightforwardly connected to a 'single social-spatial formation'.[19] Affects exceed attempts at their manipulation or orchestration. For example, a state funeral for a former prime minister will be accompanied by music from a particular repertoire and symbols such as a flag, but it will also be made up of everyday decisions to go along with something, and chance encounters that may not be rational or coherent. While recognizing the importance of tracing the manipulation of affects by the state,[20] in this book, I follow 'forms of nationalism that are ambivalent, politically ambiguous and not always coherent'.[21] I argue that 'national affects' emerge through different moments of heightened tension, ranging from terrorist attacks to refugee crises, when efforts at orchestrating national unity are especially visible. However, these moments are also composed of other affective feelings, and gatherings that reject excluding, punishing or dominating people that we consider to be different from ourselves. My interest in affect stems from a curiosity about how people go along with a political mood, even as they might also hold very different views. And overall, I am interested in the possibilities for interrupting a dominant national mood, and encouraging structures of feeling that defy ideas about 'us and them'.

Situating affect

What is appealing about working with affect when studying collectivities in world politics is that it offers an entry point that avoids group-based thinking.[22] That is, it works against the enduring assumption in the social sciences that there are coherent groups that encounter other groups. Beginning with affect means turning this assumption around to ask how we might come to think of people as belonging to distinct, separable groups in the first place.[23] My route in therefore follows Teresa Brennan's call for us to attend to the 'transfer of feelings' and how 'the emotions provoked by one are contagiously extended to another'. As she recalls, in the late nineteenth and early twentieth centuries, there was an intense interest in group psychology, by figures including Gustav Le Bon, Wilfred Trotter and Sigmund Freud. To quote Brennan, all these figures identified a phenomenon of 'we' feelings. However, Brennan argues that they did not explain its transmission.[24] Her point is that these psychologists and early sociologists either collapsed the focus on 'we feelings' back into a claim about social groups, or they undermined the *liveliness* of affective relations.[25] She sets out a challenge of addressing affective relations without reducing these to emotions that belong to self-contained individuals or groups.

The twentieth-century sociologist Émile Durkheim also paid close attention to group feelings. For example, he offers us astute observations about the emotional intensities of different social formations, such as when a belief, shared among a group, comes to assume the status of a religion. Consider the striking way Durkheim articulates the process of believing strongly in something with others, when he describes 'the heat of common conviction'.[26] Durkheim says that when a belief is shared, it gathers energy and it also becomes more difficult to challenge: it becomes 'something sacred' and 'beyond critique'.[27] This point powerfully addresses what is at stake when it comes to national affects, although Durkheim would not have put it in these terms. That is, national affects can make it difficult to imagine going against the dominant mood. Durkheim was keen to subject his empirical observations to the principles of logic and reason, to establish a scientific approach to these emotional scenes and the study of the social world.[28] But it is not my intention to prove or precisely define a national affect, so that others can test them. It is more thought-provoking to stay with Durkheim's interest in the unspoken codes and rhythms of social life, while resisting his urge for 'clarity of mind and language'.[29] In this spirit, this book engages national affects without reducing them to rules and principles that can be applied to coherent groups. My approach asks how national frames of being together emerge, become dominant and how they can be resisted and overturned.

Affect therefore names my object of analysis, and it also names a method and approach. This focus on national affects complements the work of resisting methodological nationalism in the social sciences. That is, it seeks a way in that refuses to focus on 'a map of national cultures', with each static society imagined to be differently staggered in its own advance towards capitalist modernity.[30] Or, it rubs against the view of the world as a collection of countries, each with their 'diverse national societies, each "rooted" in its proper place', by looking transversally, at movements, ideas and activisms that resonate and travel across borders.[31] Methodological nationalism involves starting from the presumption of a framework of nation-states, which is in turn informed by modern, Western knowledge and its account of reason.[32] But this idea that the world naturally falls into a nation and state-centred framework curtails our abilities to see the lively ways people organize politically beneath and across nation-states. It presents this homogenizing way of organizing ourselves as universal, ignoring how it clashes with other, rich traditions of understanding our place in the world. Opening a space for affect theory in the study of nations and nationalism can therefore be situated alongside multiple significant and long-standing efforts at enriching and pluralizing the social sciences. But this also involves acknowledging there are limits to this concept, and questions about how far affect travels.[33]

In sum, the chapters that follow all begin with moments when a transfer of feelings brings the nation-state framework, and the idea of a sovereign, bounded individual, into view – either because it is being amplified or because it is shown to be under strain. In doing so, the book seeks to show how nationalism remains a culturally specific, limited and violent way of seeing and organizing the world around us.

Method, experience and the politics of knowledge

My approach seeks to establish the connections between intimate and global politics. As such, I am following in a tradition of feminist scholars who have turned to experience to narrate their own inscription in nationalist, racist, gendered and colonial discourses.[34] For example, more than twenty-five years ago, Ruth Frankenberg and Lata Mani shared autobiographical stories recounting Mani's upbringing in post-independence Mumbai singing the Indian national anthem in school assemblies and Frankenberg described how British imperialism shaped the stories she read at bedtime growing up in Manchester, England, and informed everyday words including *pyjamas* and *shampoo*.[35] An affective approach extends this attention to 'the intimate and the global', and challenges hierarchical accounts of scale and space.[36] As such, it complements the way critical scholars in International Relations have also experimented with using autobiography as a refreshing way into the study of politics.[37] As Naeem Inayatullah writes, summoning experience can provide 'supplementary depth, urgency, and clarity to authors' preferred theoretical postures', as part of an effort to create an 'artistic science'.[38] Following both this movement of work in International Relations (IR) and a longer history of feminist scholarship, in this book I use storytelling to examine how nation, race, gender, empire and colonialism make themselves felt in the present, and shape how we come to understand who we are in the world. These stories and anecdotes appear as openings to chapters, and in short interludes. They form a moment that invited me to think about the role of affect in political life, and I use them to 'examine, explore and digress' from academic knowledge.[39] They mostly describe a sense of being enclosed in ideas about 'us and them', before the moment passed, changed or shifted. These have served a role in keeping me focused on the question of how nationalism endures.

In turning to experience, I draw inspiration from feminist, postcolonial and decolonial theorists, as well as scholars of Black studies, who turn to other ways of writing to capture moments that seem otherwise absent in academic investigations.[40] Furthermore, experience provides a good entry point for reflecting on the force of something as nebulous and vague as an 'atmosphere'.[41] This is what Yasmin Gunaratnam suggests when she uses poetry and stories to reflect on 'what can have effects but is non-manifest.' in her study of migrants' experiences of end-of-life care in the UK.[42] Telling stories in this case provides another way into knowledge, as it does for the International Relations scholar Elizabeth Dauphinee, who decided to write a fictional story about the Bosnian war, offering another kind of investigation, with a different potential for sustaining our attention.[43] In a further example, Christina Sharpe uses storytelling to recount her family's devastating histories of loss, survival, death and belonging as part of the slave trade and its afterlives, to counteract the violence of abstraction in many academic theories.[44] However, invoking experience is not always an innocent move. Wendy Brown famously describes how white women have invoked 'experience' to establish equivalence with other histories of oppression, and in doing so failed to listen to the histories and experiences of women of colour.[45] Talking about experience can therefore risk making us think we are *naturally* inclined towards a humanitarian and kind politics, without reflecting on the politics of our narratives and our starting points.[46]

Experience is relevant for this study because it allows for another approach to knowledge, yielding refreshing starting points in the study of nations and nationalism. But it also takes us to different ways of understanding being-in-common. For example, reflecting on the phrase, 'the personal is political', Lauren Berlant argues that this was never intended to advocate for a turn inwards. Rather, it was designed to show that any engagement with politics must, at some point, develop 'new vocabularies of pleasure, recognition, and equity'.[47] While studying politics requires addressing power, authority and domination, it also calls for examining ways of living and what we do to make ourselves feel comfortable in the world. Sharing experiences or anecdotes[48] can therefore yield better understandings of how domination is interlaced with the ways we seek pleasure, distraction and belonging. The anthropologist Ghassan Hage confirms this when he argues that everyday processes of nation-building must be understood alongside all the ways we have 'of inhabiting and making ourselves visible and comfortable in the world'.[49] He points to all the little ways we are involved in practising 'domination, control, extraction and exploitation' – in our relationship to others and in how we relate to animals, insects, plants, nature or trees.[50] He calls this process 'domestication'. It usefully demonstrates all the affective elements of nation-building. And it shows us that experience is about much more than attending to emotions or the inner lives of social beings. It is about understanding how we are all situated in relation to structures of exploitation and that the task of building other worlds will have to address the ways we live in common.

Mobilizing geopolitical cartographies

I draw on critical approaches to Politics and International Relations because of how they help situate the study of the nation beyond a domestic frame. This means addressing the nation as a mobile category, showing how the idea of a common culture is connected to the geopolitical system of sovereign states. As Michael Shapiro has demonstrated across several books, it takes work, in the form of policing, disciplining and bordering practices, to maintain the fiction of homogeneity between culture and territory.[51] Whether based on race, language or other markers of culture, what is consistent is the drive towards *unity* that is central to state formation, and which limits our capacity to acknowledge and live with difference.[52] The principle of homogeneity under the state has been advanced through ideas about a common language and a common race – key indicators of sameness cultivated and mobilized under modernity.[53] This is why ideas about race and nation are deeply connected: it can be gleaned in how 'familiality' remains a central principle for the nation, and in turn, for shoring up the system of states.[54]

Critical scholars of IR also help me draw the connections between processes of nation formation and ideas about personhood as bounded and enabling ideas about 'us' as different from 'them'. As Cynthia Weber demonstrates (drawing on the work of Rick Ashley), state sovereignty produces 'binary sovereign subjectivities (citizen vs foreigner; patriot vs traitor) alongside sovereign orders (domestic vs international; the West vs the rest)'.[55] Weber shows how the work of crafting political community is connected to crafting political subjectivity and is further connected to the normalization of sexualized subjectivities.[56] For example, the work of reproducing distinctions between inside and outside the nation-state is 'intimately intertwined' with the production and reproduction of gendered and sexualized figures, including the 'homosexual', the 'gender variant' and the 'trans'.[57] Weber highlights four figures that routinely appear 'perverse' in discourses of IR and global politics: the 'underdeveloped', the 'undevelopable', the 'unwanted im/migrant' and the 'terrorist'. She shows how all these figures are made to appear removed from the *familiality* of the nation, outside of the international system, or as 'arrested' in their development.[58] What her examples suggest is that the work of maintaining unity and stability inside the nation operates not only as part of an international story about development, but also as part of an intimate story about gendered and sexualized subjects.

These texts provide important context for the study of affect. This is because they allow us to reject, from the outset, the pretence that the nation is inclusive.[59] Instead, we can ask questions about how national affects exclude and marginalize. In turning to the geographies of affect, my aim is to understand how ideas about 'us and them' persist through modes of comfort and discomfort, everyday remarks, habits, journeys and dreams, and how these are connected to geopolitical cartographies. But this involves loosening a symbolic reading of the world that describes it as already heavy with meaning. Instead, I work with what Kathleen Stewart describes as 'descriptive detours', to address the elusive, intimate, haphazard and complex ways in which power works and exceeds our frameworks of understanding.[60] As Shapiro shows in his treatment of landscape, film, music and novels to understand the multiple processes of affective nation-building in global politics, we must avoid taking nation-states as 'autonomous, self-contained agents, separate from the activities that constitute them'.[61] He shows how affect provides an analytical lens not only for focusing on nation-states' activities, but also how such activities exceed statist organizations, institutions and agents. This is exactly what has drawn scholars such as Jason Dittmer and Cynthia Weber to study how the nation emerges in popular culture,[62] and how critical IR scholars more generally encourage us to look for politics beyond the usual places.[63] Following these authors, I want to maintain this awareness of the nation's place in a system of states, while pursuing an analysis that avoids giving the framework too much coherency. Structures of power are, as Debbie Lisle argues, ambivalent, full of 'fissures and gaps', through which they are contested and interrupted.[64] This approach is central to appreciating that things may become otherwise.

Finally, drawing on critical approaches in IR allows me to analyse the mobile power relations in different scenes and claims of togetherness. Critically, these literatures follow Michel Foucault's point that we remain constrained by an understanding of power as something exercised *over us* by a single sovereign authority. A more mobile frame allows us to consider power as stemming from multiple points and as entangled with the languages and forms of resistance. Indeed, in Eve Sedgwick's principal work on affect, she says she is propelled by Foucault's promise of developing a critical theory that can go beyond the 'repressive hypothesis'.[65] This is, as Sedgwick describes, the promise that critique might do something other than reveal 'oppressive historical forces' or a 'residual form of essentialism'.[66] I am also motivated by this potential. Working with the concept of affect allows us to read political events as more fragile and mobile than our analyses purport, and to consider the richness and heterogeneity of positions, subjectivities, viewpoints and actions. It allows us to loosen an understanding of power as all-encompassing in its grip on people, where it becomes difficult to imagine ever shifting, loosening or changing situations.[67] And it encourages us to attend to all that remains beyond our coherent representations and explanations of how power works. Overall, it calls for a more gentle, open and experimental way into writing about political life.

Engaging politics through the arts

In the chapters that follow, I turn to the arts – discussing novels and performances – to expand my routes into addressing the affective force of nationality. This is partly because, as Ben Highmore argues, there are inherent difficulties in writing about creaturely, experiential life.[68] But it also complements an attempt 'to write from within instead of standing outside pointing'.[69] In academia, we are trained to point. But when we point, we don't necessarily invite readers to sit and think with us. Given that aesthetic works, including music, a film or a novel, are not principally interested in educating us, so much as in moving us, they offer another approach for engaging national affects. For example, literature is 'in principle neither knowledge-yielding or knowledge-denying, but instead effectively avoids – and self-consciously avoids – or stands to the side of the *question* of knowledge'.[70] It values the experience of not-knowing.[71] This suggests starting points that are less interested in certainty than in allowing for hesitation and making room for questions.

In turning to artistic works, my point of departure is that social science's explanations of the world are often inadequate in addressing political life as it is experienced. For example, while work that helps us explain, conceptualize and historicize the structural formations of nations and nationalism remain important, they do not always help us understand how nationalism persists, returns and assumes new forms. How is it that people continue to turn so readily to explanations of a common identity to anchor their place in the world? How is it that the nation persists in offering itself as a sensible or comforting framework for navigating political crises, even when those crises reveal that they are better addressed at very different scales? Turning to affect allows me to ask how the nation remains attractive as an organizing category and how this limits our abilities to pursue a political imagination that looks horizontally rather than vertically, acknowledging plurality rather than seeking homogeneity.

In addition to providing another route to knowledge, the arts also engage the affective realm. As Elizabeth Grosz describes, art produces 'sensations, affects, intensities as its mode of addressing problems'.[72] This is because the arts work at a register that precedes 'rationality and knowledge, perception and intellection'.[73] This does not mean that the arts are in some way inherently progressive. Artistic interventions can be amusing, affirmative, but also uninteresting and conservative. However, the works I present in this book share in a desire to interrupt the dominant ways of seeing and to look at something anew. They introduce a dent in the coherency of explanations and suggest a new angle on political events. As Alex Danchev and Debbie Lisle put it in their discussion of the relationship between art and politics, it is not that artistic practice is *better* but that we have a great deal to gain from the dialogue between how scholars interpret the world and how artists respond to the times: 'Thinker-poets, thinker-painters, thinker-photographers and their kin may help us to glimpse previously unseen possibilities for thinker-politics – and actor-politics'.[74] While artists are not principally involved in producing concepts and interpretation, they are deeply involved in addressing 'problems and provocations', through their own mediums.[75] Thinking with affect across scholarly and artistic works invites us to consider different ways of listening to and engaging the world. It generates the potential of identifying passages through and away from the dominant worldviews, presenting new ways of thinking and inhabiting the world.

Accordingly, Grosz situates the arts at the register of inventing other possible worlds, or put another way, as presenting other worlds in which we might feel at home. While plenty of artistic works reflect characters, audiences and groups that we already know,[76] I am drawn to works that present new ways of speaking, seeing or being together. The works I select intervene in the ordering of the world (although this may not be a deliberate motivation). They use different materials – photography, film, novels, short stories, music, dance – to direct or redirect forces at some 'mythical sense of "the beginning"' – that is, in the 'chaos, the whirling, unpredictable movements of forces, vibratory oscillations that constitute the universe'.[77] They take this 'whirling complexity – [of] sensations, affects, percepts, intensities' and give them 'a life of their own'.[78] Grosz calls this a 'fabrication of the frame'.[79] It carries the potential of generating a new encounter.

The book

This book is organized around a series of instances of heightened nationalism, emerging across different sites and spaces, encompassing the period running from the London 2012 Olympic Games to the 2015 'refugee crisis' and 'Brexit' and the rise in nationalist governments and racist violence across much of the world. It ends with the Covid-19 pandemic and a further entrenchment of the nation as a framework for articulating political organization and belonging. The book is interested in how ideas about the nation, and necessarily race and colonialism, emerge and intensify in and through these events, making themselves felt in everyday spaces. In it, I consider the work required to interrupt ideas about 'us and them'. However, this is not an exhaustive examination and there are many significant moments from this time period that I don't address with a full chapter, such as the devastating fire at Grenfell Tower on 14 June 2017. This preventative fire, which killed seventy-two people and caused lifelong trauma for hundreds more, spread rapidly because the building's cladding did not comply with fire regulations. This horrific event raised urgent questions about the politics of housing in the UK, about inequality and racial justice. The events that I focus on do not straightforwardly represent the most significant political moments or the moments of greatest injustice in this time period. Rather, they are selected because of how the national frame seemed especially heavy, constraining and troubling at these times.

National Affects thus stages a series of encounters with the geographies of 'us and them', but it approaches these moments from the side, rather than directly. In this, I draw on Eve Sedgwick's idea of situating ourselves *beside* politics, because of how, as she puts it, *beside* suggests a non-dualistic form of thought. It invites us to look at what happens in between the categories of 'us and them'. In contrast to strong images of citizens and non-citizens, insiders and outsiders, I consider how these categories are mobile, shifting and come in and out of focus. This is because these categories often suggest something more stable, coherent and definitive than the complex ways people understand themselves in everyday life. In beginning with national affects, I'm looking to examine moments of intensification in ideas about 'us and them', using a framework that allows for movement, difference, subversion and newness. Indeed, Michel Foucault argues that to give our theoretical frameworks mobility, it is necessary to adopt 'a distant view'. This is an interesting spatial concept, as it does not suggest stepping back from personal experience. Indeed, Foucault complicates a geography that presumes distance means standing further away or which separates the personal from the world, by arguing that a 'distant view' involves looking both 'at what is nearby and all around oneself'.[80] This suggests that an event such as the 2015 'refugee crisis' took place not only on the shores of Italy, Greece and Turkey, but also on social media, at the school gate and at our local supermarket. In paying attention to these different sites and spaces, we can expand our understandings of how global politics unfolds and takes hold in ordinary spaces.

In this vein, I engage with national events ranging from the London Olympic Games of 2012 to Margaret Thatcher's funeral in 2013, to the 2015 refugee crisis and the 2016 Brexit vote, following a loosely chronological timeline. I attend to the geographies of 'us and them' as lively, mobile and part of everyday life, to prise open space for imagining other ways of seeing and relating that run underneath, across and through them. With this timeline, the book traces a shift from celebrations of an international order based around cosmopolitanism in the case of the London 2012 Olympic Games, to the politics of populism and the hardening of international borders. We might describe this as a journey from the highs of inclusive cosmopolitanism to the return of ugly nationalisms.

Certainly, the discourses used and legitimized by political leaders in the UK, Italy, Poland, Brazil and India, to name but a few countries, is increasingly racist, homophobic, ugly, misogynistic and insular. But liberal cosmopolitanism was also exclusionary. State programmes of multiculturalism were open to cultural difference so long as the differences were acceptable to the dominant culture of the state. This political consensus relied on its own forms of violence. The challenge, therefore, lies with addressing the return of global nationalism without narrating these uncertain times as representing a fall from the heights of cosmopolitan citizenship. Narratives of progress and decline are themselves intertwined with the legacy of the nation and the traditions of the European enlightenment. They rely on colonial discourses that presume the superiority of Europe and of white European man.[81] This narrative has to be questioned rather than assumed. But this also suggests something hopeful, in as much as things are never headed in a single direction.

As any critical engagement with nationalism will teach us, there is no going back to a purer starting point. A critique of ugly nationalisms must go alongside reflecting on the everyday nationalisms at work on public transport and in work environments, in public health strategies and in the frameworks of knowledge and understandings that we pass on. But these emerge in a world of endless variation, multiplicity and non-sovereign ways of making our way in the world. In approaching 'national affects' as both entrenched and fragile, as forming patterns of domination and of living otherwise, we are led to the potential for retuning the world around us.

1

The affective atmospheres of nationalism

Following the London Olympic Games in 2012, empty plastic water bottles containing 100 per cent Olympic-Bottled Atmosphere started retailing on eBay for a buy it now price of £50.[1] Indeed, the organizers spoke of the 'extraordinary atmosphere'[2] during that summer, as the event of the Olympic Games permeated several parts of everyday life – as banks and shops displayed miniature versions of the British flag, and Olympic themed events were introduced in schools and nurseries (Figure 1). What took people by surprise was just how popular the London Olympic Games proved to be, even with people who had been previously critical of them. As one commentator in *The Guardian* noted, the games 'reminded those suspicious of raucous patriotism of how great the union flag suddenly looked when it was ripped out of the hands of the extreme right and wrapped around the shoulders of Jessica Ennis or Mo Farah'.[3] In this first chapter, I reflect on the claims about an 'extraordinary atmosphere' and this short period of happy flag-waving to ask what might it mean to think about nationality as a set of feelings circling in the air. Specifically, I turn to this moment to ask how might thinking about nationality as something felt and experienced affectively also help us understand the suspension of critique by those usually suspicious of raucous patriotism.

The chapter proceeds by unpacking how the concept of an affective atmosphere builds on debates around everyday nationalism, before identifying moments through which feelings of being part of a nation together are shaped, practised, undermined and mocked. The chapter therefore also addresses the spatial geographies of nationalism, arguing that national feelings cannot be traced back to a single sovereign source but rather emanate from multiple constituencies, which are nebulous and diffuse. Taking these points about the feelings and spatialities of nationalism together, the chapter examines how nationalism takes hold and makes it difficult to voice critical perspectives, as was the case during the 'party atmosphere' of the London 2012 Olympic Games.[4]

Figure 1. The Olympic Rings near Cardiff City Hall. Photograph by Iestyn Hughes.

Of course, what we mean by a suspension of critique varies enormously by region and has different implications depending on where we are placed in the world. And the current politics of populism represents a very different political moment to the liberal cosmopolitanism that formed a backdrop to the London Games.[5] Nevertheless, this context remains relevant in reflecting on the nation's persistence as an 'object of intimacy and affect'.[6] This becomes manifest in times of mega-events, as it does in times of 'crisis', as Chapters 3 and 4 will discuss. This chapter focuses on what difference it makes to address the nation through the concept of an 'affective atmosphere', and how we might pursue the connections between the nation's affects and the challenges of resistance.

Towards the atmospherics of nationalism

While geography has traditionally involved the study of earth, land and terrain, geographers have recently invited us to turn our gaze to the air, and to look up and down along vertical rather than horizontal lines.[7] Mark Jackson and Maria Fannin ask, what might we gain in training our sights on 'aerographies'?[8] The concept of affective atmospheres complements this interest in turning our gaze to the air, to what surrounds us and lies between us. It suggests an especially interesting opening for the study of nations and nationalism, because it brings together arguments about the emotional power of national identity[9] with insights about the importance of developing a more relational understanding of national territories, attentive to the associations between people and things.[10] While the concept of atmosphere can be used to point to a broad array of phenomena, including 'transpersonal intensity', 'environment', 'aura', 'tone in literature', 'waves of sentiment' as well as 'a sense of place',[11] in this chapter I use it as a provocation for addressing the role of 'moody force fields' in the making and shaping of collective publics.[12] For example, nationality is often – if not mostly – experienced as a *feeling*. This might include feelings of togetherness experienced at a stadium or concert hall, the act of singing as part of a crowd noting the currents of energy that pass between bodies or the 'forcible affect' of sharing a language with others.[13] These examples may involve an ambivalent relationship to any particular nation, and will necessarily contain multiple experiences of togetherness. But what foregrounding 'affective atmospheres' does is place affective feelings centre stage and ask how they come to matter politically.

Writing in this vein, Derek P. McCormack argues that the concept of atmosphere can be understood both in its meteorological sense, 'as a turbulent zone of gaseous matter', and in an affective sense as 'a quality of environmental immersion that registers in and through sensing bodies while also remaining diffuse'.[14] The fact that the Olympic Games took place over a sunny two weeks in August (a change from the largely rainy British summers) suggests that the meteorological and affective aspects of atmospheres are intimately connected. Certainly, the weather made a difference to this event: although most people experienced the games as a television event, and/or through social media,[15] they watched crowds of bodies assembling in the sunshine to watch other bodies move in time. As with all Olympic Games, this event formed a performance of global politics, designed for both a domestic and an international audience, and was infused with narratives about modernity and progress, which in turn rely on imagining a colonial and underdeveloped other.[16] It is worth recalling, then, that at the turn of the twentieth century, the Olympic Games were housed within the World Expositions (such as the *Exposition Universelle* in Paris in 1900 and the *Franco-British Exposition* in London in 1908). They served to exhibit the superiority of the people and confirm a faith in progress, as famously demonstrated at the 1936 Berlin Olympic Games, but also at the 1904 Games in St Louis, in the United States, when great effort was put into comparing and classifying human types by measuring height, weight, head shape and size – an example of the connections between the games and pernicious attempts at organizing populations into racialized categories.[17]

The concept of atmosphere invites us to consider how such ideas are mobilized through 'regimes of representation', as Stuart Hall puts it in his critical study of ideas about race and otherness in photographs from the 1988 Olympic Games in Seoul.[18] That is, how text, narrative and image engage 'feelings, attitudes and emotions'.[19] But it also allows us to pay attention to materials, everyday objects, lighting, design and architecture, bringing the study of visuality and materiality together.[20] Significantly, working with the concept of atmospheres invites attention to the ambiguous, mobile and changeable forms that domination often takes. That is, ideas about a common nation intertwine with ideas about coloniality and modernity, progress, and development, and they emerge, recede, shift and move in various, often unexpected ways.

How do we account for the ways in which bodies are moved by national feelings circling in the air without reducing such moments to examples of 'mass hysteria' or of the people being manipulated?[21] These Olympic Games formed the 'most expensive security operation in recent British history':[22] at an estimated cost of 11 billion (9 billion of which was public money),[23] they were obscenely expensive, and took place against the claim that we were entering a time of 'austerity', demanded by the 2008 global financial crisis. Yet a *Guardian*/ICM poll carried out at the end of 2012 reported that 78 per cent people were still happy with the £9 billion price tag and that the Olympics 'did a valuable job in cheering up a country in hard times'.[24] However, while critical arguments about the cost of these games are powerful, they do not address how many people were moved by this event. Indeed, arguments about economic costs seem to wash away when presented with the emotional tides of sharing in a mass event with others. While explanations of how the nation is constituted through a common experience of time,[25] or as the invention of tradition,[26] are valuable, they do not prioritize a 'sensorial approach' that addresses 'the mobilizing potential of a place', 'the articulatory value of a gesture' or 'the implicit in ordinary practices' in the way that J. P. Thibaud argues the concept of *ambiance* or atmosphere does.[27] What happens then, when we use the idea of national affective atmospheres as an opening for engaging how national feelings touch us, take hold and become infectious – how they are felt through bodies but surpass one individual body? How might such seemingly 'banal' feelings – moods that we 'go along with' – be identified as both political and yet not all determining?

Beyond everyday nationalism

The affective qualities of nationalism are extensively discussed in the literatures on everyday nationalism. Take for example Michael Billig's comment that there is an 'aura [that] attends the very idea of nationhood'.[28] As Billig notes, there is something affective and auratic about sovereign nationhood which makes it difficult to pin down and to consider how we might think outside of it. Approaching nationalism atmospherically builds upon Michael Billig's argument that nationalism should not be understood as involving 'dangerous and powerful passions' and 'extraordinary emotions' but rather as a background noise that is always already there and which erupts from time to time.[29] While Rhys Jones and Peter Merriman argue that Billig unwittingly reproduces the distinction between 'hot' and 'mundane' instances of nationalism,[30] the case of the London Olympic Games shows us that distinctions between the 'hot' and 'mundane' are difficult if not impossible to maintain. These games resonated with people in both spectacular and ordinary ways and involved a combination of macro and micropolitical moments. As Achille Mbembe describes in relation to ceremonial displays in post-colonial Cameroon, occasions which 'state power organizes for dramatizing its own magnificence' reveal the difficulties of distinguishing between the state and civil society, resistance and passivity, as well as between hegemonic and counter-hegemonic discourses.[31] Indeed, what is interesting about the spectacle of the London Games is how they seemed to draw so many people in, albeit to different degrees, making it difficult to determine the boundaries between the orchestrated displays of sovereign power and various efforts of 'going along' with the games. This suggests that binary categorizations would be better replaced by an attentiveness to the many varying tonalities and intensities of nationality. The concept of affective atmospheres better captures 'the messy dynamics of attachment'[32] as well as the messy dynamics of power. It suggests that national feelings can move between the happy and the ugly, but also contain ambivalence, curiosity or detachment.

For example, not all of the feelings of being together released by the London Olympic Games are reducible to nationalism. This event involved the co-presence of national, developmental, military, capitalist and cosmopolitan narratives, which all have historic links with sport.[33] These narratives often travelled together, and could include progressive elements while simultaneously revivifying colonial images and storylines. For example, the Opening Ceremony, directed by film-maker Danny Boyle, struck a cosmopolitan tone, including a scene celebrating two women kissing, but it also revived imperialistic themes about how the whole world could be visited through a journey to London.[34] However, I want to try and move away from a discussion of the representations of the nation, circulating in and through that ceremony and the games more generally, to consider how the provocation of affective atmospheres prompts new openings for engaging nationalism's everydayness and everywhereness. I'm interested in how it invites us to consider the ways sound, music, colours, patterns, postures and gestures work to generate national affective experiences. This presumes that collectivities do not *precede* events, but rather, as Sara Ahmed argues, are produced through the circulation of emotions.[35] I also want to consider how the nation was not only seen, experienced and felt through the rhythms, memories and affects of this mass sporting event, but also through feelings that skipped between different sites and moments. This means considering affect as not only an 'object-target', as Ben Anderson puts it: that is, the ways 'states, institutions and corporations' work 'directly and indirectly on people and their environments'.[36] It means addressing affect as involving relations, feelings and life that exceed their manipulation.

Identifying affective atmospheres

Significant amounts of energy and capital were spent on securing happy feelings at the London 2012 Olympic Games. From the British government's perspective, as well as the London Organising Committee of the Olympic and Paralympic Games (LOCOG), it was critical that people enjoyed the games. Given the lack of enthusiasm in the run-up to the event, people's emotions needed to be worked upon, and in the course of the event they were continuously monitored and reflected back to the nation by way of opinion polls, images, graphs, collected tweets and even art installations. For example, the Mood-o-Meter formed a collaboration between McDonalds, the fast food company, and the *Sunday Times* and was designed to record the emotions for each day of the games, which could range between awestruck, delirious, drunk, jubilant, excited, hopeful, bothered, sulky, gutted and inconsolable.[37] This resonated with an interactive online art installation by a group called EMOTO, which drew on twitter feeds to chart an emotion graph, ranging from 1 – slightly negative to 6 – enthusiastic.[38] Sound was also an important atmospheric, and the BBC made regular reference to the decibel count in the stadium and how close it came to 140 decibels, or equivalent to a plane taking off.[39] These kinds of emotion graphs and polls resonate with new governing initiatives such as the Well-Being Index of the UK Office for National Statistics and the Organisation for Economic Cooperation and Development's (OECD)'s key priority of measuring well-being and progress. It can be understood as a mode of governing where 'affect becomes a mode of categorizing, classifying and coding' populations.[40] They were not designed to register negative feelings about the games. They could not record disinterest or silence. These examples point to how national affects might be measured and as such, treat emotions and feelings as substances that derive from a community that is already assumed to exist.

The focus on affective atmospheres attends to those unpredictable affective encounters that cannot be traced back to the feelings or emotions of an individual or group. Affect necessarily exceeds attempts at engineering and directing feelings and can, momentarily at least, seem outside attempts at control.[41] This is why ideas about nationality can be mobilized through fun and laughter as much as through the politics of fear.[42] Affect therefore invites us to begin our analyses of national collectives not with the 'psychoanalytically informed criticism of subject identity'[43] or the idea of 'human individuals coming together in community'[44] but with 'the ebbs and swells of intensities that pass between bodies'.[45] This approach draws our attention to the transmissions between the singular and the collective,[46] how 'waves of affect are [both] transmitted and received' and significantly, how this comes to matter politically.[47] It helps us to understand 'the behavior of groups and gatherings'[48] but in a way that refuses the taken-for-granted notion that emotions and energies go 'no further than the skin'[49]. Attending to the affective transmissions between subjects means addressing 'surges of emotion or passion'[50] and their contagious qualities, and how, for example, smells, sounds, chemicals, rhythms and vibrations work to align people with others and against others.[51] These interventions are significant for the study of nationalism which has struggled to break free of assuming national groups that pre-exist political relations.

This suggests a difference between studying attempts at stage managing an atmosphere and examining those 'rhythmic qualities' that escape highly orchestrated moments, but which nevertheless resonate alongside them.[52] The distinction demands that we address those unpredictable moments of attachment and detachment, generated through waves of intensity, which might include ways of being that are generous and hospitable as well as competitive and hostile.[53] Take for example the moment when the then chancellor of the exchequer George Osborne, when presenting the medals for the Men's 400-metres T38 Paralympic event, was booed by the crowd – 'the first booes to be heard all week'.[54] This moment formed a break from the codified emotions of the games, and echoed with protests against cuts to public services and disability benefits, driven by the then chancellor, and made in the name of 'austerity'. Here is an example of something unpredictable that escaped 'the overcoding machine' and disrupted the otherwise carefully choreographed atmospheres.[55] It formed a moment when the people were able to articulate a critique of the government, in terms that took the media and other institutions involved in coordinating the games by surprise.

This act of booing may be understood as a moment that contested Osborne's claim to represent the nation. But in seeking to make sense of it, we might also miss how the participants didn't necessarily set out to stage a protest. Something happened, and the work of 'interpretive sense making' can be 'inadequate to the task of apprehending the affective and processual logics of the space-times in which moving bodies are generative participants'.[56] The collective affects, energies and noise of this moment might thus be read as *generative* of nationhood, or what Kathleen Stewart describes as a 'weirdly floating "we" snap[ping] into blurry focus'.[57] How do we attend to *these* sorts of minor ways of being political? Rather than seek to record and document feelings about a nation that is already assumed to exist, the provocation of affective atmospheres invites an alternative way in – one that requires a 'haptic description in which the analyst discovers her object of analysis by writing out its inhabited elements in a space and time'.[58] It calls for a thick description of what it was like to encounter the event of the games.

Relays

Although the London Games officially began with the opening ceremony held on 27 July 2012, they were preceded by the torch relay, which ran from 19 May to 27 July 2012, forming a countdown towards the games and toured all parts of the UK – from Derry to Aberystwyth to the Shetland Islands. The relay proved surprisingly popular, as enormous crowds gathered to watch it pass through towns and villages, and each street in the journey was mapped in advance on local authority websites as well as on the BBC and official Olympic Torch website with a precise timetable outlining when the torch would arrive at each location (e.g. Day one, 07:15 Land's End; 07:31 Sennen; 08:00 Newlyn; 08:20 Penzance; 09:01 Marazion; 09:26 Rosudgeon.) The seventy-day relay began in Cornwall (having arrived from Olympia, Greece, on a British Airways aircraft), travelled to 1,018 towns, villages and cities and was carried by '8,000 inspirational torchbearers'.[59] The torch came within ten miles of 95 per cent of the population[60] and approximately one-third of the British population watched the torch visit their communities.[61] By way of the torch, the idea of a bounded nation was performed through a journey, as it travelled to the most northern isles in Scotland, parts of Wales and Northern Ireland, and even crossed beyond UK borders from Belfast to Dublin.[62]

As such, the torch relay worked to smooth over some of Britain's colonial histories yet it resonated with the state's ambitions as a global power. Britain's current role as a colonizing force was seen and sensed in the injured bodies of soldiers back from Iraq and Afghanistan selected to carry the torch through their hometowns. Ideas of an imagined community were performed by way of this journey which affirmed London's position – the torch's final destination – as the 'presumptive location of "the national"'.[63] Feelings of happy belonging were reinforced on the ground with bunting, flags and *Your 2012* merchandise – with 'almost 25 kilometres of bunting … and 638 square metres of building decorations' on display in London by the time of the games.[64] This atmosphere was not produced within an architectural building such as a sport stadium or concert hall,[65] and it didn't rely on being there on the ground. Rather, the BBC played a crucial role in building the sense of excitement by showing pictures of the torch's progress on its daily news, launching maps and street by street routes on their website, and blogging and tweeting about the torch's journey. They played a role in 'semiconducting' the affective atmospheres of the games, an idea developed by Derek McCormack from Michael Serres's work. As McCormack argues, sport commentators do not only mediate or represent a state of affairs to the viewer/listener; rather, she (but often, a he) leans into the flow of activity, and in doing so 'performs the liveliness of affective modulation by operating upon the virtual cusp of the event'.[66] We can read this process of performing the liveliness of the event in the BBC blog updates as they followed the torch on its journey:

May 28, Day 10, Aberystwyth to Bangor

.0746: Morning everyone … It's day 10 of the torch relay and we're still in a very sunny Wales, with the first flame hitching a ride on Aberystwyth's Cliff Railway … it's already 20C in Aberystwyth so sun hats to the ready.

.0801: We are relying, as ever, on you getting involved. Are you going to watch the torch today? Don't forget you can e-mail yourpics@bbc.co.uk or text 61124, tweet us at @BBC2012 or visit our Facebook page at BBC London 2012.[67]

Other corporations including relay sponsors Samsung, Coca-Cola and Lloyds
TSB played similar roles – with Samsung inviting people to tag pictures and
post videos of themselves with the torch on their website. In this sense, the
feelings of national belonging created through the torch relay were produced
and reinforced by several different institutions, each with a different relationship
to the state, and it was enacted materially as well as virtually, through hashtags
such as #olympic, #torch, #relay, #torchbearer, #london2012, #day35. What is
significant here is that the feelings of national togetherness cannot be traced
back to the work of a single sovereign authority directing people's feelings but
rather must be understood as emanating from several different constituencies.
They worked as part of what political theorist William Connolly describes as
a 'qualitative assemblage', involving 'affinities of spirituality' that jump across
'different professions of creed, doctrine and philosophy' and acting as part of
a 'resonance machine', drawing people together despite creedal differences.[68]
It built a sense of unity, but was held together provisionally. The semblance of
unity was achieved by appealing to multiple forms and genres of affinity.

Connolly's vocabulary and concept of the 'resonance machine' is useful in
considering the complex connections between austerity politics, capitalism,
the British military, popular culture, media organizations such as the BBC
and LOCOG, working in association to crystallize and amplify the affective
atmospheres of the London 2012 Olympic Games. Arguing that it is insufficient
to portray political leaders as manipulating their followers, Connolly points to
how 'motivations and sentiments whirl in a hurricane out of heretofore loosely
associated elements'.[69] This concept of the resonance machine and its spiritual
dimension is in part developed by Connolly through the work of Max Weber,
who famously described how nationalism emerges against the mounting sense of
the rationalization of social and economic life and to offer a sense of *meaning*.[70]
Of course, the contemporary conditions of capital are very different, but Weber's
attempt to situate the nation as a 'value orientation' that can provide meaning
in meaningless times is significant for understanding the emergence of these
games against the backdrop of austerity. For Weber, nationalism also emerges
alongside the idea of the heroic individual, an idea that is equally important in
reflecting on London 2012. Ideas about individuality based around striving, self-
reliance and self-control worked in tandem with ideas about the nation, both at
the games, through sport, as well as in the broader political context of 'austerity'
as a *moral* response to financial crisis. Taken together, these ideas had a broad
appeal. They were central to both the Olympic and Paralympic Games in 2012,
as ideas about self-determination combined with governmental ideas about

austerity were anchored *physically* in objects such as the torch, and experienced viscerally in the act of watching bodies move at speed and compete in carefully measured segments of time.

Accordingly, when we consider an event such as the torch relay, it is inadequate to understand its popularity by dismissing it as a state engineered event. Although it required enormous amounts of state sponsorship, corporate funding and media support, the fact that exceptionally large gatherings of people went to see it, and got up at early hours in the morning in order to do so, suggests a coming together of microelements that flowed beyond a centralizing machine. How can we appreciate the collective enjoyment experienced at national events such as this one while simultaneously developing an argument about it? The relay worked because it followed a recognizable national-territorial journey and therefore offers a good example of how the spectacles of state nationalism cannot be separated from everyday life. In the case of this relay, the macro and the micropolitical operated together: while the journey wouldn't have been recognizable without macropolitical elements including state sponsored marketing campaigns, as well as the work of semiconducting carried out by the BBC among other institutions and corporations, it took hold through affective forces which resonated in excess of attempts at engineering feelings. As the anthropologist Kathleen Stewart puts it, 'a world of shared banalities' can simply appear as the relief of being 'in' something with others[71] and these 'little experiences' of feeling part of a 'we' take place before any conscious decisions.[72] The micropolitical moments of feeling part of a collective 'we' might be prosaic and ordinary, but they matter politically. In the event of the London 2012 Olympic Games, it was these 'little experiences' of 'shared banalities' that enabled the sense that national affective atmospheres were penetrating 'every cell of society',[73] and making it difficult to imagine going against the national mood.

Attractors

Key figures such as Mo Farah, winner of the 10,000-metre and 5,000-metre races at this event, emerged as central to ideas about British identity in cosmopolitan times of austerity. Farah was born in Mogadishu, Somalia and moved to the UK when he was eight years old to live with his father who was born and raised in London. Farah was repeatedly asked in television interviews about his feelings of belonging to Britain. He emerged as an 'attractor', to borrow Jasbir Puar's term,[74] that not only focused ideas about an 'inclusive' British nation, but also, Britain's anxieties about its everyday cosmopolitanism. The social commentary wavered between celebrating him as *emphatically* British and yet queried him about the *depth* of his Britishness, confirming Stuart Hall's point that ideas about difference vacillate between the positive and the negative.[75] It also shows how racism works in accordance with the nation, seeking to determine a 'stable distribution of places, times, identities and competencies'.[76] The shift to affect enables us to extend these critiques: for example, Jasbir Puar draws on Sara Ahmed's work to discuss how emotions 'stick' to certain bodies, materials and objects under particular conditions. Discussing the stickiness of race allows us to displace the idea that particular bodies will *in each case* be understood as potentially 'other' – be that as exceptionally high achieving, or as threatening. In the case of the London Games, ideas about striving, working hard and playing by the rules temporarily stuck to images of Farah's highly athletic body, to the perceived sensation of pressing a body to its limits, and combined with flashes of red, white and blue in a swirl of ideas about British values. But there were also familiar 'racially-coded regimes of intelligibility' at work.[77] In the constant questions put to him about his feelings of *home*, he was anticipated as *potentially* other,[78] as part of attempts at fixing the lines between inside and outside.

In addition to high-profile figures, seventy thousand people who worked as volunteer Games Makers at these Olympic and Paralympic Games emerged as 'attractors' and were honoured by the British prime minister David Cameron for their contributions towards citizenship and nationhood.[79] Alongside objects such as the torch, the Games Makers gathered and radiated particular ideas about belonging, nationhood and responsible citizenship, ideas that of course travel beyond the specific individuals themselves. This was useful in a context where the current Conservative-Liberal Democrat coalition government in the UK was cutting jobs at local libraries and children's centres, and shifting the work onto volunteers. But the idea of ordinary people taking their place and playing their part is also central to the activation of feelings about a nation. Consider for example the list of 'ordinary people' read out by the US president Barack Obama in the aftermath of bombings in Boston on 15 April 2013:

> The brave first responders ...
> The race volunteers ...
> The determined doctors and nurses ...
> May God bless the people of Boston and the United States of America.[80]

Chapter 3 will go on to discuss how a national community is conjured in response to cases of terrorist attacks. But I draw attention to this extract for the images of 'ordinary people' summoned, in ways that resonated with the ordinary people featured in the Olympic Games (doctors and nurses in the opening ceremony, volunteer games makers), and also for the recognizable cadence, the distribution of accents, syllables and silences that form this distinctive rhythm. In hearing the list, 'we ... pre-hear ... a foreseeable sonic context'.[81] Focusing on the rhythms helps explain why the speech given by Obama in response to the bombings in Boston echoes with the rhyming couplets of a McDonalds advert that ran throughout the London 2012 Olympic Games.

McDonalds, as part of its sponsorship of the London Games, ran a marketing campaign titled 'We All Make the Games'.[82] The advert evoked distinctive groups of 'ordinary people', representing different backgrounds, ages and occupations – echoing the cosmopolitan theme of the games. It was set to background music that featured a reworked version of the *Tears for Fears* song, 'Everybody Wants to Rule the World'. It formed another element in the resonance machine that activated and amplified national feelings during the London 2012 Olympic Games. The text, spoken to the rhythms of the music, included the following images:

> The punchers, the peekers, the hero-meeters;
> the snogger, the blogger, the relive the week-ers;
> the clapper, the napper, the 'xcuse-me-squeeze-paster;
> the whistlers, the quenchers, the sat-down-at-laster;
> ... the glued-to-the-screen-er, the edge-of-seat-leaner,
> the snapper, the chatter, the not-really-keen-er ...
> We All Make the Games.

The combination of text, images and music worked according to a distinctive rhythm of accents, sounds and silences. And it configured space in a way that drew the lines between inside and outside. While some listeners with cultural memories of 1980s Britain will have been aware of the *Tears For Fears* song, many more will have known the song by anamnesis – that is, by the 'effect of reminiscence in which a past situation or atmosphere is brought back to the listener's consciousness, provoked by a particular signal or sonic context'.[83] The advert is expertly designed to evoke, stir and produce the sense of a distinctly national audience, but any sense of *disagreement* evoked by the atmospheric memories of 1980s Britain is forgotten as the affective national community is in this case affirmed as a space of 'happy feelings'.[84]

'We All Make the Games' formed a powerful television advert. But as with the torch, it must be read in the context of a broader 'resonance machine',[85] and therefore, not as a straightforward source of national affects. Indeed, studying the nation atmospherically encourages us to move away from looking for a cause or a direct source of national feelings. These lines and refrains worked and travelled because they echoed with other images and songs. For example, the refrain 'We All Make the Games' echoed with the British chancellor George Osborne's claim that, under austerity, 'We're All in This Together'.[86] None of us can position ourselves as completely outside of or untouched by these refrains. We may or may not find ourselves moved by them. But my point here is not so much about how this advert represented the nation in a particular way (as cosmopolitan, as inclusive, even as it also sanitized the nation of its histories); it is about how it worked as part of many different elements to 'semiconduct' the affective atmospheres of London 2012 by performing the liveliness of the event. The handheld cameras, used to produce the adverts, and to record spectators in different parts of the country enjoying themselves in real time further reinforced the lively feel. They ensured that the adverts had an improvisational tone. The original advert was updated, several times, as new versions of the basic melodic motif, sequence of images and final closing motto were released at key stages in the course of the games, such as Super Saturday – when Britain won its highest number of Olympic medals in one day. New text was added to the lyrics to capture the event as it unfolded, referring to a group of spectators called 'The 9.63ers', to acknowledge Usain Bolt winning the 100-metres sprint in this number of seconds. The idea of a national community was produced through this repetitious and performative experience of time, and by tapping into historical moments, refrains and moods, to produce the sense of a 'continuist, accumulative' temporality.[87] While McDonalds might not seem the most appropriate sponsor for a global event that also purports to celebrate fitness and health,[88] both McDonalds and the games shared in 'a dominant cultural form'.[89] This much is understood by the advertisers – who worked to position McDonalds as 'The People's Restaurant', as 'democratic' and 'populist', and who significantly, understood that the games were about more than sport.

Resonance, amplification, interruption

In contrast to studies of nations and nationalism that approach particular images, bodies or objects (e.g. the flag) as symbolic of the nation, the provocation of affective atmospheres suggests ways in which we might think about the circulation of key figures, images, sounds and moving images as more than symbolic. Firstly, rather than read the emergence of nationalist affects as traceable to an essence, we can read them as a temporally and spatially specific encounter of swirling affects, memories, sounds, rhythms and images sticking to particular assemblages of bodies and materials.[90] Secondly, we can say that images, songs, lyrics, bodies or objects do not operate in isolation, and don't in themselves project a national aura. Rather, they work as part of an assemblage of constituencies and elements that assume different intensities at various moments and localities. This means that an image or an object does not assume the same political charge in each context and may not be charged at all. It also implies that national feelings and affects can stick to many different kinds of objects, materials and bodies – far beyond the familiar examples of flags, monuments and memorials offered in most studies of nationalism. Ideas about nationality, autonomy, austerity and self-determination did not congeal around one object – such as the torch – but rather worked by 'skipping from point to point',[91] resonating and amplifying in relation to different parts and constituencies.

The affective atmospheres of the games echoed, then, in gestures such as Mo Farah's trademark 'M' victory sign, which was copied and performed in several sites including workplaces and children's playgrounds. This 'M' gesture took off in a way that was not predictable in advance and which is not reducible to nationalism. However, it activated ideas about being-with-others that resonated alongside the affective atmospheres of the games. Together with the objects, materials, sounds and gestures discussed, it offers a glimpse of some of the ways in which the nation might be seen, heard and felt.[92] But none of these examples can be understood as simply symbolic; their meanings were multiple. They carried their own affects, and if and when they assumed an affective charge, they did so because of the reverberations that jump between the different parts of the assemblage, activating national feelings at periodic moments. Finally, the reverberations did not in each instance play into, or heighten a national affective atmosphere; they also, on occasion, interrupted the mood, or dispersed into the formation of other affective communities. They suggested the potential of alternative experiences of being together, which were co-present throughout the games.

What happened to the atmospheres of these games? On 7 February 2014, Prime Minister David Cameron returned to the Olympic Park in East London to make a speech to the people of Scotland in advance of a Referendum on 18 September 2014 asking whether the people of Scotland wanted it to become an independent country. In his speech, David Cameron decided to spell out the 'emotional, patriotic case' for staying in the UK, by stating: 'We want you to stay'.[93] National leaders are well aware that the nation has profound 'emotional legitimacy'.[94] But Cameron's decision to return to the Olympic Park suggests that the idea of bottling the atmospheres of the London 2012 Olympic Games is not so far-fetched. The feelings of nationality associated with London 2012 can be recalled and claimed for other political causes – a subject I return to in the next chapter on the funeral of Margaret Thatcher. National feelings take hold because they are familiar, and because they tap into past emotions and affects, which return by way of pictures, musical refrains, combinations of colours, gestures and postures. Overall the provocation of affective atmospheres therefore offers ways of loosening the grip of the language of identity, essence and belonging in the study of nationalism, and attend to the currents and transmissions that pass between bodies and which congeal around particular objects, materials and bodies in specific times and spaces. But it still leaves us with the question of how to challenge national affects at work.

To address this question, I want to turn to a short experimental film project called 'Swandown', developed by the film-maker Andrew Kötting and the psychogeographer Iain Sinclair (Figure 2). This formed one of the more unusual response to the games. In it, Sinclair and Kötting set sail on the back of a giant

Figure 2. Swandown, directed by Andrew Kötting and Iain Sinclair. Photograph by Anonymous Bosch.

fiberglass swan (called Edith), travelling up the river Thames from Hastings to Hackney and the site of the Olympic Park.[95] This voyage forms an alternative kind of Olympic journey which could be followed on Facebook, Twitter and the project website. Although it drew on similar mapping tools to the torch relay, it questioned the sovereignty of that vision. For example, although the swan's journey had to be scheduled to time, this was not a finely calculated schedule but a celebration of slow time, evident in the fact that they kept getting stuck on mudbanks and that the swan is at the beginning of the film overtaken by a UK Border Agency boat. Pedalling this plastic swan is visibly hard work, but it is not hard work that has recognition as a sport; it draws gasps of delight from those who encounter it and indirectly raises questions about the absurdity of many of the Olympic competitions. While both this film and the London Olympic Games celebrate endurance, they do so in different ways. In the film, endurance is more about humility than super strength. Kötting argues that the journey does not represent a protest against the Olympics, so much as a reflection on the ridiculousness of pedalling a plastic swan. But the film does of course form a critique: it shows the difficulties of resisting the at times all-encompassing atmospheres of enjoyment at work during the course of the London 2012 Olympic Games. This slow journey forms a perturbation that briefly escapes the 'overcoding machine'.[96] And it is unrecognizable within the terms of order, precision, speed, heroism and national virility promoted by the event of the games.

The swan does not rely on the language of uniting *against* the Olympics. After all, being against the Olympics was, in this context, next to impossible. What it does is launch a humble yet defiant disturbance into the consensual affective atmospheres that defined the London 2012 Olympic Games. It interrupts the national affects circulating, and shows us that other structures of feeling are present and latent. This question of how national affects work to unify, and how they can also be unsettled, is now explored further in a chapter that turns to the funeral of Baroness Margaret Thatcher, British prime minister from 1979 to 1990, and a key figure in the global politics of neoliberalism.

2

Consensus and resistance at Margaret Thatcher's funeral

On 17 April 2013, Margaret Thatcher, British prime minister from 1979 to 1990, and a key figure in the globalization of neoliberalism, was accorded a ceremonial funeral in London following her death at the age of eighty-seven. According to the right-wing journal, *The Spectator*, she died while reading in her room at the Ritz, a 5-star hotel in Mayfair, London.[1] The Ritz had been her home since she moved out of her own house in 2012. On 10 April, the British Parliament was recalled from its Easter recess so that members could pay tribute to Baroness Thatcher.[2] The then prime minister David Cameron described her as 'an extraordinary leader and an extraordinary woman' and emphasized the 'thickness of the glass ceiling that she broke through' – from her early upbringing as the daughter of a grocer in Grantham to becoming the first woman to lead the Conservative Party and the first female British prime minister.[3] However, Cameron also acknowledged the political struggle around her legacy. He borrowed Thatcher's own description of herself, pronouncing her to be a 'conviction' rather than 'consensus politician'.[4] He even praised the opposition MPs for turning up to pay their respects, despite having profoundly disagreed with her.

Thatcher was a polarizing figure; she attracted both love and hatred, admiration and disgust. But in her death, Thatcher was rendered a national figure. While acknowledging disagreement, there was an effort to establish a national consensus, where we could all celebrate her hard-working ethos and her success as a woman in a man's world. These efforts demonstrate how national affects are mobilized in the pursuit of unity by establishing points for directing patriotisms and passions. However, this chapter aims to show how fragile such efforts are and how people express their doubt about political narratives of unity, progress, self-determination and conviction. As such, the chapter explores the contradictory texture of national affects, drawing on moments from the day of the funeral, from my perspective among the crowds

Figure 3. The cortege, Baroness Margaret Thatcher's funeral, 17 April 2013. Photograph by Ronnie Macdonald. Available via Flickr under Creative Commons License.

on Fleet Street, London, where I went to conduct fieldwork (Figure 3). I show how despite the efforts put into celebrating Thatcher, the mood on this day was above all, indifferent.

The chapter draws inspiration from the work of Lauren Berlant on 'cruel optimism', and what happens when good-life fantasies (of faith in a political system or project, alongside other fantasies, including upward mobility, romantic love, the perfect family or job security) begin to fall apart. Berlant describes these fantasies as cruel, because they involve a promise of change, while making it impossible to 'attain the expansive transformation to which a person or a people risks striving'.[5] I identify such cruelty in the promises of free-market economics made by Thatcherism, which recurred through austerity, in the line that 'We're all in this together', and again through Brexit.[6] The figure of Thatcher loomed heavy in this new context because of how she famously argued that businesses, governments and housewives all have to 'add up the figures', equating a government's spending policies with those of running a household.[7] This idea reminds us of how neoliberalism involves more than economics (e.g. the privatization of services and utilities; the deregulation of labour markets and repression of organized labour).[8] These ideas were achieved then as they are now through intimate and affective narratives about progress, self-advancement and self-improvement – be that doing up a home, measuring our fitness or going shopping. Prime Minister David Cameron had a point when he claimed in a radio interview after her death that 'we're all Thatcherites now'.[9] How do we begin to resist a system that we're all so immersed in?

The chapter explores how we interrupt claims of national consensus by following the mood of indifference felt on this day. Drawing on my field notes, I emphasize the role of ambivalence and doubt in people's claims about the promises of Thatcherism. In contrast to Thatcher's model of politics as adversarial, involving strong actions and conviction, I examine how so much of political life is in fact composed of people going along with things. This has two implications for thinking about resistance. First, it emphasizes how resisting Thatcherism must also involve resisting this model of a politics of 'us and them'. Second, it argues that thinking beyond an adversarial model of politics allows us to imagine resistance in more creative, plural and lively terms. The chapter does this by turning to an example of creative resistance offered by performance artist Tim Etchells, called '55 funerals' and concludes by discussing Hilary Mantel's short story, *The Assassination of Margaret Thatcher – August 6th, 1983*. While the figure of Thatcher suggests an understanding of politics as involving strong actions, a sense of purpose and clear direction, this chapter draws on a combination of field notes and creative works to unpack other understandings of what it means to be political.

Politics after Thatcher

Thatcher's death had long been imagined, anticipated, even summoned. Yet given the extensive work being put into consensus-building around her death, it was difficult to guess what form resistance would take, or whether the people were particularly moved or bothered. This figure that had once, for some, represented the zenith of neoliberalism and British nationalism was dead. As oppositional parties were manoeuvred into saluting her nominally *extra-political* values – her achievements as a woman in a male-dominated profession, and as someone that had crossed the class divide – the political question that emerged was how critique might break through the consensus being established between government, media, and other professions and establishments. How does resistance break out of the forms that are already being anticipated for it? The process of establishing consensus forms what Jacques Rancière describes as the evacuation of politics.[10] By relinquishing that which lies at the heart of politics, 'the dispute of the people', it advances its own 'legitimization processes'.[11] Yet as Rancière argues, it is impossible to relinquish politics completely. This is what he describes as the 'miscount of politics'[12]: 'There is politics – and not just domination', because the 'people are always more or less than the people'.[13] That is, the people will speak or make themselves visible in ways that cannot be fully anticipated.

Resistance around the event of Thatcher's funeral was nevertheless anticipated, discussed, and planned through police operations and a full-dress rehearsal carried out on 15 April. *The Telegraph* claimed that 'anti-Thatcher campaigners' would be lining the route of the procession to 'turn their backs on the coffin as it passes'.[14] *The Spectator* described that on hearing the news of Thatcher's death: '200 people gathered at Easton, in Bristol, celebrating the death and setting fire to dustbins after dark'[15]. This is what the authorities expected. Yet in the event, evidence of the spectacles of resistance were thin on the ground and the people were largely uninterested. As one leading broadsheet commented: 'It was a day of both respect and rancour but one which went off with very little disruption in the end, the significant protests confined to former mining towns in the north'.[16] The broadsheet's narratives reactivated ideas about resistance stemming from specific geographical sites – Easton in Bristol and 'the North', drawing on familiar imaginative geographies, of places that had been centre points of protest and revolt in the 1980s. But in the event, resistance took very different forms, such as when a remix of *The Wizard of Oz* song, 'Ding Dong, The Witch Is Dead!', entered the pop charts at number 2, selling 52,605 copies.[17]

We can say that these accounts of protest assume an understanding of a 'resistant subject'.[18] But how does this claim about confrontation between power and its opposite mask the ways in which the people are already entangled in power's languages, styles and structures of feeling? As Stuart Hall was quick to note in the 1980s, Thatcherism's success lay with how it was more than a political and economic movement involving a profound restructuring of the state; it also formed an affective force.[19] It included a set of 'ideological discourses' and stories that people could connect with, if only provisionally. Doreen Massey further describes neoliberalism's success by way of its capacity to govern as 'sophisticated common sense'.[20] This is not a process that unfolds separately to us: we are deeply embedded in it. Thinking about resistance as 'always already entangled with power'[21] allows us to acknowledge how neoliberalism is not something we can get outside of but something that shapes our understandings of politics and resistance.

One of the problems we therefore face under neoliberalism involves knowing what to do with how scandalized we are, outside of the co-opted, reified and solidified mechanisms of being political, which are often caught up in the problems they seek to oppose. What forms might resistance take, given that neoliberalism is 'more termite like than lion like ... its mode of reason boring in capillary fashion into the trunks and branches of workplaces, schools, public agencies, social and political discourse, and above all, the subject'?[22] How might we consider the plurality of ways in which being scandalized and politicized might materialize – including, through refusing, staying with, joking, interrupting and remaining present?

Thinking with Thatcher leads us to imagine a powerful figure, acting on conviction, engaged in politics as confrontational opposition, where one group is right and the other wrong. As such, she is a face for what Michel Foucault describes as an adversarial model of politics.[23] Treating Thatcher as a figure that is 'both subject and object, indeterminate container for meaning, and affective conduit', allows us to contemplate this model of politics.[24] It suggests that power and resistance spring from distinctly *separate sites*, assume *completely different forms*, and generate different kinds of *active subjects*. But what if power and resistance are more intermeshed, compromised and entangled than this model implies? What if thinking against Thatcher involves thinking beyond this presumed separation between 'us and them', between action as politics and vulnerability as its opposite. Addressing Thatcher as 'at once material body, media image and cultural signifier' that 'can testify, attract, alienate, repulse and captivate'[25] allows us to consider what is at stake when we treat politics as war.[26]

In the next section, I go on to describe how politics and resistance were entangled from my perspective on the street on the day of Thatcher's funeral. In doing so, I address pervasive ideas about agents, action and conviction by attending to the politics of 'little things'[27] to generate other ways of thinking about how political positions, decisions and authorities are arrived at and assembled. This approach draws on Sedgwick's method of generating thought from a position of placing ourselves *beside* politics. It offers material for thinking politically beyond an adversarial model.

The politics of little things

The funeral of a former prime minister provides an opportunity for the state to present a view of itself as coherent, grand, majestic and a view of the people as united in their respect.[28] But what does such unity and coherency look like from the perspective of the street? The legacies of Thatcherism could be heard in ideas about the nation in a time of austerity, in ideas about virtue and morality, in ways that revivified post-war imagery of a nation pulling together against an enemy.[29] Another of Thatcher's refrains, used by former prime minister David Cameron in a tribute made to her in parliament, was that 'she made our country great again'.[30] Authority secures its own authority by appealing to nostalgic fantasies. How do these elements work together, in an event such as this ceremonial funeral,[31] to 'protect the (affective) fantasy of the nation as a powerful anchor'?[32] Paul Gilroy describes this process as one where the 'lines of inclusion and exclusion which mark out the national community are redrawn', during times of crisis. The nostalgic fantasies of belonging had lost their cosmopolitan tone from the London Olympic Games and were animated by racialized fantasies of a white nation acting morally during times of austerity. Here, Gilroy's description of how the nation is homogenized in times of crisis, a point he made in relation to deindustrialization in the 1980s, remains relevant. As he puts it: 'Britons are invited to put on their tin hats and climb back down to the World War II air-raid shelters. There, they can be comforted by the rustic glow of the homogenous national culture … That unsullied culture can be mystically reconstituted, particularly amidst national adversity when distinctively British qualities supposedly emerge with the greatest force and clarity'.[33] At this funeral, such images and narratives were animated anew.

Lauren Berlant articulates this as a process of assembling refrains, flags, symbols, style and gestures into a fantasy of national belonging. But her account of this, as a combination of macropolitical narratives and micropolitical background noise is useful for addressing the question of resistance. She reminds us of how this process of converting 'a historical moment into an iconic event' preserves it 'from history's contingencies, people's memories, and ambivalence'.[34] In the context of austerity, the hugely damaging cuts to disability benefits, child support, the national health service, maternity grants, housing allowances and working tax credits were accompanied and in part enabled by the atmospheric register, composed through ideas about 'paying our way' and the 'deserving and undeserving poor'.[35] These represent powerful accounts of how we make sense of our lives, and in this context, took hold rapidly, because they tapped into ideas that were already familiar. How can such ideas, which emerge as a hum, be interrupted?

Engaging affect allows us to address this register of the background noise through which political ideas take hold, and through which they might also be diverted and contested.[36] It reveals the incoherence and tensions within many of these ideas, as well as their temporariness and ephemerality. An affective approach allows us glean uncertain accounts of how power operates; for example, on this register, we become better able to hear how authority trembles in its attempts at holding on to authority, or how the everyday 'beliefs' of the people quietly wobble as they are repeated but *also, doubted*. This approach allows us to move away from ideas about intention, purpose and action in political life to become interested in how people *happen* to turn out to particular events, or just end up *going along* with something, perhaps to temporarily break with boredom or the whirr of anxiety. The point here is not to underplay the force of power, but to remind ourselves that power sometimes fails to do what it is supposed to do.[37] In terms of thinking about resistance, it suggests that decisions are made and governments supported, not always because people have signed up to a consistent ideology, but because we have, on judging the balance of awful options available, decided to go along with something, or aligned ourselves with one set of affective forces over another. What does it mean to address politics through *this* register?

Attuning to how power and resistance are entangled involves listening to the contradictions expressed in political desires and acknowledging the complexity of different positions and subjectivities held. It also invites us to tease out ambivalent moments, figures or stances in the study of politics.[38] In her field guide to attuning to this 'in-between' register, Debbie Lisle reminds us of the 'seductive power of laws, limits and order' – how these inform both theories of power and its 'uncritical opposition'.[39] Seductive as it may be to chart resistance as a process of moving from outside of power to inside of it, or as a question of taking over institutions and replacing one form of government with another, such 'comfortable and orderly forms of resistance' risk serving only to 'reinforce the ruthlessness of the laws being opposed'.[40] What happens if instead we trace the possibilities and efforts of resistance in 'experiences, conditions, things, dreams, landscapes, imaginaries, and lived sensory moments'?[41] This means loosening the possibility of resistance from that figure of the active agent and instead looking for dispersed, less spectacular efforts at altering the refrains.

Geographically, this means tracing an account of resistance as something other than springing from a clearly identifiable place or distinct social group. Instead, drawing on Eve Sedgwick's productive spatial category of thinking 'beside', we can consider resistance outside of a dualistic model: 'Beside comprises of a wide range of desiring, identifying, representing, repelling, differentiating, rivalling, leaning, twisting, mimicking, withdrawing, attracting, aggressing, warping, and other relations'.[42] What happens when we think about resistance through this category? Spatially, it means refusing to chart the problem as one of moving from outside to inside, and enquiring into the complex interdependency of inside and outside in political movements. Temporally, it means thinking against ideas about redemption. And finally, it means thinking beyond the figure of the oppositional subject – deemed to be acting from a place of conviction. The next sections turn to the event of Margaret Thatcher's funeral from my position among the crowd on the street. Through these snapshots, I want to show how the day was not only composed through the state's efforts to manipulate nostalgic national affects but also assembled through affects that exceeded their purpose and design.

Funerary atmospheres

Waiting

Several different institutions were involved in the organization of the funeral on 17 April of 2013, including the Conservative Party; the British Army, Navy and Royal Air Force; the BBC; the Church of England; the Cabinet Office; the City of London Police; the Metropolitan Police and Baroness Thatcher's Estate. Before her death, Thatcher had reportedly been consulted about the plans.[43] At 10.00 am, the coffin was transported in a hearse from the Palace of Westminster to the Church of St Clement Danes on The Strand. It was then transferred to a gun carriage, drawn by the King's Troop Royal Horse Artillery and taken in procession to St Paul's Cathedral. The route was lined by more than seven hundred armed services personnel, led by the Band of HM Royal Marines Portsmouth, who covered their drums in black cloth.[44] A gun was fired every minute from Tower Wharf for the duration of the procession, and Big Ben was quiet for the proceedings.[45] Through the use of symbolism, music, imagery, rituals and uniforms, this event was designed to press the impression of national unity. But such unity felt both fractured and fragile from my perspective among the crowd:

> Standing on Ludgate Hill, looking down toward Fleet Street on one side and St Paul's Cathedral on the other, over several hours, the space I'd carved out for myself on the side of the street had become narrower and tighter. Whereas

earlier it was still possible to move around and take my camera in and out of my bag, my arms were now stuck in place, looking for whatever moment would offer itself as evidence of the event. I sensed that an event was about to unfold from the feeling of bodies pressed beside me, sheltering me a bit from the rain that had just begun, and the broken murmurs of police radios on this unusually silent London street. (Edited field notes, 17 April 2013)

On this street were a mix of touristy pubs, steakhouses, souvenir shops, which for this day had moved displays of union-jack-coloured mugs to the front of shop windows. More people joined us in the crowd until it was about seven people deep. Others took advantage of vantage points above the street – leaning out of windows, crowding on to balconies, or jumping onto bins: (Edited Field notes, 17 April 2013)

Looking up, I could see three armed policemen on the roof of St Paul's and another policeman with a video camera recording the crowd. I could hear the bells of St Paul's ringing and the sounds of media and police helicopters overhead. Already this seemed to be a scene replete with the force of the state. Yet amongst this largely acquiescent crowd, there was only the odd shout or heckle that carried across the air. I glimpsed a red t-shirt under someone's coat with the words: 'Thatcher: good riddance'. (Edited field notes, 17 April 2013)

What is suggested here is all the different elements and rhythms that go into composing a 'national event', from hanging around for something to take place to the tiny shuffling movements involved in waiting and watching a public event with others. This is the 'live background' that Kathleen Stewart discusses.[46] In this case, it involved the sounds of media and police helicopters circling overhead; the distinctiveness of British weather and rain in particular; and the objects, equipment and postures of the policewomen and men on duty. The event was composed both through the hushed whispers, the shouting of the odd military order, the clip clop of the horses' hooves along with the occasional heckle. These minor elements gave the event its charge. However, this background material did not take place underneath or behind a more coherent politics. These were the thousand tiny organized and unorganized ways through which a sense of unity and coherency was established.[47]

Debbie Lisle encourages us to attune to the performance of sovereign fictions alongside the 'mundane realities of everyday life'.[48] This might mean that, as soon as we are drawn towards identifying power, we also recognize that moment as 'always-already punctured by contingency'.[49] Such an approach complements an understanding of affective power, as exerting a force that is vague and diffuse, ephemeral and indeterminate.[50] Certainly, this funeral displayed the full wealth of ceremonial power – in the hearse that eventually passed wrapped in a British flag, and in the music of Beethoven, Chopin and Mendelssohn played by the military bands – clear identifiers of 'institutional hierarchies' and military power.[51] But what is at stake when we imagine a determinative sovereign that is successful at inculcating these ideas in the people? As Achille Mbembe argues in his study of ceremonial power in Cameroon, there is not a 'fundamental conflict between worlds of meaning that are in principle antagonistic'. On the contrary, 'officialdom and the people have many references in common, not least a certain conception of the aesthetics and stylistics of power and the way it operates and expands'.[52] Put another way, there is, here, a shared community of sense through which power and the people are assembled.

> After the hearse and full procession passes, and the dignitaries, politicians, celebrities and members of Thatcher's family make their way into St Paul's cathedral for the ceremony, I go into a nearby pub. The multiple screens above the bar are showing the BBC broadcasting live from within St Paul's. The cathedral itself is no more than 100 metres away from us. I watch people watching the screens – which they don't do in full, with purpose or concentration, but rather indifferently, and intermittently, during a pause in conversation, or as they take a swig of beer, or a sip of hot coffee. There is nothing eventful or especially political about this gathering. But it might also tell us something about how people engage the political in their everyday lives. They do not participate as fully conscious, active agents: they tune in briefly in between other demands, and they absorb a scene that is already recognisable as part of the stylistics of power. (Edited field notes 17 April 2013)

Working with affect is illuminating for describing these indifferent but felt accounts of the political, which rarely add up to evidence of a collective subject or position. They allow us to think about those thoughts, inclinations, and views of the world arrived at in the middle of ordinary life, and from 'under the radar of politics':[53]

> After the ceremony finishes, I walk down Fleet Street towards Holborn, tracing the journey of the gun carriage. There is sand and horse shit along the route, and what I see are the remainders of the event. Traffic is now allowed back onto previously cordoned off streets; workers are taking down the security barriers with the odd poster, flag, or message of protest written on them. Off Fleet Street, a line of trucks await, ready to go and do the clean-up. In walking just a few

streets, it becomes impossible to recognise that any significant event has taken place: the city returns to its usual midday rhythms and noises. Several thousand other appointments, decisions, and encounters go ahead. The markers that signified the event are being disassembled and driven away. (Edited field notes, 17 April 2013)

Melissa Gregg and Greg Seigworth describe little experiences as 'intimate and impersonal'[54] and that they exceed their symbolic status – as, for example, an identifier of the nation, or of neoliberalism. The point here is that the affective feelings register 'before the mind can think' and before something is recognizable as any coherent political formation.[55] An account of power as hegemonic and all-encompassing might identify this scene as already occupied by particular identities and aligned with a clear set of values. But while power is undoubtedly at work, these people are not all united around a shared memory or cause. The communities of sense are plural. While the news reports on the morning of the funeral had led me to expect to see the force of Thatcherism's reach, as well as defiant subjects challenging the crowds, in standing with the crowds, what I saw were temporary gatherings of mixed publics, alongside the purposeful attempts at establishing unity, hierarchy and order. The gatherings gradually dissolved back into the multiple flows of the city (Figure 4). I encountered minimal 'actions' from the people watching and half-watching, the newspaper-sellers

Figure 4. Dismantling the event. Baroness Margaret Thatcher's funeral, 17 April 2013. Photograph by the author.

making an income on the back of a special issue of the papers. What I heard was the odd shout from the crowd and message of objection on a t-shirt.

Being political

I asked the people standing around me in the crowd to describe why they had come along and people were keen to offer me their reasons. Interestingly, those reasons shuttled back and forth between expressing some curiosity or respect for Thatcher, or at least for the occasion, and suggesting that they were simultaneously quite indifferent. For example, one couple told me that they had only come along because they were on holiday in London: 'We live in France. We wouldn't have come but we were in London. And it's historic isn't it?' Two more of those who stood alongside me insisted that this event was not for them about politics at all: one middle-aged man said: 'Today's about respect isn't it. She's a mother. A grandmother.' A middle-aged woman said, 'I'm not political, you'd be better off talking to my husband.'

As part of this effort to engage resistance, we can dismiss these claims of being apolitical by pointing out that these people *were* participating (if that is not too strong a term) in this political event. As Rancière argues, there is nothing more political than the claim that something is not political. However, these lines that were repeated to me do not necessarily belong to these 'participants': they were already circulating in the public sphere, spoken in parliament and on the airwaves. They were part of how the event was being framed as something *above* politics, and thereby belonging to the nation as a whole. Yet, I don't want to dismiss these words too quickly either. What *is* this insistence that 'I'm not political', so eager to refute? What does it acknowledge and yet refuse to say? What if this statement indicates how so many people go about being political, suggesting the very terrain we need to address for thinking resistance? That is: that being political often involves going along with something, nodding and refusing to interrupt the consensus.

We expect politics to be about conviction, strong feelings, purpose and action. But on this day, people simply described to me how this would fit into the general pattern of the day. What if a great part of being political is going along with something to keep a domestic situation intact? Or deciding to back something because no other ways of articulating a felt experience seems readily available? This account of politics is not animated by an account of a better land that we can get to, or a common identity. It is politics as a process of figuring it out amongst the compromises, histories, desires, disappointments, laughs,

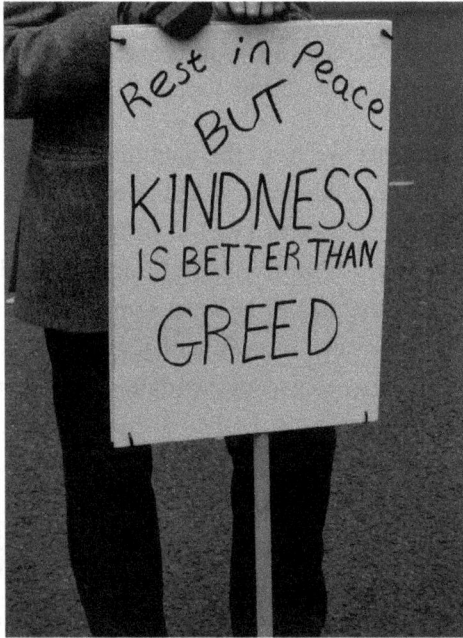

Figure 5. A moment of resistance. Baroness Margaret Thatcher's funeral, 17 April 2013. Photograph by the author.

thrills and multiple obstacles of everyday life. But if so much of political life takes places through happenstance, a relationship, or a community of feeling, then this also suggests that the possibilities for resistance are more plural, multiple and frequent than we might imagine them to be. More than conviction, this is politics at the register of tipping the balance in one way rather than the other (Figure 5). Thinking in these terms makes it possible to begin thinking about power as less all-embracing and mighty, revealing openings for resistance.

Doing something

One person standing alongside with me was very specific about his political allegiance to Thatcher. He said: 'Politically, I'm a libertarian not a Tory. I'm a fan of Thatcher but not the Tories. I've come down from Colchester. I came here because I admired her as a woman.' This account confounds a politics that wants to organize political positions into the 'left' and 'right'. But the refrain about her womanhood, as something superseding disagreement, was persistent. Other comments involved saying how they admired her strength and her determination to 'do something':

You either love her or you hate her don't you. But at least she got something done.'

'She was not to be bossed around by the men. She was there to do something. I don't agree with everything she did but I admired her.'

Again, in these comments we hear the shuttling back and forth between acknowledging and denying the political nature of the event. Lauren Berlant describes this as an enduring hope that we *will* arrive at an authentic connection through politics.[56] Certainly, I heard calls for a more 'immediate, seductive or binding' politics on this grey day in London: something that can lift us from an ordinary life to a better state, something that can offer us redemption. But haunting the comments about conviction, strength, determination was the sense that *people already knew* these desired solutions mostly disappoint and that big promises often have violent outcomes. Is this not part of what is being said when we insist that 'we don't agree with everything that she did'?

Accounts of politics as strong actions and which rely on the fiction of self-sufficiency is enough to put many off politics ('I'm not political'). However, these narratives from the street are combined with ordinary desires and pull factors – to interrupt the day, to dwell in memories, to follow someone else who wanted to do something, or to look to people that we find to be more extraordinary than ourselves. These ordinary affects are assembled 'out of forms, flows, powers, pleasures, encounters, distractions, drudgery, denials, practical solutions, shape-shifting forms of violence, daydreams, and opportunities lost or found'.[57] As a form of *politics*, they are 'hard to grasp'.[58] They nevertheless confirm the plural, affective, often contradictory reasons *why* people find themselves part of political and populist movements. For all the work that goes into maintaining the coherency and grandeur of a national fantasy, it seems that it often, simply offers a distraction.

'55 Funerals'

Performance artist Tim Etchells is interested in troubling the narratives that we associate with Thatcher. Etchells is artistic director of the performance group, Forced Entertainment, who are based in Sheffield, England. His work, '55 Funerals' formed a response to Thatcher's death which engaged with the refrains, memories, histories, slogans and images that circulated as part of her government, and which returned under austerity. This work formed a text that was available to download on the day of her funeral, only. It formed part of a larger work called *Vacuum Days*, a series of absurd, playful and political announcements, initially published every day throughout 2011.[59] Styled as 'a kind of Dadaist yearbook', *Vacuum Days* is organized around various events that took place in 2011, ranging from the royal wedding of Prince William and the Duchess of Cambridge, to the triple disasters of the earthquake, tsunami and ensuing failure of the Fukushima Daiichi nuclear power plant on 11 March in Japan, the killing of Osama bin Laden by the US Navy SEALs on 2 May and the rioting in English cities that summer.[60] *Vacuum Days* featured a mixture of absurd, offensive and fantastic announcements, forming a 'distorted process of call and response with unfolding political situations and events'.[61] '55 Funerals' follows in the same style: it absorbs the key words, figures, styles, gestures, catchphrases that we associate with Thatcherism and scrambles them to generate an alternative affective encounter at the time of her death. As such, it forms an especially apt work for considering the relationship between affect, politics and resistance.

'55 Funerals' engages the event of Thatcher's funeral using the technique of political announcements. Etchells borrows some of the 'figurations' associated with Thatcherism, but turns up the volume on them, distorting them to make them appear strange and grotesque, as well as to force new images and meanings. The announcements reference key images and symbols, including Port Stanley (in the Falkland Islands or Malvinas), miners, emphysema, economics, class war, greengrocer's daughter, North/South divide, Pinochet, poll tax, privatization, the Irish Republican Army (IRA), riots. These are cut and pasted together in unexpected ways, designed to provoke a new encounter (Figure 6). They also include directions about colour, music and shapes. Each announcement closes with the words, 'NO FLOWERS'. Overall, this work is interesting for thinking about the relationship between affect and politics because it does not engage the political through opposition (although Etchells's anti-Thatcherist politics is clear). Here, resistance is not framed within a register of agency, purpose or conviction. Rather, Etchells demonstrates how embedded we all are in the refrains, images and desires of the nation and neoliberalism – the point that 'we're all Thatcherites now'. Rather than frame resistance from a spatial position that purports to be outside Thatcherist politics, it acknowledges how these attachments, structures of feeling and ways of organizing the relationship between present and future are part of us. '55 Funerals' suggests that Thatcherism has to be resisted at this affective register.

The project works with the affective force of words, images, slogans and rhythms that congealed around this national event. Etchells's methods are thus

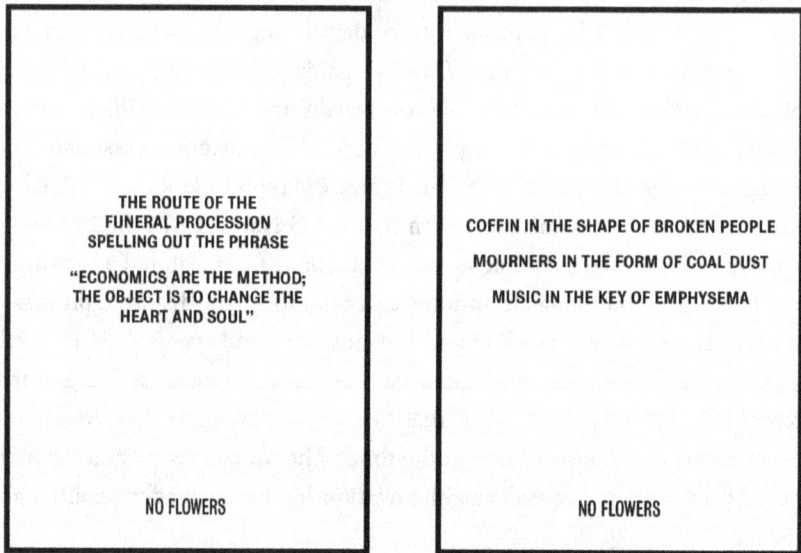

| THE ROUTE OF THE FUNERAL PROCESSION SPELLING OUT THE PHRASE "ECONOMICS ARE THE METHOD; THE OBJECT IS TO CHANGE THE HEART AND SOUL" | COFFIN IN THE SHAPE OF BROKEN PEOPLE MOURNERS IN THE FORM OF COAL DUST MUSIC IN THE KEY OF EMPHYSEMA |
| NO FLOWERS | NO FLOWERS |

Figure 6. 'Economics are the method'. Sample material from '55 Funerals'. Photograph from the work of Tim Etchells.

to some extent aligned with those of the media, in particular the process of pickup and affective amplification.[62] As Etchells puts it:

> Often I was trying to grab the hyperbolic language of the media space – amplifying its blood-lust, its desire for spectacle, its thirst for drama and suffering. The project wanted to turn up the volume on all of those things.[63]

However, in contrast to forms of resistance that are concerned with revealing these as 'common sense' or getting to see their 'true meanings', Etchells takes them, mashes them up and presents them again in new and provoking ways. In doing so, he says that the project shares something with that desire to shout at the television. In a comparative example, Scott Sharpe, J-D Dewsbury and Maria Hynes discuss how the comedian Stewart Lee uses repetition to produce differences. As they put it: 'repetition is 'the mechanism for the production of difference'. 'The richness of the situation … is increased, and divergences created.'[64] For example, in repeating the slogan 'MAKING BRITAIN GREAT AGAIN', Etchells invites us to appreciate the ridiculous incongruity of this claim. Because the announcements are also written to be performed, they are written in a way that slows down the message, emphasizing how claims of greatness have been used to destroy people and places: 'THE ROUTE OF THE FUNERAL

PROCESSION SPELLING OUT THE PHRASE "MAKING BRITAIN GREAT AGAIN"'.

The arbitrary ideas, words, images and rhythms that compose the affective life of a nation are always bubbling 'near the surface of contemporary life'.[65] This is why they appear 'banal'. But these 'background' refrains are also anything but: they are central to the process of authority establishing its own authority. In positioning himself *beside* them, to echo Sedgwick, and working with techniques including repetition, amplification, noise and juxtaposition, Etchells's approach moves beyond questions about how such 'lies' might be believed to consider how these ideas, refrains and figures are embedded and enmeshed in our everyday lives and form part of how we have come to understand who we are.

Etchells acknowledges the felt intensities of these memories, words and images and projects them in different directions, sending them awry. In working on the 'soft tissues of affect, emotion, habit' this work challenges an unreflective, nostalgic account of the 1980s.[66] '55 Funerals' also suggests that none of us are able to stand outside of the affective force of these structures of feeling, but that they might be interrupted to generate an alternative political response. In this sense, Etchells shows how we might 'work experimentally to alter the machine'.[67] In resurrecting, and distorting these materials, 'affective amplification' is being used to 'change how people experience what potentials they have to go and to do'.[68] What we can take from this work is a sense of the playful ways in which affective forces can be steered and reworked as they circulate, altering a sense of what seems possible politically.

While '55 Funerals' demonstrates how affects can be worked on and amplified, this is not to say that they are forces that can be trained, manipulated and directed. In contrast to the idea of the agent that manipulates emotions, Etchells weighs into the circulation of affects with little appetite or capacity to command. This form of interruption is better aligned with the view that change takes place anyway, that power is more fragile than we assume, 'tied more to contingencies than necessities'.[69] Put another way, he is not directing the event but 'semi-conducting' it.[70] However, unlike a television anchor whose role in covering national events is to amplify national affects, Etchells's role is to interrupt and distort the signal. Critically, this is not a form of politics concerned with fostering oppositional affective feelings. In contrast, Etchells works *with* ideas about Britishness, ceremony, music, rhythms – but with the aim of distorting the expected conventions, meanings and connotations. This performance does oppose Thatcherism, but rather than present politics as involving coherent accounts of conviction, it affirms the arbitrary jumble of practices that keeps power in place, how these are full of ambivalence and open to change and distortion.

Against the politics of conviction

'What do you think this is about?' he said.

'Ireland'.

He nodded. And I want you to understand that I'm not shooting her because she doesn't like the opera. Or because you don't care for what in sod's name do you call it – her accessories. It's about Ireland, only Ireland, right?

'Oh I don't know', I said.

'You're a bit of a fake yourself, I think'.[71]

In this extract from Hilary Mantel's short story, *The Assassination of Margaret Thatcher*, two characters discuss the different reasons why someone might want to kill the then prime minister. However, the reasons do not seem to matter, or rather, they keep slipping away in the course of the dialogue. In the exchange, the would-be assassin presents the 'cause' of injustice: 'Ireland'. However, this is shadowed by all sorts of seemingly trivial, affective, everyday life worlds that threaten to undo what should be a straightforward action: killing Thatcher. The would-be assassin presents many other reasons for his anger: 'three million unemployed',[72] her 'fake femininity', 'the way she loves the rich', 'her philistinism'.[73] However, in the course of chatting and waiting with the woman whose flat he has arrived at in order to carry out the attack, he begins to hesitate. She has let him in thinking he's the plumber, then thinking he's a cameraman, who has arrived to take a shot of Thatcher:

'How much will you get for a good shot?'

'Life without parole', he said.

I laughed. 'It's not a crime.'

'That's my feeling'.[74]

In this humorous exchange, Mantel introduces doubt in the idea that there is 'another society, another way of thinking, another culture, another vision of the world' that can *straightforwardly*, or in one fell swoop replace the horrors of this world.[75] As they wait around, and 'the hours stretched ahead',[76] Mantel teases out the broader textures and affects of political life – desire, indifference, inaction, comfort and discomfort. None of these are 'comprehensible within the strong idioms through which politics is meant to be practiced'.[77] But in this short exchange, Mantel suggests these are also part of the fabric of political life, as doubt is introduced into an otherwise adversarial account of politics.

In this chapter, I've argued that thinking against Thatcher involves moving beyond an adversarial model of politics to consider how political life takes place at this everyday register. Seen as emblematic of strong political action, and as engendering transformative and irreversible change, Thatcher galvanizes ideas about power and resistance as springing from different sites and involving 'us and them'. I have argued that these ideas, heard around Thatcher's funeral, remain persistent. However, Thatcher's death and the event of her funeral offers an opportune moment for asking: what does it mean to think about politics without the haunting image of 'strongly resistant action in the idiom of political agency as it is usually regarded'?[78] What is at stake if such accounts miss forms of resistance already taking place?

Ideas about individuality, animatedness, heroism and redemption infuse the ways we think about politics – and resistance. These themes return in Chapters 3 and 4, where I address how the nation comes into view in response to terrorist attacks and in relation to a refugee crisis. To conclude this chapter, I have sought to bring to the fore more ambiguous accounts for why people turn out for national events or align themselves with one 'cause' or another. In leaving aside ideas about heroism, leadership and actions, I have tried to think through the minor ways in which people are moved politically or find themselves aligning with various structures of feeling. Doing so allows us to appreciate how political identities, positions and ideologies are never as all-encompassing as they may seem. Listening closely to how people live and what they have to say suggests other accounts of being political and of how people might yet resist domination.

Interlude: A night at the cinema

Later in the year that I moved house, I was invited by a new friend to the cinema. An independent arts centre was showing *In This World* – a film by Michael Winterbottom. The film follows the treacherous journey made by a father and son from Pakistan to the UK. They were showing it to raise money towards refugee support groups in Samos, Greece, as well as people living in Aleppo, Syria, which had just been heavily bombed. The room was packed. We sat in close proximity sharing sofas made from used wooden pallets. We had all been persuaded to attend in the hope we could *do something* in response to this humanitarian emergency, and the largest forced movement of people since the Second World War.

The film is harrowing, as you might expect. But we liberal-minded audiences are used to being shocked in these ways. People were also keen to stay after the film and ask – what could they do? The team organizing the evening had arranged that a father from Syria, recently arrived in the city through the UK Syrian Vulnerable Persons Relocation scheme would speak about his own journey from Syria, via Calais to Swansea. He spoke eloquently and gently, but as the minutes rolled on, his young children started climbing up his legs, eager for the seriousness to end so they could get back to playing. So far, we had been able to locate the problem as something happening far away. We could return to our homes angry about the world but comforted that we were good citizens. But I'm sure I was not alone in feeling discomfited by the jarring experience of watching horror on the screen and then 'meeting' this family.

It must also have been a strange – and not untroubling experience – for him, his wife and young children to be introduced to this earnest audience. But what stayed with me for months after this evening was how fragile the generous feelings about *doing something* were. For although all of us had willingly decided to turn up, and pay our entry fees accordingly, what emerged in the discussion after the screening was disagreement. Once the family had shared their experiences, we were asked by the organizers whether we could donate large items such as ovens and carpets to other families who had just arrived in the city. It was at this point that the atmospheres in the room began to shift. One person in the audience said that she had also been saving for new household items and was still waiting for her landlord to make repairs. Amongst this great desire to be generous, questions emerged about why 'poor nomads' should be prioritized over 'poor residents'.[1] How had we moved from such good will to what felt like borders hardening in various microscopic ways?

In leaving the cinema, I felt irritated with myself for not saying something. I was a university lecturer teaching migration, national identity and global politics. How could I have nothing to say? And yet, who was going to listen to someone 'from the university', telling other people what to think?

In This World is part of a genre of films that claim we only need to see more horror to be moved to act. But at what point does good will tip into rejection, keeping the stranger in need at bay? How does generosity, and an eagerness to think of Europe as a place of sanctuary, tilt back into the idea that we have an obligation to 'our own kind' first? William Walters and Barbara Lüthi argue that there are risks in relying on 'the idea that exposing scenes of violence and domination to a public will generate movements of reform'. They claim that such exposure can have the opposite effect: that is, it can 'serve to fuel the border spectacle', further entrenching ideas about 'us and them'.[2] This complements Emma McCluskey's point that practices of security are often 'intertwined with notions of hospitality, generosity, and even solidarity'.[3] The imaginative geographies of 'us and them' were not initiated by this film, but they may have been oxygenated by it. What emerged was the fine balance between feeling shocked, jolted, and moved to do something, and feeling overwhelmed, sickened and inclined to return to more comforting norms of belonging.

Most accounts of global politics tell us that borders are marked on the ground. But they also emerge in our minds, guts, nerve endings and in the energies that pass between us. Nevertheless, the lines that crystallized on this evening were not as sharp and clear cut as theories of world politics might suggest.[4] The presence of this family in the room jarred with representations of victims on the screen. The family spoke for themselves and did not expect charity. It wasn't possible for us, the audience, to wallow in feeling outraged or sad for too long. Someone needed to decide who would sort through the donations, and drive items to people that needed them. Hands shot up, people moved around the room, swapping phone numbers and addresses. One person was introduced to another and they suggested more ways they could contribute. While the film had invited strong and often unequivocal emotions of outrage, shame and guilt, as these ebbed, the generous as well as 'ugly feelings' that emerged were less coherent and more ambivalent.[5] While politically, the film left many of us feeling blocked, the act of gathering people together and allowing disagreement led to new openings. Stuff happened, connections were made and people got on with it.

What I encountered at the cinema was an atmosphere of discomfort, but it involved 'multiple senses and experiences',[6] and led to political closures as well as openings. This was not resolved with a cathartic sense of political action.[7] However, it led to conversation, movement, energizing those that wanted to think more creatively about ways of acting. Ultimately, it initiated something different from the 'certainty of despair',[8] as the writer Rebecca Solnit describes it. In the politics of discomfort, there was 'room to act'.[9] Yet no doubt, the feelings of generosity, altruism, and open-mindedness were fragile. It was easy to tip the balance in another direction.

How do we work on atmospheric thresholds that include the impulse both to give and to refuse? How do we, in circumstances such as these, contribute in ways that tip the balance in favour of empathy? What preoccupied me following this evening was how the *same* people who had questioned giving to 'them', later mucked in, collecting used clothes. People's behaviour jarred with the ways academics talk about political standpoints and points of view – as though these are fixed stances that belong to people who are consistent and constant. What I learned was that sometimes, ideas about 'us and them' travel lightly, and fail to stick. Such ideas can be *diffused* and *destabilized* This in turn suggests different modes of intervening to the work of *exposing, proving* or *explaining* a political reality.

Chapters 3 and 4 explore more experiences of discomfort, in relation to responses to the 2015 Charlie Hebdo attacks in Paris and the European refugee crisis. In both chapters, I seek a different way of engaging and understanding the politics of action.

3

Mourning and the transversal geographies of terror

In response to the shooting of twelve people at the Charlie Hebdo magazine offices in Paris, France on 7 January 2015, which was followed by the police killing two suspects on 9 January 2015,[1] the digital hashtag #jesuischarlie circulated between several social media platforms, including Twitter and Facebook. In sharing the hashtag, users expressed their affective solidarity with those killed. By 'tweeting in alliance',[2] they affirmed a view of themselves as belonging to a community in mourning for others in distant places. But they also performed a sense of community that marked themselves as different from the enemy. The imaginative geographies of 'us and them' emerged through this hashtag, echoing ideas that had been widespread and vociferous in response to the events of 9/11 more than a decade earlier.[3] For example, expressions of empathy travelled alongside hostile, historical and colonial ideas about what makes 'us' European, and different from those that do not share the same values. Such ideas have effects, as can be gleaned in the heightened abuse and harassment experienced by Black and Arab minorities in the aftermath of these attacks.[4] This chapter addresses these national affects of 'us and them', where empathy and grief combine with ideas about advanced and peaceful societies in opposition to their colonial others. I want to argue that these ideas reveal a dominant national frame that comes into view in response to terrorist attacks. In reading two novels written in response to other instances of terrorism, Chapter 3 explores the resources necessary for developing a different politics of grief, compassion and belonging.

Writing in response to the *Charlie Hebdo* attacks, Tariq Ali argues that what was significant about the #jesuischarlie hashtag was that it became almost obligatory – that we were almost compelled to share it.[5] This echoes the context following 11 September 2001 when declaring love for America also became almost obligatory.[6] In 2015, #jesuischarlie was accompanied by images of people

Figure 7. A broken pencil at a temporary site of memory, Paris, 31 January 2015. Photograph by Rhodri Davies.

holding pens and pencils (broken and unbroken) in the air, and with home-made pencils left at temporary memorial sites (Figure 7). Placed together with the #jesuischarlie hashtag, these images of pencils made a uniquely European statement about the value of 'free speech', and about Europe as a place where journalists should be able to write freely without fear of reprisals. This may sound like a straightforward demand, even a moment when Europe rediscovered some of its founding values. These attacks took place in Paris after all – capital of the principles of *liberté, equalité* and *fraternité*.[7] However, 'free speech' also became a way of marking distinctions between 'us and them': less to do with questions of writing, publishing and the circulation of ideas than a way of animating racialized distinctions.[8] Tariq Ali's point about how this hashtag became almost obligatory is important because it highlights what is at stake in the affective atmospheres that follow violent events that get described as terrorism. As Judith Butler remarks in relation to the aftermath of the 11 September 2001 attacks, atmospheres of 'heightened nationalism' matter because they make it more difficult to voice critique, and to question the frame that suggests people must choose between 'civilization and terrorism'.[9] Indeed, in this case, it became difficult to raise critical questions about who gets to feel that they belong in Europe and embody Europe's values.

Accordingly, this chapter examines how responses to terror are typically articulated within a national security frame, which affirms the unity of the people against an enemy, and civilization against difference.[10] Terrorist events and matters of security often get framed as outside of, or beyond, the 'normal' political realm, thereby legitimizing a unique and exceptional set of policy and media responses.[11] We find ourselves part of these dominant framings when we suddenly feel compelled to express our solidarity as a nation. The chapter begins by discussing critiques of this national frame by Jenny Edkins and Athena Athansiou before turning to Saba Mahmood's work, to ask what, in these expressions of grief, do we remain unable to hear? By foregrounding affect, the chapter pivots around developing another understanding of personhood, which rejects ideas of self-mastery and sovereign will. In this regard, the chapter turns to two novels that develop an alternative response to terrorism from the perspective of the atmospheres of everyday urban life to yield other accounts of subjectivity. The two novels I turn to, Hanif Kureishi's *The Black Album*, set in 1980s London, when the Thatcher government was at war with the Irish Republican Army, and Teju Cole's *Open City*, set in New York in the aftermath of 9/11, generate other understandings of being and belonging, drawing on the urban landscape. These complement Saba Mahmood's call that we investigate other structures of affect, beyond the dominant forms made available. I go on to argue that this allows us to develop a different ethical response to terrorist events, through a transversal geography that connects different histories of suffering and of violence, offering another perspective to the national frame.[12] It also questions the relationship between acknowledging violence, extending sympathy, and responding politically and ethically. Overall, the chapter draws on resources offered by these novels, as well as on theories of urban life, to develop the possibilities of a different ethical response to terrorism.

Mourning and the national frame

The national affects that unfolded in Europe in response to the 2015 Charlie Hebdo attacks were unique not only for how a national frame came into view, but also for how European ideas about identity articulated through colonial logics were reanimated. This was evident in the motif of the pencil, the #jesuischarlie hashtag and in striking images such as that of a photograph of European and world leaders marching through Paris on 11 January 2015, in a public demonstration of 1.6 million people – reported to be one of the largest public demonstrations in Paris since the end of the Second World War – all holding a banner with the word 'Charlie' written on it. The images reinforced the idea of a common European public standing against an enemy.

Mustafa Dikeç writes that, at the time, it was hard not to feel moved by 'the extraordinary mobilisation of citizens'. Yet, the horrors of what had happened should trouble us enough 'to inquire about the conditions that made such a mobilisation of hate possible'.[13] The events raised questions about how grief and mourning can work in alliance with ideas about Europe as a site of civilization, mobilizing ideas about 'us and them', even when the very aims are to contest violence.

In her sustained engagement with trauma and the politics of memory, Jenny Edkins demonstrates how the dead routinely get co-opted into nationalist narratives.[14] For example, she discusses the difference between practices of remembering that use commemoration to tell a story about the founding of the state, and practices that are more 'insurrectionary and counter-hegemonic'.[15] She offers several examples of sites of memory that tell both an official story, and also a counterhegemonic story about war. For example, in her reflections on the Cenotaph Memorial in Whitehall, London, built as a memorial to the Great War of 1914–18, Edkins describes how the ceremony held in the UK on Remembrance Day – 11 November – around the Cenotaph is today a formal event in the national calendar, but that it was not always so. The memorial was originally designed to be plain, rather than ostentatious, signalling that this was no celebration of war. And while the original plans intended for the memorial to be moved to a London park, it became such a popular site that it was kept in the middle of the city. For Edkins, its location signals its potential in keeping open the question of how we commemorate victims of war and violence. It forms 'a point around which Londoners and tourists endlessly circle in the course of their daily business ...'.[16] In contrast to how the nation remembers its dead by placing them in a well-rehearsed historical timeline, with the effect of closing those stories from further interrogation, Edkins uses the example of the Cenotaph to consider how memorials can operate as 'a hindrance that reminds us of the impossibility of closure'.[17] Sites of memory can therefore contest self-certain narratives of national unity.

Arguing in a similar theoretical vein, but drawing on a very different moment, Athena Athansiou recounts the extraordinary work of the 'Women in Black' movement, which was organized in Belgrade during the time of the Yugoslav wars in the 1990s. Like Edkins, Athansiou highlights how practices of remembrance tend to work within a latent national frame, and are often based upon ideas about gender, kinship and national normativity.[18] However, 'Women in Black' used a different language from that of national belonging. Firstly, they wore black to show grief not only for their 'own side' but to remember *all* victims: 'We wear black because people have been thrown out of their homes, because women have been raped, because cities and villages have been burnt and destroyed.'[19] Secondly, in gathering in public space to demonstrate their mourning, they claimed that as a space of difference rather than identity, as an: 'inconvenient plurality as opposed to absolutist homogeneity'.[20] Thirdly, they reclaimed the language of victimization, through which women are usually situated as silent and subdued mourners. In contrast, 'Women in Black' performed motherhood in terms that refused their co-optation as nurturers of the nation.[21] Drawing on the work of Judith Butler and Saba Mahmood, among others, Athansiou casts this as a non-sovereign form of political agency.[22] The courage shown by the 'Women in Black' movement challenges the familiar terms of response to loss in times of war, and operates outside narratives of heroes and victims. They trouble the familiar accounts through which lives are made grievable. As Athansiou argues, this is important because grief is often fetishized by sovereign power as *the* form of 'intimate sociality' that legitimates patriotisms and familialisms.[23] This is relevant because it shows us how ideas about grief and mourning are deeply intertwined with ideas about a national society.

What is relevant and far-reaching about Athansiou's argument is that the 'Women in Black' movement presented not only a challenge to nationalist responses to war and suffering, but also to 'liberal sensibilities'.[24] That is, she ties her critique of nationalism to ideas about individuality and freedom as constituted through 'self-mastery and sovereign will'. This is relevant because – as we see in the response to the Charlie Hebdo attacks, ideas about 'us and them' combine with ideas about liberal freedom. Atmospheres of response to terror bring to the fore not only powerful ideas about a united community, but also colonial ideas about personhood, citizenship and what makes us modern.[25] In the next section, I consider these latent ideas about modernity and citizenship further.

What are we able to hear?

The anthropologist Saba Mahmood articulates an original response to another moment of violence and tension in Europe when claims about a constitutive difference between Christianity and Islam were again in the air. She writes in response to the 2005 (and 2008) Danish Cartoon controversies, when depictions of the prophet Mohammed were published by the Danish newspaper, *Jyllands-Posten*, and then reprinted by Norwegian newspaper *Magazinet*, as well as by

Charlie Hebdo and *Liberation* in France. It is considered highly offensive in Islamic cultures to visually represent the Prophet,[26] and the publication of these cartoons in 2005 prompted large protests in many Muslim majority countries as well as across Europe. Mahmood's critique focuses specifically on the political response to the publication of these images, which in many ways mirrored that of the aftermath of the Charlie Hebdo attacks in January 2015. This is because, in both cases, there was a focus on ideas about 'free speech' and on 'European values'. What she argues is that this response demonstrated a failure to understand the texture of hurt felt by Muslim communities in response to the publication of these images of prophet Mohammed.

Saba Mahmood's critique is powerful because it highlights our enduring, limited understanding of religious attachment in public life in Europe as well as in the social sciences.[27] She articulates how cultural and religious experience is not represented in the well-meaning political categories made available for it. For example, Mahmood argues that framing religion as a *choice* suggests an inability to address religion and faith as particular forms of affective attachment, and in turn, the form of injury being narrated in the objection to the publication of these cartoons. Muslims objected to the publication of these images on the grounds that Islam strictly prohibits all images, pictures or depictions of Mohammed or any of the prophets. But as Mahmood explains, when Muslims felt injured at the publication of these photographs, it was not only because a law, rule or commandment had been breached. Rather, these images wounded an entire 'structure of affect, a habitus'.[28] Describing the events as 'blasphemy', a 'hate crime' or even 'racism' captures some elements of this controversy, but these terms also fail to capture a broader experience of what exactly had been hurt.[29] The point here is about how, in the battle of ideas between 'free speech' and 'religion', there is an inability to hear accounts of everyday faith, belonging and attachment. This is helpful for thinking about the responses to the Charlie Hebdo attacks with which I opened this chapter. This is because the speed with which people adopted and shared the #jesuischarlie hashtag meant there was little time to listen to the histories of offence caused by this magazine – which was thoughtlessly discounted when people adopted the hashtag or stood behind 'Charlie' banners. The responses were claiming that people should be allowed to live freely, but they were also making some ways of living and being European feel delegitimized, marginalized and silenced.

What I appreciate in Mahmood's critique is that she asks us to listen harder to these claims of injury. In the context of the 2015 Hebdo attacks, this might mean listening to the communities who are hurt and placed at risk when loud declarations of European identity as a predominantly Christian community gather pace. It might also encourage us to reflect on values we might take to be universal, secular and available to all who choose them, but which have their limits when it comes to acknowledging and reflecting the plural structures of affect that compose European cities today.[30] Mahmood locates her critique within a broader problem, and that is, of how under modernity, questions of religion are cast out of the sphere of aesthetic experiences compatible with modern citizenship and national identity. Under modernity, religion is given the status of a value or special interest. In assuming this status, we fail to appreciate forms of cultural and religious feeling and attachment. For example, in interviews with people about their personal responses to the published images of the prophet, one respondent describes them as more painful than if someone had mocked his closest family. Mahmood argues that we are largely unable to hear these experiences of injury, because they indicate a community of sense that is rendered out of joint with modern citizenship. This confirms Madeleine Fagan's argument that many conceptions of ethics include 'an occlusion of otherness' where ideas about morals, and about our identities as 'civilized societies', leave us unable to hear other experiences.[31] There are, however, other experiences of intimacy, community and belonging at work under modernity, and many of those alternatives are captured and articulated in narratives of urban life. The next section turns to two novels set within a particular tradition of writing about the urban condition, positioned at the edges of liberalism, which pluralize questions about what it means to belong.

Urban atmospheres: Reading *The Black Album*

How might a focus on the affective atmospheres of urban life rework and redraw the imaginative geographies of 'us and them'? Matthew Gandy argues that theorists of urban life have long written about the non-visible but nevertheless formative register of an atmosphere.[32] For example, Georg Simmel's idea of a 'nervous life' suggests some of the atmospheric and bodily effects of fast-paced, multisensory life in the metropolis. Ash Amin and Nigel Thrift turn to Simmel to describe the urban landscape as a 'sensorium', a 'habitat' and a space of 'escalated atmospheres'.[33] For these authors, cities are identifiable by the atmospheric feeling of bodies pressed together and the swirl of colours, materials, smells and textures that press on the senses. Cities have an affective life, and significantly for our purposes, this has connections to ideas about how we understand who we are and come to know the world around us. Urban life suggests ways of being-with-others that defy images of bounded, autonomous subjects and instead affirms the ties between us, as well as the constitutive relationship between people and the material infrastructure of the city.[34]

The city's habitat and sensorium are key characters in Hanif Kureishi's *The Black Album*. This novel is set in late 1980s London when the Irish Republican Army (IRA) were in a violent struggle against the British state and Iran's Ayatollah Khomeini had pronounced a fatwa on the author Salman Rushdie, accusing him of blasphemy for his novel, *The Satanic Verses*. I turn to it for how it addresses the theme of a struggle between Western liberal values and fundamentalism – a theme that returns in the context of the Charlie Hebdo attacks. I want to offer a reading of this novel that departs from this dualistic framing to instead emphasize how a plurality of structures of affect come into view through urban life. What I pursue here is a reading that suggests the city's atmospheres contribute towards undoing the self-certain identity categories that come into view through the geographies of 'us and them'.

The novel takes its title from Prince's album of the same name and follows the life of Shahid Hasan, who lives in a bedsit in Kilburn, North-West London, in a house 'filled with Africans, Irish people, Pakistanis and *even* a group of English students'.[35] Shahid's story begins as he befriends Riaz, Chad and Hat: these are 'the first people he meets in the city, and the first people he recognises as "like him" and to whom "he didn't have to explain anything"'.[36] But one of these new friends, Riaz, also claims he sees Shahid as someone that he already knows. Riaz, it transpires, is seeking to build a world in his own image. This is not immediately a stifling experience for Shahid. But gradually Shahid seeks something other than the fundamentalism of identity politics. While Shahid is attracted to the group, he is also suspicious of this desire for purity. This belief in pure identities is mocked in a scene where the new friends go to a café that Riaz champions as a place where 'ordinary people' eat. This Indian café is situated 'between a Carribean wig centre and a Romanian restaurant', and Riaz tells Shahid that he 'will really feel at home' there. Shahid wonders how Riaz would know he would feel at home 'in a place with five Formica tables and screwed-down red bucket seats, all as brightly lit under white neon as a police cell'?[37] Riaz's celebration of an originary, pure and culturally distinct 'Indian people' is ridiculed by pointing to the 'ordinariness' of plastic tables, chairs and neon lighting.

Kureishi is well known for his persistent critique of different forms of fundamentalism. This leads Sara Upstone to admonish him for critiquing 'fundamentalist Islamism without recourse to alternative manifestations'.[38]

However, his account of fundamentalism is not confined to religion: family, is also considered fundamentalist. The city emerges as an archive of alternative manifestations of how we might live together. In contrast to the novel's characters, who can take on a didactic role, assuming a position in the battle between liberalism and fundamentalism, the city complicates the options, and unravels the cramped spaces that Shahid otherwise encounters. When he begins to want to escape his new friends, he says that: 'He figured it would be easier to get out, out of this whole thing, whatever it was, and disappear into the city'.[39] In the city, distinct and orderly ideas about 'us and them' become undone. In these moments, Kureishi reworks ideas about freedom as mastery to invoke what Athansiou calls 'non-sovereign forms of political agency'. These are forms of being together that are based on something other than purity or the certainty of a common story. For example, this is glimpsed through an image of a togetherness between strangers, which does not add up to a group that shares something in common. As Shahid comments in the aftermath of a bomb going off at Victoria station: 'The proximity of others comforted him: they all sat guarded, scared, wet. Such a tragedy was the closest a city like London could come to communal emotion'.[40]

The novel draws on experiences of urban life to develop alternative indexes of conviviality, including what Sarah Nuttall describes as 'stranger intimacy'.[41] Using the backdrop of the urban experience, Kureishi develops new vocabularies of connection and separation.[42] As Shahid learns to give up on dreams of purity and opt for an uncertain life with his on/off girlfriend Deedee, it requires him give up a belief in his own self-sufficiency: 'He had never relied on anyone before'.[43] This is not a pain-free process, and it requires a leap of faith on Shahid's part. However these new and emerging communities of sense represent something other than his sister-in-law Zulma's embrace of Thatcherism, or his mother's refusal to acknowledge that racism exists. Through the city, he encounters other ways of seeing and being in the world, reinforcing what he says he felt as a teenager on reading Malcolm X and Maya Angelou. Shahid's experiences of the city allow him to extend his initial instincts that belonging could involve something outside of the orders of intelligibility already made available for him.

Knowledge, certainty and ambivalence

Kureishi's *The Black Album* contrasts self-certainty and the desire for absolute knowledge, with ambivalence, uncertainty and doubt. This extends a long-standing theme in urban literatures, which celebrate and place a spotlight on

informal forms of knowing, including everyday tactics and improvisation.[44] For
example, as Thomas Blom Hansen and Oskar Verkaaik suggest, quintessential
urban figures – artists, taxi drivers, detectives, cops – all rely on unique skills
and unconventional knowledge bases.[45] Achille Mbembe and Sarah Nuttall
similarly highlight the figure of the black migrant worker in Johannesburg, for
whom 'nervous discomfort and improvisation became essential elements of a
tactical repertoire'.[46] As Ash Amin and Nigel Thrift argue, these urban accounts
of informal approaches to knowledge suggest an alternative archive for the social
sciences.[47] For example, the city rewards forms of knowing that involve 'sensory
and bodily perception, conversation and storytelling, memory and archive,
formal and informal expertise, symbolic and computational intelligence'.[48] Cities
involve and evolve from 'a science of different nervous systems'.[49] In contrast
to how the national atmospheres that emerge in response to terrorist attacks
travel with ideas about our own distinct identities, and self-certain ideas about
belonging to a unique cultural tradition that is distinct from a pre-modern
world, or a world that is external to Europe, cities reveal the value of everyday
diplomacy, adaptability, improvisation, transversal thinking, just as they also
present the art of working out how to live with others non-violently.

The city's dynamic pluralism seeps into Shahid. It provides over time the
conditions that allow him to trust other ways of being and knowing. In contrast
to the magnetic pull of a narrative of truth, as presented by some of his new
friends, another form of truth, and another relationship of care, materializes
through the urban atmosphere, as this quote captures:

> The problem was, when he was with his friends their story compelled him. But
> when he walked out, like someone leaving a cinema, he found the world to be
> more subtle and inexplicable.[50]

These urban atmospheres cannot be straightforwardly understood in
opposition to fundamentalism. Although liberal cosmopolitanism emerges in
this novel as a preferred alternative, it does not escape critique. For example,
Shahid's girlfriend, Deedee Osgood, personifies liberal cosmopolitanism, not
least in her position as a college lecturer. But this is not straightforwardly
presented as more progressive than religious belief. When Deedee discusses
Shahid's friends – Riaz, Chad and Hat – with him, she asks: 'Don't they scare
you?' He shakes his head and says: 'Some people have anger and passionate
beliefs. Without that nothing could get done'.[51] When she asks whether he
also feels angry and has passionate beliefs, he responds: 'The thing is, Deedee,
clever white people like you are too cynical … Why would you want to change

anything when you already have everything your way?'[52] While she is the
one with a string of university degrees, he emerges as the one that has lived.
Urban experience emerges as another form of knowledge while her cynicism
is presented as its own religion.

In this novel as in Kureishi's other works, what ultimately appears as the
opposite of fundamentalism is 'live culture' and imagination.[53] He describes a
live culture as 'our endless curiosity about our own strangeness and impossible
sexuality: [where] wisdom is more important than doctrine; doubt more important
than certainty'.[54] It is these qualities that Kureishi advocates. They emerge in *The
Black Album* through the depiction of London's urban atmospheres. But they
also emerge in his films, *My Beautiful Launderette* and *Sammy and Rosie get Laid*
(both directed by Stephen Frears, with Kureishi writing the screenplays). As the
film critic Leonard Quart argues, it is Kureishi and Frears's passion for 'ambiguity
and contradiction' that characterizes their collaborative style.[55] In the oppressive
context of 1980s Thatcherist Britain, the point here is that critique went beyond
positing a contrasting set of values, suggesting that we need only persuade and
educate others of our better morals. Rather, in these films, as in *The Black Album*,
there is no pure politics, and no set of good values that we can subscribe to. In
the films, the 'victims of racial prejudice and economic deprivation could, at
the same time, be either exploiters or barbaric racists' just as 'idealistic leftists
could espouse politics which are essentially rhetorical or futile, or become with
their ascent to power, murderers and torturers'.[56] The refusal to offer a story of
redemption is also reflected in the filming style, which makes use of 'split screen,
rapid, rhythmic cross-cutting, shock cuts ... to help disrupt our sense of order'.[57]
In this case, as in *The Black Album*, the geographies of 'us and them' are cut up
and scrambled to prevent simplistic ideas about one set of people holding one
set of values over another. Instead, we are left to make our way in acceptance of
the multiple imperfect options around us, and acknowledge our own complicity
in chains of violence.

Partial illuminations: Reading *Open City*

Teju Cole's *Open City*[58] forms a response to a different time of terror, and is
set five years after the events of 9/11. It follows the impressions and walks of a
flâneur, Julius, a Nigerian American that lives in New York. Unlike *The Black
Album*, where we follow the main character along a coming-of-age journey,
this novel has 'hardly any scenes, few characters, and no plot'.[59] Echoing a

modern theme, the mental life of the main character is reflected in and shaped by the environment of the city. What is similar to Kureishi's novel is that the urban experience presents another approach to subjectivity. For example, the novel offers images of togetherness informed by 'stranger intimacy', in contrast to a community held together by common values. These include reflections on the experience of 'standing with thousands of others in their solitude'.[60] Or how the birds play as much of a role in urban social life as other people, suggesting that being-with-others includes more than humans. In this novel, the urban experience again yields another approach to knowledge. For example, Julius talks about his habit of walking the city to offset his work at the hospital, where he is training to become a psychiatrist. His work at the hospital involves a 'regime of perfection and competence [that] does not allow for improvisation'.[61] But in contrast, his urban walks follow no particular direction. He can digress, get lost or repeat. The city becomes a site in which he can lose himself, a task that Rebecca Solnit describes as requiring being 'capable of being in uncertainty and mystery'.[62] This recalls Amin and Thrift's point about forms of knowing that draw on sensory and bodily perception, conversation and storytelling, memory and archive, formal and informal expertise. Overall, these combine to offer a different meditation on how we respond collectively to acts of terror.

Accordingly, this novel is best read as a series of cinematic encounters. Julius's first-person reflections move between questions about birds to taste in music, in a continuous process of cutting between different scenes. Using this style, Cole exploits the position of the detached, ambivalent flâneur to address the event of 9/11 from the side, rather than head on. Indeed, one of the significant stylistic aims of this novel is to keep the central event (9/11) at a distance. For example, through a conversation with Professor Saito, we encounter Saito's experiences as a survivor of a Second World War detention camp, suggesting how the novel juxtaposes different histories of violence. We then meet Julius's neighbour Seth, and Julius is shocked on learning that he did not know Seth's wife died months previously. These encounters exploit a familiar theme of the city as composed of a 'society of strangers'. But it also presents the possibility of an ethics of care that is 'decentred from considerations of interpersonal obligation and civic orientation'.[63] In contrast to forms of society based on familial obligation or a civic mission, which Ash Amin argues, are 'increasingly impossible to achieve in a hyperdiverse and fluid community',[64] the novel asks how we engage the ethical work of responding to different and ongoing histories of violence.

Through his encounters in the city, Julius learns about different moments from the past. Yet this relationship to remembering and forgetting takes a different form to that made possible by a national frame, which remembers 'our' country's people ahead of other people. As Sarah Nuttall and Achille Mbembe argue in relation to the memory of apartheid in Johannesburg, events are neither fully remembered nor fully forgotten; they emerge as traces or interruptions in the urban landscape. In this vein, the event of 9/11 reveals itself in the novel slowly, and without assuming a central focus. Unlike so many other 9/11 novels, in *Open City*, we encounter the site of the former World Trade Center quite late in the book, on page 52, and only in passing. Julius is sat in a restaurant near the site, and a stranger, Kenneth, starts a conversation with him. Kenneth wants to talk to Julius about his 'roots'. Julius tries to get away from this conversation, which is set on defining him by place. He therefore walks from the restaurant to the waterline and sees the Statue of Liberty and Ellis Island. Ground Zero, the site of the former World Trade Center, emerges into view, but significantly, it does so alongside these other histories, of migration, belonging and loss. On this walk, Julius also encounters the burial site for enslaved Africans, who died between 1690 and 1794 in Lower Manhattan.[65] Through these cinematic scenes, the event of 9/11 is remembered but also decentred from its position as the main history of suffering remembered. It takes its place among many different, and uneven, histories of violence made visible and invisible through this city.

The first encounter with the word 'terror' comes through an event taking place on the streets beneath his flat, where a crowd has gathered, and drums are beating. He listens from the window and hears the slogan: Women's bodies, women's lives, we will not be terrorized. 'I watched them, as their faces came in and out of the spotlight of the streetlamps'.[66] This comment about the spotlight is more than descriptive because it reflects Cole's approach in this novel: that is, different forms and histories of violence are brought into focus through partial illuminations, using what Michael Shapiro describes as a 'transversal eye' that juxtaposes various histories of suffering and terror.[67] This is instructive for social scientists who tend to approach crises through a single frame, rather than according to the ways crises intersect. It also suggests an alternative to a national frame that elevates a united subject responding to one event or a common enemy. Using a 'transversal eye', we are invited to address terror in relation to other ongoing atrocities, including the forms of violence implicit in ideas about 'us and them'. Cole experiments with this indirect approach by way of the distracted urban walker. A transversal eye allows us to question how some people's deaths are remembered more than others, and address the ethical possibilities of unravelling a national frame.

Transversal lines and the possibility of ethics

Cole's method, where different events are juxtaposed and partially illuminated, draws transversal lines to make connections.[68] *Open City* encounters different events through the city's atmospheres – which are constantly moving and shifting. This atmospheric approach suggests a perspective that does not order crises into a hierarchy. Rather, crises come in and out of focus. This approach takes us beyond the nation to consider the transnational geographies of violence and suffering. Against the almost obligatory expressions of grief and solidarity that emerge at some moments of crisis, and the silence around other histories of violence, Cole questions the overwhelming focus on, or full illumination of, some moments of suffering and asks what is the connection between complete knowledge and an ethical response. For example, in one scene, Julius goes to watch *The Last King of Scotland* (2006) at the cinema – a film about Idi Amin's reign of Uganda (1971–9). The film recounts the story of a young doctor from Scotland that goes to work for President Amin, and who becomes a witness to the unfolding horror of mass killings and violence. Julius tells us how he remembers spending hours watching *The Rise and Fall of Idi Amin* as a child, in a film where 'no detail was spared to present the callousness, insanity, and sheer excitement of the man'.[69] He says: 'we enjoyed the shock of it', and so they would watch the film again and again.[70] Cole tries to unpack how it is that horror emerges as something that we routinely disavow, such as in the command 'never again', and yet how we keep watching spectacles of violence. What does this desire to look at violence *directly* mean in terms of developing an ethical response?

> I wondered, as Coetzee did in *Elizabeth Costello,* what the use was of going into these recesses of the human heart. Why show torture? Was it not enough to be told, in imprecise detail, that bad things happened?[71]

In this moment at the cinema, as well as in the novel's circumambulatory style, Cole asks what difference it makes to address horror and violence directly, as opposed to indirectly and with a 'transversal eye'. This question, posed at the cinema, connects with the whole method of the novel, which experiments with approaching terror and violence through the perspective of a distracted, but sensitive urban walker. This approach offers another vantage point that connects different instances of suffering.

Teju Cole's novel addresses the event of 9/11 using a transversal eye, made possible by Julius's submersion in the city's atmospheres.[72] And Cole's method examines this event indirectly. Indeed, Cole has written about how it took him a long time to work out how to address this event in his writing, and how it involved working: 'Circumstantially, circumambulatorily. Still hesitant to get any closer'.[73] This circumambulatory approach to knowledge, drawing on the archive of urban life, offers an alternative ethical response to urban terror by expanding the frame of what we can see, to include transnational geographies and different histories. This ethical imagination, fostered 'through an indirect eye',[74] also questions what is achieved by the intensive attention given to some moments of terror and suffering. This is raised by juxtaposing some histories that get remembered with those that receive less attention, and by asking what does *knowing* achieve, when it leads only to confirm dominant ways of seeing the world as composed of civilized people and outsiders? By addressing different scenes of violence in passing, Cole achieves a refreshing encounter that questions some entrenched narratives. A circumambulatory approach asks us to question what we already claim to know, as the cinematic, atmospheric approach unravels ideas about 'us and them'. In developing a form of thinking moved by the affective atmospheres of the city, we shift from the ruminations of the main character to a critical reading of the world around us.

Approaching terror through the city

Writing in response to the events of 9/11, which became a global political crisis as the United States promised to retaliate through war, Jacques Derrida wrote that some responses to terror 'produce, invent, and feed the very monstrosity they claim to overcome'.[75] Examining 9/11 from both a psychoanalytical and a political angle, he argued that efforts to 'attenuate or neutralize the effect of the traumatism … be it through the police, the military or the economy – ends up producing, reproducing and regenerating the very thing it seeks to disarm'.[76] With these words, Derrida marks what is at stake in the popular responses to the 'Charlie Hebdo' attacks in 2015. While the rush to declare sympathy with those killed, injured and traumatized is well meaning and ethically important, this chapter shows how the politics of mourning also does other work. For example, declaring a common 'European' community serves to establish some people as insiders and others as outsiders. As this chapter has shown, a focus on urban atmospheres yields a perspective that can look across different forms, durations and instances of violence, and involving spectacular acts what passes as mundane or necessary uses of force. Adopting a 'transversal eye' allows us to ask what exactly is being declared when we share different hashtags, memes and profile pictures, as ways of declaring modes of belonging in a heightened context of violence such as that which followed the 'Charlie Hebdo' attacks? How might our responses to violence become complicit in the very forms of violence that we claim to object?

Urban writings have long generated alternative ideas about ways of being together. The two novels discussed here tell more complex stories than what can be shared in a hashtag or meme, understandably. But notably, they alert us to the risks of some vocabularies of response to terror when collective empathy, fear and shock become entangled with claims about a common European identity or civilization, standing against the other. Kureishi's novel, *The Black Album*, touches upon how oppressive a liberal outlook that imagines itself as free from cultural attachment can be. In that novel, the plurality of the city undermines self-certain viewpoints and identity positions. The urban air somehow supports him in investigating other ways of being-in-the-world. Yet this novel remains enamoured by the idea of a liberal individual that chooses his way in the world – a self-sufficient, detached way of living that feels alien to anyone walking the city with children in tow, or mindful of how their paths through the city are obstructed by stairs, potholes, traffic, a lack of elevators and everyday racism. In contrast, Saba Mahmood's work allows us to discuss how dominant affective responses to terror make it difficult to listen to other structures of affect and habitus. Responses to acts of terror demand reflection on European narratives about 'our' own values, sense of civilization and development. In contrast to the hashtags, cartoons, images, editorials and headlines that shored up the sense of a European identity that is different from the enemy, what is required is acknowledgment of the plural structures of affect that compose European cities today.

What I've unpacked in this chapter is how urban atmospheres make possible different ideas about being-with-others to those that harness ideas about a collective identity standing in mastery against an enemy. In *Open City*, which pivots around the figure of the urban flâneur and the city's rhythms, ideas about proximity and distance are reworked to draw transversal connections between different forms and moments of pain and suffering. This suggests another response to terror, one that responds to moral standpoint with doubt and asks questions about our own place in relation to violence. In decentring the event of 9/11, we address other histories of violence across this city as well as the geographies that connect us to violence in other parts of the world. While Kureishi pursues the ethical potential of doubt rather than certainty, Cole advocates a political standpoint of ambivalence. This is not an ambivalence to the horrors of the world. Rather, the scale of the horror is precisely why violence cannot be addressed directly. But this sideways, distant perspective reorients ideas about 'us and them', and invites us to consider our complicity in chains of exploitation and violence.

Finally, both these novels touch on how people find ways of carrying on and responding to violence through telling other stories. In 'The Word and the Bomb', Kureishi argues that 'in an age of propaganda, political simplicities and violence, our stories are crucial'. Firstly, because they form a way for the political to be interrogated, and secondly, because it is through stories 'that we can speak of, include and generate more complex and difficult selves'.[77] Indeed, it is because of our plurality that Saba Mahmood cautions against appealing to the state and its categories to resolve pain, fear and hurt. The state is unable to acknowledge plural experiences of living. While the narratives of 'us and them' posit the European subject at the centre of the world, a transversal geography looks across from here to there and remains uncertain when faced with the question of how we seek justice.

4

Vulnerability and the politics of action

As I write, thousands of migrants are being held in overcrowded camps in Greek islands. One of the camps, Moria, on the island of Lesbos, has in September 2020 suffered a devastating fire, leaving several thousand people living on the side of the road. Closer to home, and roughly fifty miles from my house, hundreds have gathered on a beach in Tenby, Wales, to demonstrate their welcome for new refugee families, and anger at news that these families will be housed in an army base camp, behind barbed wire.[1]

Six years on from the 2015 'refugee crisis', there are ongoing horrors, both far away and nearby. Knowing what to do and what might be the most effective way of acting in the face of these can often leave us feeling dizzy, frustrated and inadequate. Digital technologies offer new modes and genres of response and a need to feel 'compelled to act'.[2] But they also recall Susan Sontag's point about how images of suffering can rouse an emotional response and make us feel we 'ought to care more', while also making the possibility of change appear epic and hard to reach.[3] The wave of sadness and horror prompted by the publication of the image of Alan Kurdi on 4 September 2015,[4] whose small body was photographed lying face down on a beach near Bodrum, Turkey, was one such instance that made 'suffering loom larger'.[5] However, it also led people across Europe to take action by setting up cities and towns of sanctuary, establishing multilingual libraries,[6] taking theatre productions to the Calais refugee camp,[7] staging protests at football matches[8] or working as volunteers in Greek and Italian coastal towns and villages. The staggering inaction on the part of European governments and the European Council was met with thousands of creative actions in different localities, suggesting a range of different ideas about what it might mean to act politically.

This period of response to the 2015 'refugee crisis' in Europe[9] was therefore accompanied by many calls about wanting to *do something*. It demonstrates how responses to major political emergencies such as this one can energize and lead to a form of 'awakening'. However, such affective responses also have a specific temporal duration: they run out and people move on. They carry no guarantees in terms of what comes next. And as we explored in the last chapter, empathetic action can sometimes include its own forms of violence, suggesting a need to combine action with thought. For these reasons, this chapter addresses affective responses to crisis and their relationship to forms of political action. After all, beyond the visible and audible affects of anger and outrage, political work relies on a range of emotions and affects, including calmness, determination, the art of endurance,[10] and seeking enjoyment even in the most desperate and inhuman of situations. Yet the familiar ways in which we understand being political – speaking out or standing up, and putting ourselves in a position of discomfort, remain persistent.[11] In contrast to the figure of the heroic actor, this chapter considers what action might look like when we detach it from sovereign ideas about self-sufficiency and mastery.

While the dominant affects heard in response to the 2015 refugee crisis included anger, outrage, fear and hatred, these were not the only feelings shared. People also reported weak feelings and affects, which do not lend themselves to a clear direction, and where the relationship between the original cause and the ensuing feeling is less clear.[12] For example, the steady flow of images, glimpsed among the strains and distractions of everyday life over a number of years might incur different affects, including sadness and negativity, and involve a different temporality. Yet these 'weak affects' carry their own force, such as an amplified capacity to diagnose situations.[13] Accounts of political action as animatedness may therefore obscure other ways we pursue change in the world, such as by making ourselves present and staying alongside others, or by *enduring* long-term political work without becoming 'hardened, calloused and indifferent to life'.[14]

Given how ideas about action tend to presume an animated, detached, sovereign person, this chapter turns to the concept of vulnerability to ask how it informs other ways of being political.[15] The chapter unfolds through a discussion of some of the visual images that accompanied the 2015 refugee crisis, how these relied on powerful ideas about caring for others in distant places and substituted a national frame for an appeal to our common sense of humanity. However, the chapter argues that the distinctions drawn between proximity/distance, and a national/human community can be problematic. I argue that the work of responding critically and ethically to suffering needs to involve more than shifting the lens from the proximate to the distant, or from the national to the human scale. Both these methods can fail to challenge underpinning ideas about a sovereign actor and romanticized ideas about action that remain unavailable for most people. This chapter therefore navigates the terrain between the distant and the proximate, the national and the human, by way of a novel that addresses Brexit and the 2015 refugee crisis together: *Autumn* by Ali Smith. In discussing scenes from this novel, I look for ways of writing against animated ideas of action, and to present non-sovereign ideas about what it means to be political, swapping the image of the striving individual actor with the fact of our constitutive vulnerabilities and interdependence. Drawing on Judith Butler, Zeynep Gambetti and Leticia Sabsay's work on 'vulnerability and resistance' and Lauren Berlant's idea of 'crisis ordinariness', the chapter indicates alternative, non-sovereign accounts of political action that replace ideas about heroism, virility and getting from 'here' to 'there', with a focus on vulnerability, friendship, endurance, and small acts that involve courage and muddling through.

Crisis, nation, action

As we saw in the last chapter on responses to terrorism, crises bring the nation into view. They form moments when dominant ideas about who we are and how we relate to others are on display.[16] In August 2015, when scenes of people trying to cross the Mediterranean Sea on small unstable boats were repeatedly in the news, the then UK prime minister David Cameron spoke about people trying to 'break into our country', and in one interview, described the people attempting the crossing as a 'swarm'.[17] Charities and non-governmental organizations were quick to criticize Cameron for his dehumanizing language. Certainly, his language was dehumanizing, but it also served to remind us of another point: that is, how heightened attention to 'refugees' quickly takes us back to the 'national order of things', as Lisa Maalki argues.[18] In further explicating, and not apologizing, for using the word 'swarm' to describe this mass movement of people, Cameron reinforced an image of refugees as different and separate from 'the people' that belong to the political community. But whether it be through objecting to people crossing borders, or through the wish to rescue them, a 'refugee crisis' heightens ideas about 'us and them'.

Many critical scholars of migration question the definition of the 2015 refugee crisis as a 'crisis'.[19] They rightly argue that the use of 'crisis' can mask the regularity and persistence with which people die at the state's borders. For example, Peter Nyers reminds us that people have always moved or been forced to move across international borders: the history of refugeeness is diffuse and enduring.[20] Situations described as crises or emergencies are therefore interesting, in Nyers's view, because they reveal ideas about what we think the *norm* is. For example, we assume global politics conforms to a sedentary norm, where displacement forms but a temporary aberration.[21] The visual frame that posits people attempting to cross borders as a 'problem' naturalizes distinctions between 'citizens' and 'migrants', 'refugees' and 'locals'.[22] Indeed, as Lilie Chouliaraki and Tijana Stolic argue, visual representations of the 2015 refugee crisis contributed to this sovereign framing by working to 'massify, infantilise, or vilify refugees', through racialized snapshots of groups at a distance and close-ups of children, making possible regimes of empathy that cast people either as risky others or as others in need.[23] Kathy Burrell and Kathrin Hörschelmann concur that there was a 'benign and malignant power' to many of these images, which reanimated colonial legacies.[24] The images and narratives that emerged in shaping these atrocities into a 'crisis' therefore promoted a national frame, and projected 'a self-centred form of civic agency',[25] positing a political actor that was either able to or who refused to reach out to vulnerable others in distant places.

However, there are risks in positioning active citizens in opposition to vulnerable populations. For example, this can lead us to political responses grounded in pity, which Vicki Squire argues is limiting when this does not also 'challenge wider relations of privilege'.[26] Pity can dovetail with forms of 'pastoral caretaking', which is quick to 'support the innocent victims of migration, while [nevertheless] preventing the passage of criminal others'.[27] In this sense, a national frame supports a distinction between 'deserving' and 'undeserving' migrants.[28] While pity may bring together a community in feeling, it refuses to acknowledge the broader issue of state bordering practices, and the sovereign politics that makes it possible for us to distinguish between the 'deserving' and 'undeserving' person. To interrupt this national and hierarchical frame, I turn to the concept of vulnerability. Vulnerability means being capable of being physically or emotionally wounded. The populations attempting dangerous border crossings and living in temporary refugee camps where they are contained and divided are without doubt in extremely vulnerable situations.[29] But thinking about vulnerability is useful for developing an ethical and political response that potentially allows empathy without positioning the other as *lacking* in agency. It can adjust the framing through which we respond to the needs of others.

For example, focusing on our common – and yet highly uneven – vulnerabilities allows us to contest the presumption of 'animatedness' that is bound up with images and narratives of political action.[30] While the image of awakening to vigour and activity has its uses, being animated and active is not always an option for all people.[31] It suggests that states of drowsiness or numbness, which may form part of living with long-term pain, conditions of anxiety or structural and long-term precarity, cannot be compatible with doing politics. Ideas about political action therefore often carry a set of presumptions about able bodies and positive energies, which present their own forms of exclusion. In contrast, vulnerability suggests another consideration of personhood. As a concept for thinking politically, it takes us to literatures and debates on disabilities, the experiences of new mothers, situations of precarity arising from low-paid or insecure work, the experiences of populations described as migrants or refugees, and the situations faced by people living with long-term illnesses. These are vastly different life experiences, which sometimes also overlap. But as a framework, it allows us to consider people beyond their position as 'migrant' or 'citizen', and as inside or outside the nation. While 'pity' maintains a distinction between 'us and them', vulnerability suggests potential lines of connection.

Of course, vulnerability is also a risky category and feminist theorists are especially attuned to the risks of suggesting that a social group such as women (or migrants) are especially vulnerable.[32] Embracing a united, shared identity risks failing to acknowledge intersectional experiences of racism, disability, gender and sexuality. However, in contrast to using vulnerability to shore up and defend an identity, Judith Butler argues that vulnerability presents an opening towards considering the ties between us. In this case, we can consider all the different aspects of vulnerability, ranging from frailty to precarity and uncertainty.

Judith Butler, Zeynep Gambetti and Leticia Sabsay therefore ask us to stop treating vulnerability as a condition that needs to be *overcome* in order to act. For them, framing vulnerability in opposition to resistance presents a narrow consideration of what it means to be political. Recalling Sontag's sense of the epicness of suffering, it is only a giant of a person, with enormous reserves of emotional and structural support that can easily step forward and 'act' in times of crisis. We might say that one of today's challenges is working out how to keep acting when living under the enormous weight of heightened neoliberalisms, authoritarianisms, inequalities and the ongoing destruction of the environment. In thinking with Butler, Gambetti, Sabsay, we can ask: what does it mean to consider vulnerability as *part of the act* of resistance? How does changing our view of the subject of action change our view of what it means to be political? Butler, Gambetti and Sabsay argue that vulnerability requires rethinking ideas about the body 'as discrete, singular, and self-sufficient'.[33] When we begin with ideas of personhood as discrete and independent, we rely on a framework that begins with the separation of myself from the other. Instead,

Butler's understanding of personhood starts from the condition of being-with-others. This aligns with an affective approach that begins from the ties between us. For Butler, the condition of being social is fundamental and originary. The implication is that we are always part of the frame, and already involved and implicated, as witnesses, consumers, educators, citizens and neighbours.

Rather than adopt a linear equation then, where crisis invites action, vulnerability points to the ongoingness of crises. While the act of fleeing one's home and country, and traversing state borders necessarily puts people in emergency situations, and demands urgent responses, this does not always address what happens next. As scholars of migration Jennifer Hyndman and Wenona Giles argue, often when a crisis is out of the news, it is assumed that human suffering has ended, but this is not the case for populations described as refugees and asylum seekers.[34] People find themselves living in make-shift camps at the edges of a state's territory, as different governments refuse to identify long-term solutions. This is evidenced in the dozens of refugee camps in Greece today, funded by the United Nations High Commissioner for Refugees (UNHCR) and European Union, where people wait for years before being moved along to another temporary settlement. The capacity to bear such situations must call for enormous resilience, as well as mental, spiritual and physical resourcefulness. But as Hyndman and Giles put it, the term 'refugee' often strips people of these capacities and their identities as 'people who work, raise families, go to school, and live in communities of their own making', who laugh, play and build lives with others.[35] Centring vulnerability allows us to move from a framework that posits us as different from them to consider the ways our lives are entangled.

Distance/proximity and visualizing the 2015 refugee crisis

The photograph of the toddler Alan Kurdi that dominated the front pages of UK and European newspapers in September 2015 formed a 'rupturing moment' in the steady stream of images of people crossing the Mediterranean Sea.[36] The image of Kurdi (who died along with his mother and brother) was reproduced with the permission of his father. It was published in all the main UK newspapers and many of the newspapers across Europe; many more people encountered it as an image online – on a Facebook or Twitter timeline. However, as Debbie Lisle argues, photographs are not 'still objects' that deliver 'a static moment to the viewer'.[37] They are lively and take on new life and meanings in different contexts. What turned this photograph into a significant moment is that the photograph was shared again and again – it became one of those photographs of horror and suffering that we collectively agree needs to be seen, just as we also cannot bear to look.

On 1 February 2016, an image was released of the political artist Ai Weiwei lying face down, on an otherwise empty beach, dressed in a kagool and pair of trainers, in an image that restaged the image of Kurdi. This image was taken by Rohit Chawla, published in *India Today*, and shared widely via twitter.[38] It is a shocking image, and deliberately so. But it also raises a series of ethico-political questions. The photo asks us: does your empathy extend to me? Four months after the original image of Kurdi, are we still moved to act?

We are familiar with a framework that understands photographs as evidence, or as a true document of events. But this image of Weiwei disrupts such a framework as we know it is not a genuine image of suffering. Indeed, it may be that because it flaunts its *inauthenticity* that the image can also be read as uncaring. This restaged photograph – a familiar artistic technique – asks us to consider empathy and its limits. Most public commentaries on this photograph have focused on the question of whether it represents art or activism, whether it forms a justifiable political act or is unacceptable and repulsive. These are familiar questions and often applied to artistic work that emerges from crises, including this crisis. Take for example how the skeleton of a ship that sank on 18 April 2015 on route between Libya and Italy killing between 700 and 1,100 people was put on display at the 2019 Venice Biennale International Art Exhibition as a 'sombre reminder' of this horror.[39] Rather than focus on what category we should assign the work, we are better placed asking about the form of encounter staged between the photograph (or art work) and the embodied viewer, and therefore what the work does politically. The question to ask of these works is do they trouble or do they leave intact the dominant frameworks of response to crisis, including powerful ideas about 'us and them'.

While the original photograph of Alan Kurdi invites pity, empathy and horror, and the second photograph by Chawla invites outrage and disgust, neither leads us to 'connect the dots' between the passage that Kurdi's family made from Syria to Turkey, and the ways Europe allows free movement for some on the condition of keeping others out.[40] Neither photograph allows us to move much beyond a framework of passive victims and active agents. This dualistic framework is often applied to refugees, as the migration scholar Anne McNevin argues. Often, she says, a migrant is portrayed either as a 'bare life', or as exceptionally active, resistant and adroit. This framework avoids offering a fuller understanding that appreciates the multiple tensions that characterize migrants' struggles, and proceeds by acknowledging ambivalence.[41] McNevin's point complements Butler, Gambetti and Sabsay's efforts to explore ideas about subjectivity that surpass images of active agents or passive victims, allowing us to consider different forms of activism, resistance and endurance, involving both the people crossing borders and the people situated in witnessing them, assisting them, talking about them or welcoming them.

In swapping the subject of the original horrific image of Kurdi with an image of an adult man, the image of Ai Weiwei experiments with ideas about distance and proximity and seeks to bring the crisis closer. A similar method is employed in Weiwei's own extensive number of works in response to this crisis, after he moved his studio temporarily from Berlin to Lesbos to get closer to these events.[42] In one work, he wrapped the pillars of a Berlin concert house in illuminous orange life jackets, transported from Lesbos, Greece to Berlin, Germany, during the 66th Berlinale International Film Festival in 2016 (Figure 8).[43] This work formed an attempt to collapse the distance between two points: that is, a global art event taking place in a beautiful building in Berlin and the beaches where people were arriving at the edges of Europe in small boats with next to nothing. In this vein, Weiwei challenges what migration scholar Nick Gill calls the 'moral distance' we place between ourselves and migrants.[44] However, bringing an event closer, or pressing for more empathy, does not necessarily shift stubborn sovereign ideas about 'us and them'. Although the distance between two points

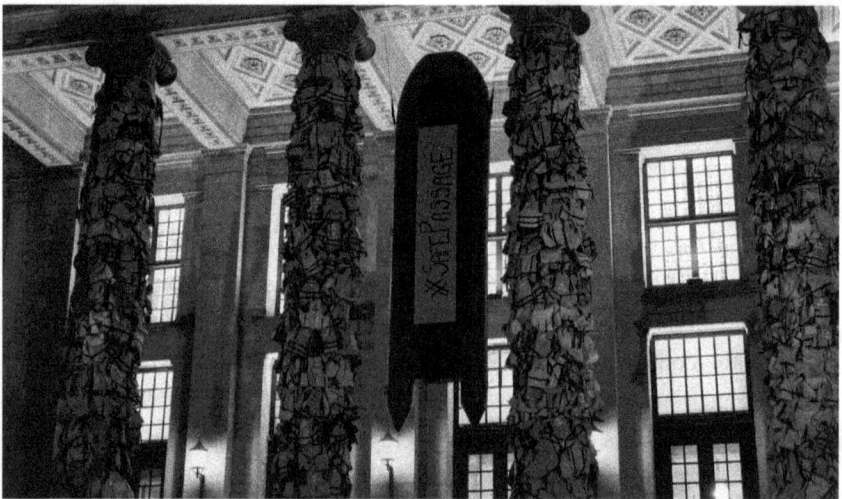

Figure 8. #SafePassage from Ai Weiwei, Konzerthaus Berlin. Photograph by Felipe Tofani. Available via Flickr under Creative Commons License.

is challenged, the works operate within a discourse of crisis that potentially only affirms ideas about capable and independent European citizens as the inverted image of passive victims. While calls for action are therefore noble and necessary, the question is whether these works move people in the ways they are designed to do?

We can nevertheless consider different understandings of the relationship between distance and ethics. As we examined in the last chapter, distance does not necessarily present a problem for ethics. Distance can suggest the possibility of another ethical response. Rather than imagine distance as a gap that must be overcome, this gap can also be circled, or approached from near and far simultaneously. While the repeated and ongoing atrocities of the European refugee crisis demand urgent political responses, they also call for sustained action, which include challenging the framings that make it possible to position 'migrants' as different from 'citizens'. This work may not always require getting 'closer' to scenes of suffering. Indeed, in their work on 'distance' in the context of security politics, Lara Coleman and Hannah Hughes argue that the relationship between distance and proximity is often marked by a relationship of comfort – where we presume getting closer will overcome the discomfort we feel.[45] However, they argue that there are also problems with 'getting closer'. For example, there are risks in presuming there are more authentic understandings of a crisis available, or that we can access an untainted, subaltern view of what is going on. Coleman and Hughes remind us that all crises are mediated to us and suggest that working at a distance is not incompatible with being fully engaged or immersed in a site of study.[46] This is because distance can bring other perspectives and considerations into view. Accordingly, they advocate moving between different standpoints, drawing on positions of proximity and distance, to avoid becoming too comfortable and attached to any one framework of knowledge and understanding.

The suggestion that we move from passivity to action, distance to proximity is often connected with the idea of acting beyond the nation, and on the basis of our shared humanity. For example, at the heart of Ai Weiwei's film, 'Human Flow' (2017), also about the 2015 refugee crisis, lies the idea that 'humanity is one'. He uses his position as a citizen in exile to call on us to rediscover what *makes us human*, and this again forms part of a broader repertoire of responses to this crisis. Take for example the work of artist Bern O'Donoghue, who in the artwork, 'Dead Reckoning' (2017), made a paper boat in memory of all the people lost in the Mediterranean Sea in 2017. The boats were personalized with the words 'son', 'daughter', 'neighbour', 'friend'. When I saw them, they were displayed on the floor of the Tate Modern in striking colourful circles, as part of a collaboration with scholar Vicki Squire.[47] Weiwei uses a comparable method of acknowledging and naming victims, returning to them a sense of their humanity. This comes through most forcefully in 'Human Flow' where impersonal aerial photographs of migrants walking are interspersed with scenes of people enjoying taking selfies with him. Yet while this strategy of making the crisis personal and making people feel part of a common humanity are important, they again do not necessarily displace the figure of the heroic and separate political actor, who is poised to actively respond to others, and who stands in a hierarchical relationship to the migrants who mostly do not speak for themselves.

As Squire argues, then, in the context of a large-scale project she directed documenting the stories of those crossing the Mediterranean Sea,[48] many calls to help have been framed in the context of 'human dignity'. However, Squire shows how historically, this has also formed an *exclusive* category – humanity is not considered available to all. For example, in the Roman idea of *dignitas hominis*, dignity was 'limited to those of reputation and with particular privileges' and used by Cicero to distinguish humans from animals.[49] This prompts Squire to question the critical potential of using 'human dignity' as a preferable framework for responding to this crisis, given it presents its own set of exclusions, as some people are considered to be outside of, or to belong further down in the hierarchy of humanity. Switching the emphasis to humanity may therefore work to overcome the problem of distance or insular nationalism, but the issue is that these powerful sovereign framings are not undone so much as swapped with new coordinates of inclusion and exclusion. We can therefore join Squire in questioning the critical potential of this term as a framework for engaging this particular crisis. It either suggests that some people deserve more human dignity than others, or it reasserts a distinction between humans and other species, including animals that are considered secondary and less significant.[50]

In contrast to shifting the framework from distance to proximity, and from passivity to attention, I am seeking to expand our understandings of political action. The next section returns to the idea of vulnerability for the ways it offers a different framework of response to this crisis, presenting non-sovereign ideas of personhood from a sense of crisis as ongoing. Through a discussion of scenes from Ali Smith's novel *Autumn*, I examine other affects that emerge as part of a politics of response and how these might generate alternative accounts of action.

Approaching crisis from the side: Reading *Autumn*

Ali Smith's *Autumn* opens with a scene evoking the 2015 European refugee crisis, but it comes into view in relation to other crises, including Brexit, austerity, and the after-effects of the 2007–8 global financial crisis. Smith's approach therefore addresses this crisis from the side, that is, hesitantly and indirectly. This recalls Teju Cole's method in *Open City* and Eve Sedgwick's provocation that we take up a position *beside* politics. Rather than place the figure of the refugee – and therefore the viewer/actor – squarely in the frame, Smith arrives at events through the liminal space of the beach, and with a man, Daniel Gluck, who is said to be lying somewhere in between life and death. Smith attunes to what Yasmin Gunaratnam describes as 'two of the most radical thresholds of bodily estrangement and vulnerability: the movement across territories and from life to death'.[51] As this character looks around him, he sees dead bodies lying in between people who are sunbathing. The scene emphasizes how we are never looking with full attention at a single scene of suffering, but looking from different standpoints and from different relations of complicity in terms of chains of violence and suffering. It also reminds us of global inequalities, in the sense that some are suffering while others are sunbathing:

Just along from this dead person, there is another dead person. Beyond it, another, and another.

He looks along the shore at the dark line of the tide-dumped dead.

Some of the bodies are of very small children. He crouches down near a swollen man who has a child, just a baby really, still zipped inside his jacket, its mouth open, dripping sea, its head resting dead on the bloated man's chest.

Further up the beach there are more people.

These people are human, like the ones on the shore, but these are alive. They're under parasols. They are holidaying up the shore from the dead.

There is music coming out of a screen. One of the people is working on a computer. Another is sitting in the shade reading a little screen. Another is dozing under the same parasol, another is rubbing suncream into his shoulder and down his arm.

A child squealing with laughter is running in and out of the water, dodging the bigger waves.

Daniel Gluck looks from the death to the life, then back to the death again.[52]

This depiction of the diffuseness of suffering replaces an account of crisis as inviting immediate action. The sense of the crisis as enormous and seemingly without end also substitutes a linear and sovereign narrative that distinguishes between inactive victims and active responders. Instead, the people who are sunbathing are encountering the deaths of others from the affective state of 'dozing' – which cuts across ideas about passivity/activity. In contrast to a direct view of the crisis, the act of 'sitting in the shade reading a little screen' suggests another form of looking – indirectly, and without full attention. This better captures how many of us absorb what is going on in the world, and from where ideas about acting (and not acting) may potentially begin. Smith's opening scene replaces a single, discrete frame that depicts refugees and asylum seekers as a known and separate population, with a rapid juxtaposing of images and varied affective states. While the scene recalls Susan Sontag's point about the epicness of suffering, there is less sense of discernable groups: the language of crisis is replaced by that of the everyday.

* * *

Autumn's main character, Elisabeth Demand is a young lecturer in Art History working on an insecure contract at one of London's large universities. Daniel Gluck turns out to be her old neighbour, and we accompany Elisabeth as she visits him at a care home, as he nears the end of his life. This is where we also learn about their long-term friendship, based around a shared love of books, ideas and art. In caring for him, she also reads to him, and recalls her upbringing living with her mother, next door to Gluck. But this story is interweaved with the challenges Elisabeth faces without security of income or housing. We follow her going to the post office to renew her passport, and where she encounters the state's regime of documentation, censuses and taxes, and recalls the World State's motto from *Brave New World*, 'COMMUNITY, IDENTITY, STABILITY'.[53] In a story within the story, the novel also describes the life and work of Pauline Boty, one of the first female British pop artists in the 1960s, whose paintings include: 'It's a Man's World I' and 'It's a Man's World II'. All these stories told at once represent a fusion of many different presents, in a style that is distinctive to Smith. It also fits Lauren Berlant's concept of a 'crisis ordinariness', which refuses the logic of the exception – that is, a crisis presented as a structural break with the past, inviting tales of heroic agents responding to change.[54] In contrast, Elisabeth represents a 'crisis-shaped subjectivity' that lives 'amid the ongoingness of adjudication, adaptation, and improvisation' that characterizes many young people's lives today in Europe, and the growing numbers of those in precarious work since the financial crisis.[55] Berlant multiplies the language for discussing experiences of subjectivity and crisis, by working with the 'mess of temporalization'.[56] For Berlant, people find many different ways of 'managing being overwhelmed', and this can manifest in a whole range of different emotions: 'I might be flooded and feel numb, overwhelmed, teary, angry, detached, capacious, sleepy, or *whatever*, for those things that we call traumatic events do not always induce traumatic responses'.[57] How might this approach to crisis inform another kind of political and ethical response, as the focus shifts from a 'tipping point' that demands 'action' to consider instead all kinds of potential 'situations of living on' and living an ethical life?[58]

Through Elisabeth's precarious job situation, the backdrop of Brexit and heightened nationalisms, and thousands of people dying trying to cross the Mediterranean Sea, *Autumn* situates itself within scenes of multiple crises, suffering and vulnerability. Of course, this begs questions about the scale, degree and the measure of suffering. Living in makeshift camps, such as those that Amnesty International has criticized for trapping thousands of people in unsafe and unsanitary conditions, with no permanent right to remain in any country, presents a much more desperate humanitarian emergency than what this main character faces.[59] But the point here is not to compare different experiences: it is to return to the question of *what can we do*. How might this different framework, which begins with the uncertainties and precarities of everyday life, yield other languages of action which bypass ideas about heroic actors saving vulnerable others?

Elisabeth's position as a subject capable of being wounded, and engaged in caring work, suggests a different kind of acting subject. Her relationship with Daniel Gluck borders on that of teacher and pupil, as he initially ignites her interest in art, and the capacity of art to take her across borders when she does not have the capacity to travel. He invites her to be curious about the world around her. But he is not a teacher that explains and provides her with answers: the premise of the friendship is that they are equals, and he shares his passion for art with her in a way that challenges her to appreciate her own intelligence. Of course, this relationship invites suspicion, including from Elisabeth's mother, as indeed it should. It is nevertheless not recognizable within familiar understandings of love, desire, friendship (or harassment); it emerges as central to Elisabeth's emancipation. In the course of the friendship, Elisabeth learns that forgetting is as important as remembering, and that resting is essential for living on more daringly. Elisabeth's version of 'living on' is therefore mirrored in the depiction of Autumn, the title of the novel, the season of 'a million billion flowers bowing, closing their heads again, [and] of a million, billion new flowers opening instead, of a million billion buds becoming leaves then the leaves falling off and rotting into earth, of a million billion twigs splitting into a million billion brand new buds'.[60] Change here appears pervasive and takes multiple forms, rather than something condensed into a single turning point. While not underplaying the multiple crises around us, Smith nurtures a sense of the capacities we all have to act, if we could only acknowledge our own power.[61]

Slow actions

Ali Smith develops alternative understandings of acting to those that abide by a sovereign framework. In attuning to vulnerability, Smith moves us to a different terrain to the language of 'us and them', made audible through ideas of pity or animated action. The relationship between Elisabeth and Daniel, formed around shared knowledge, and a refusal to presume that one of you is the one that knows, makes other ways of living available for her. Meanwhile, Elisabeth, in her relationship of care for him at the end of his life, makes a limiting situation marginally more comfortable. From this, we arrive at a formulation of agency that bypasses ideas about striving, mobility and what Bonnie Honig calls the 'vertical posture' typically associated with ideas about autonomy.[62] Instead, it is attentive to the lively, minor and playful ways in which we adapt, navigate and improvise around the different degrees of intolerable conditions around us. This approach considers forms of action that are not developed by overcoming vulnerabilities but rather emerge from different efforts at enduring.

To elaborate, Bonnie Honig points to Adriana Cavarero's work on the gestures of maternal or caring bodies, positioned 'in the dirt of experience',[63] as alternative gestures to those of the autonomous actor that embodies a 'privileged upright posture and ethics of moral rectitude'.[64] Cavarero develops corporeal choreographies that are drawn from experiences of care. The patriarchal view may see these caring figures as subservient, but Cavarero argues that caring does not always equate with self-sacrifice. Drawing on examples ranging from Antigone to Sara Ahmed's 'The Willful Girl', Cavarero offers different postures of strength and power, which include using an arm to help hold another body up. These alternative postures suggest other ways of being political which go beyond standing upright or speaking out as an autonomous actor. This chimes with several of the images developed by Ali Smith of what it means to live and to act in concert with others. For example, Elisabeth's friendship with Daniel suggests a different account of agency, where they develop a shared strength. Daniel is confined to a bed at the end of his life, and even in earlier times, does not seem to venture far from his house. But in talking about the work of different artists with Elisabeth, he takes her all around the world. Daniel's relationship with Elisabeth offers a model of being political that bypasses the bias towards mobility and 'agentive corporeal potentialities'. While 'slower or stilled bodies' are often interpreted as being less active and as not being in an agentic state,[65] Daniel and Elisabeth lean on each other, and act as an extra set of eyes, ears, and legs for each other. They grow without travelling far and they suggest ways of collaborating that rely on something other than a dominant posture.[66]

In mobilizing vulnerability, the point is to question the image of the animated political actor that is full of moral certainty, which comes into the frame in response to crisis, and images of victims given minimal opportunities to tell their own stories.[67] What might it mean to develop an account of acting politically that avoids ideas about heroism on the one hand or the moral charge of not acting on the other hand, both of which reproduce an upright moral posture? How might we instead form ideas about acting politically from the dirt of enduring hardships? This might be gleaned in a scene where Elisabeth and her mother discuss and then undertake a slow, uncertain action in response to a new fence that will be built in the village.

It is through Elisabeth's mother, who enjoys watching game shows, that we learn that this electric fence will soon be built. As with all border fences, it goes up swiftly but not unexpectedly, quickly establishing itself as part of the banal backdrop of everyday life. At home, Elisabeth's mother goes to get an old Ordnance Survey map and nails it to the kitchen wall, to show her daughter the precise location where the fence has been built. Elisabeth's mother then asks her daughter to do something about it:

> That's where the new fence has gone up, she says. Look.
>
> She is pointing to the word *common* in the phrase *common land*.
>
> Apparently a fence three metres high with a roll of razorwire along the top of it has been erected across a stretch of land not far from the village. It has security cameras on posts all along it. It encloses a piece of land that's got nothing in it but furze, sandy flats, tufts of long grass, scrappy trees, little clumps of wildflower.
>
> Go and see it, her mother says. I want you to do something about it.
>
> What can I do about it? Elisabeth says. I'm a lecturer in the history of art.
>
> Her mother shakes her head.

You'll know what to do, she says. You're young.

Come on. We'll both go.[68]

This extract offers such a refreshing alternative to the calls for 'action' that we hear in times of crisis. Elisabeth feels what many of us feel – what can *I* do? Perhaps we have been so trained in an idea that politics must involve strong, purposeful, heroic actions that we have forgotten how much we are able to do with others. Perhaps the whole emphasis on 'us' as different from 'them' makes us also doubt our own capacities to get past these false distinctions. Elisabeth's mother, who has a different vantage point on life, knows just how much Elisabeth is capable of, and the vast resources that her daughter already has: 'You'll know what to do'. This scene suggests the possibility of acting from uncertainty and opting for a modest decision to *do something*.

Elisabeth's mother places her faith in two advantages that they have: first, Elisabeth's youth; and second, that whatever they do, they will do it together. This is an improvised doing, where what they do will be worked out in the doing of it. It will be grounded in shared understanding, trust and history. This sense of action rubs against a sovereign politics where action suggests strong subjects driving purposeful change in a clear direction. In contrast, this position suggests we do not necessarily know what positive change might involve. It aligns with a longstanding assumption in political thought – stretching from Machiavelli to Hannah Arendt – that no political act carries a guarantee as to what might come of it, or a guarantee that it will be 'good'. To act politically is to take a risk, to put something into motion, even as the outcome remains unpredictable.[69] Elisabeth's mother encourages them to use whatever resources they have to hand, and trust in their capabilities, which are vast. They don't have to share a common vision or objective; they proceed uncertainly, but in concert. In improvising, they operate from the middle of life and not with a full perspective. However, what matters is that Elisabeth's mother offers to stay alongside her daughter, as they work out what resistance might involve between the two of them. What her mother knows is Elisabeth's potential, and perhaps also women's potential, as they set off to figure out what their bodies can do.

A capacious politics of response

Too often, critical work bemoans the fact that not everyone can be convinced to see the world differently, or in the ways that 'we' see things. But it seems to me that a creative, open understanding of political action cannot wait for a time when people 'become awakened'. By moving away from images of the strong actor that comes into focus in response to crisis, I have sought to extend ideas about acting politically, so that we can see the opportunities for acting that are already around us, and which endure when the headlines change. Focusing on vulnerability as a framework leads us to the necessity of acting with others in imperfect, everyday ways. The aim of this chapter has been to shift from a framework of 'crisis', which alongside a national frame invites a restrictive, 'heroic' account of action, to consider other corporeal understandings of what it means to act and generate other possibilities for responding and feeling that we can do something.

While calls for action can leave people feeling overwhelmed, the 2015 refugee crisis was marked by thousands of happenstance decisions, across Europe, to muck in and act. These decisions relied on ways of 'thinking and feeling outside of the usual repertoire'.[70] For example, a huge mural depicting Alan Kurdi was painted on a wall in Frankfurt, in another re-staging of this photograph, designed to interrupt people's daily journeys to work, reminding people of the ongoingness of this crisis.[71] Adler-Nissen, Andersen and Hansen discuss another mural featuring an image of Kurdi, in Sorocaba, 90 km from Sao Paulo, Brazil.[72] Meanwhile in Swansea, the Glynn Vivian has become the first UK 'Gallery of Sanctuary', for its work hosting creative and artistic events between new arrivals and more long-term residents in the city.[73] Beyond the loud affects that emerge in response to crisis, these different efforts seek to maintain affective and political responses to the issues at stake. They also suggest the potential of weak affects and less spectacular, everyday actions. Yet people are still dying, regularly, in attempting to cross the Mediterranean Sea, and the European Union remains complicit in actively blocking a safe passage.[74]

This chapter has addressed how a capacious politics of response accommodates a plurality of life experiences, acknowledges intersecting crises, and seeks ways of being political that bypass ideas about specialist knowledge, heroic capacities, or spectacular acts, which in turn often rely on a distinction between 'us and them', the deserving and the undeserving, or the citizen and the human. The idea of daring to respond otherwise is summed up in Chancellor Angela Merkel's response to those who criticized her decision at the height of this crisis to provide residency for one million people seeking asylum in Germany.[75] In response to the question of how the country would manage with such large numbers of new arrivals, Merkel said, without fanfare: '*Wir schaffen das.*' (We will cope).[76] Sidestepping the opposition between sensitivity and might, vulnerability suggests a different kind of strength – involving the courage and tenacity to keep going.

Interlude: A hot afternoon

On a hot summer's day in July 2016, two weeks after the UK voted to leave the European Union, I sat on top of the garage roof with my children watching the Wales National Airshow, organized by Swansea City Council. The then prime minister David Cameron had recently announced he would be resigning; the Conservative Party were yet to choose a new leader. No politician was able to capture the national mood. We sat on several blankets as the fibreglass roof was too hot to touch. The children wavered between being awestruck and terrified and looked to me for reassurance. I made the appropriate noises of admiration as the Red Arrows – the Royal Air Force's Aerobatic Team – gathered speed by flying the Hawk T1's into the countryside before sweeping back across the seashore to mark the sky with the colours of the Union Jack. My children were too young to know the significance of the colours. And anyway, here was an opportunity to try and name them – *coch* (red), *gwyn* (white), *glas* (blue). The Spitfire, the Hurricane and Lancaster Bomber – cultural icons from the Battle of Britain (1940) and the Royal Air Force (RAF)'s role in the Second World War – flew alongside Eurofighter Typhoons (built by British Aerospace (BAE) systems) and Chinook helicopters (used in the Falklands, the 1991 and 2003 Gulf wars, the Balkans and Afghanistan). These killing machines drew beautiful circular patterns on the clear blue sky. Tens of thousands of people watched the show for free on Swansea beach front. Later, I learned that a handful of adults and children were admitted to the Burns Centre at Morriston Hospital: flying planes can be dangerous, and sitting in the blazing sun can cause injuries too.[1]

What might this story tell us about national affects? This moment took place in 2016 but I could be describing a scene from several different decades in the twentieth century – the 1950s or 1970s perhaps. This was a 'national' event, deemed to be the largest air show in Wales, assembled around icons of Britishness charged with memories of empire. Yet 'the people' did not necessarily interpret the event according to these narratives. While we can read the event through the registers of identity, difference and coloniality, doing so would miss 'the affective field of potential' through which the event took place.[2] For the three of us, the event was felt in the waves of clapping and cheer that erupted from the beach, the thundering noise of the planes rattling the roof we were sitting on, and the resonances that travelled between our skins, the fibreglass and each other. While the show was a visual spectacle, it also involved twisted stomachs and tensed limbs. It operated through a combination of wonder, boredom, anxiety and surprise. Engaging the politics of affect invites us to address the intricate entanglements of war and tourism in urban spectacles.[3] It also asks us to consider how this event was felt, as well as the lively unfolding of the event itself.

In the run up to the air show, I had encountered murmurs of resistance – such as among the networks that welcome populations described as refugees and asylum seekers to the city. A 'City of Sanctuary' since 2010, Swansea is home to many people that have arrived to escape the sounds of low-flying planes. There was also some resistance to symbols of Britishness among Welsh language activists. However, these are both marginal constituencies in the city, and anyone who hid indoors disgusted by the event risked being called a 'killjoy'.[4] Indeed, it is difficult to find ways of opposing the force of the state without reproducing identities and differences that are themselves creations of the state. Reading this air show therefore requires a multiple and mobile frame. The question of how to resist calls on us to acknowledge different forms of affective communities. A study of this event would therefore need to draw connections between national affects and heteronormative cultures, city branding, the particular rhythms of individual cities and their imperial geographies, public space and the armed forces – at least. This would enable us to ask how some 'communities of sense' are reproduced, funded, enlivened and legitimated over others.[5] It would allow us to ask how dominant communities of sense enrol new populations and re-entrench ideas about what it means to be a citizen.

Eve Sedgwick argues that the prevailing way in which we think about power is still as something *exercised over us* by a single sovereign authority. But in considering the everyday ways we enjoy spectacles of violence, we have to acknowledge power as something that is *embraced by us* as well as exercised over us.[6] For Debbie Lisle, ideas about 'us and them' operate in ways that 'do not simply enrol and exclude particular bodies and populations, [but] also make themselves felt – and indeed, achieve their power – by enrolling and excluding objects, landscapes, infrastructures, atmospheres and materials'.[7] At this air show, affect was evidently a 'mechanism for power',[8] in the sense that the event was staged in ways that required skill, practice, funding and organization. But affect also names how this event cannot be explained through accounts of power as repression, coercion, or prohibition. For this was also a spectacle that was accepted and enlivened through cheers, clapping, selfies, bodies gathering together on the sandy beach and children running for ice cream. How, then, do we intervene politically when spectacles that celebrate the everydayness of military weapons, and Britain's superiority as a victorious nation, appear so *enjoyable*?

Reading this event according to identities cast and power imposed risks 'making the world seem more coherent and more resistant to political intervention than it might otherwise be'.[9] The everyday, imaginative geographies of 'us' and 'them' are multiple and contradictory, composed through strong and weak attachments. This story about the air show invites us to address how national attachments are felt, sensed and embodied as well as structured, organized and performed as they emerge and dissolve across the everyday urban landscape. It asks us to consider how particular structures of feeling maintain their force but also how they might be contested and interrupted through new vocabularies of pleasure and togetherness.

5

Feeling 'Brexit'

In the aftermath of the 2016 Brexit vote in the UK, the prominent psychotherapist Susie Orbach spoke about how this was all people wanted to talk about in her therapy room.[1] Patients shared feelings of shock, fear, dismay, shame, anger, alienation and of 'mourning what one didn't realise one quite had'. These feelings belonged mostly to middle-class, well-educated, cosmopolitan and urban populations who had voted to 'remain' in Europe. For example, the novelist Zadie Smith describes reading essays by 'Londoners speaking proudly of their multicultural, outward-looking city, so different from these narrow xenophobic places up north', and blaming people in poorer northern cities for the vote to leave. Indeed, Smith reflects on the problematic assumptions underlying these feelings of shame, shock and regret, and how they animated ideas about 'us and them':

> 'What have they done?' we said to each other, sometimes meaning the leaders, who we felt must have known what they were doing, and sometimes meaning the people, who, we implied, didn't.[2]

Smith concludes that a useful consequence of Brexit was to 'openly reveal a deep fracture in British society that has been thirty years in the making'.[3]

The idea that middle class urbanites felt ashamed at the result of the Brexit referendum formed a strong narrative, as the UK decided on 23 June 2016 by a margin of 51.9 per cent to 48.1 per cent, to leave the European Union. It was reworked by the journalist David Goodhart to argue that the 'remain' vote belonged to people from 'nowhere', while people from 'somewhere' had voted to 'leave', an argument that animated older ideas about globalization creating 'non-places' in contrast to 'real places'.[4] This simplistic geography was adopted by the British prime minister Theresa May in her speech to the Conservative Party conference on 5 October 2016.[5] The geography of 'somewhere' and 'nowhere' romanticizes and misconstrues so-called 'left-behind' cities and towns as somehow less cosmopolitan, erasing the ways these are also made up of transnational connections in how people live, work, love, study, buy goods and enjoy themselves. What Theresa May's picture did was give further weight to the idea that the UK was split between cosmopolitan and national citizens, an idea congealed in the blunt tool of a referendum.

In this chapter, I follow Sara Ahmed's invitation to 'feel our way' into how emotions work to shape individual and collective bodies through racial and gendered discourses of nationalism and cosmopolitanism.[6] However, I use affect to reorient the debate beyond this postulation of a split geography of 'us and them' – an idea that, through Brexit, had become heavy and stifling. By starting instead with ideas about shame and the starting point of the urban street, I discuss how we can reconfigure ideas about 'the people' beyond nationalist narratives. Through an engagement with affects as involving 'forces of encounter' that draw bodies together and apart, the chapter points to different ways of understanding being-with-others, prompting new imaginaries of what bodies can do.[7] The chapter pursues this through a discussion of a theatre performance that addressed 'Brexit' through this figure of 'the people'. While acknowledging that this category of 'the people' is central to any politics that works within the system of nation-states,[8] I argue that we can approach it as something other than a category that pre-exists politics. Rather than think of politics as what affects otherwise still bodies, this chapter contributes to an understanding of politics as involving 'bodies already in motion',[9] orienting us towards the micro-possibilities of interrupting or shifting a particular mood.

The performance that I focus on, 'The Populars', was created by Volcano Theatre Company and performed in April 2017 at the company's temporary headquarters in a disused supermarket building in Swansea (Abertawe) (Figure 9). It was directed by Paul Davies (co-founder of the company) with movement director Catherine Bennett. Davies wanted to address Brexit through questions of feeling, and 'family, lovers, quite human things really, rather than policy or GDP'.[10] In this, the performance broke away from assuming different group identities. I followed the company's rehearsals between February and April 2017 and went to watch the performance with my second year 'Political Geography' students. In exploiting the theatre's position in this old shop building on a run-down urban high street, I argue that the performance offered a refreshing perspective on 'Brexit', by exploring positions in between the self-certain, noisy identities of 'Leave' and 'Remain' voter, urban and rural citizen, cosmopolitan and national citizen. By refusing to treat 'the people' as an already settled concept, this production went about putting the people in motion.

Figure 9. Volcano Theatre, High Street, Swansea (Abertawe). Photograph by Volcano Theatre.

While affects, feelings and emotions were subjects explicitly addressed in this play, they were also engaged as a different way in to understanding 'Brexit'. While certainly, Brexit can be explained by pointing to the effects of declining living standards in the UK,[11] and as an example of how the histories of Empire and colonialism continue to shape understandings of British national identity in the present,[12] Brexit is also multiple things.[13] While socio-economic conditions, identity politics and the legacies of the British Empire all play a role in it, an affective approach asks what more might be said about this event. This matters because many responses to populist politics risk borrowing from the language of populism, asserting another version of 'the people' as preferable. The problem with such responses is that they risk reproducing that which they set out to oppose, presenting a narrow understanding of politics as involving the triumph of one social group over another. What I am seeking here are ways of avoiding becoming complicit in the violent geographies of populism.

The chapter proceeds with a discussion of the shame and shock people felt at the outcome of Brexit, and how ideas about shame are connected to the nation and resonate with colonial histories. It engages with how the vote to leave formed a 'perverse politics' according to many academics and political commentators.[14] The chapter then addresses the figure of 'the people' from somewhere new, namely, from the perspective of this theatre's temporary home on High Street, Swansea, and the South Wales valleys more generally – a poor region of Europe, in which a majority of people voted to leave. The next section asks how thinking with movement helps unsettle identity politics and carries the potential for transforming ideas of the people, drawing on Erin Manning's work in *The Minor Gesture*. In it, she posits movement as 'capable of opening experience to new registers and creating new modes of existence'.[15] Overall, what I chart are forms of response to Brexit that interfere with the geographies of 'us and them'.

Shame, racialization and the nation

As Zadie Smith's Brexit essay suggests, feelings of shame have a moralizing tone. In this case, shame was mapped onto familiar distinctions between 'London' and 'the North', the city and the countryside, the educated and the uneducated. However, on closer inspection, all of these distinctions failed to provide convincing explanations of the vote. As geographer Danny Dorling makes clear, of those who voted Leave, 59 per cent were 'middle class' (A, B, or C1 social groups) and 41 per cent were 'working class' (D and E social groups – categories derived from the British National Readership Survey).[16] The proportion of leave voters in the lowest two social classes was just 24.9 per cent. This meant that 'leave voters among the middle class were crucial to the final result'.[17] Yet despite the statistics, 'poor people' were often blamed for the outcome. Yet as Robbie Shilliam argues, this vote cannot be understood as a 'rational choice made by a working class', because it must be read in the context of long-standing efforts at distinguishing between the 'deserving and undeserving poor'.[18] As Shilliam puts it, the very idea of a deserving and 'left behind' English (or, Welsh) working class is a racialized construct, which relies on the image of an 'English genus' created in relation to its non-white double. However, the Brexit vote was carried by a 'melancholic racialized nationalism',[19] among those who were relatively privileged in relation to the broader population, and mostly those in professional occupations and who owned their own homes.

The event of 'Brexit' is shot through with Britain's colonial pasts. As Gurminder Bhambra argues, the question of whether Brexit should be understood in relation to *identity politics* or in the context of *socio-economic inequality* misses the ways it must be read in relation to the histories of Empire.[20] For example, collective affects of 'shame' are powerful and comforting because of the ways they rely on ideas about how some people are more progressive, developed and enlightened than others. The feelings of 'shame' that travelled through this vote achieved their affective resonance because they reverberated with colonial figurations of 'the other' – imagined as both *within* and *beyond* the nation. Indeed, writing in another context, Elizabeth Povinelli addresses the intersection between feelings of shame, nationality and coloniality in the context of public debates around the rights of indigenous communities in Australia.[21] In a critical reading of the 1992 Australian High Court ruling on the native title rights of indigenous Australians, Povinelli shows how racial and cultural intolerance were projected as shameful things *belonging to the past*, in order to constitute the idea of a new multicultural Australia. Ideas about mulitculturalism continue to exclude the 'perverse differences' that do not fit the nation's ideal image of itself. Povinelli's analysis is significant because it shows that emotions are never disregarded by the state, but that the affective languages of shame and love are intimately connected to the abstract language of law, citizenship and rights.[22] Shame reveals how the logics of nationality, multiculturalism, coloniality and racism connect – not only in the context of Brexit, but also in many different articulations of the nation.[23]

Feelings of shame have also powerfully informed debates about Britishness. This includes the public mood that greeted the publication of the Parekh report on the *Future of Multi-Ethnic Britain* in the year 2000, and the political consensus that was shared at that time around 'multicultural tolerance'.[24] Anne-Marie Fortier reminds us of how the then Conservative Party leader William Hague responded to the publication of the report claiming his 'pride' in the fact that Britain was 'a nation of immigrants' – a claim that is hard to imagine a British political leader making post-Brexit. Fortier then documents the shift in public debate during the 1990s towards a British version of multiculturalism and how the British press were indignant at the fact that the Parekh report urged people to embrace a 'British' identity, arguing that 'Englishness' was too wrapped up in ideas about white supremacy and imperialism.[25] This prompted cries that Britain should not be 'ashamed of its history'. Tracing these debates, Fortier shows how shame was 'evoked, rejected and projected onto particular subjects',[26] and repelled as something 'we' did not want to feel. Imperial and colonial histories are in these ways deeply interwoven in Brexit, as evidenced in the persistence of racialized nationalism, and a complete ignorance of the histories of Empire among the broader British population, including that of England's relationship with Wales, Scotland, Northern Ireland and Ireland. However, shame brings these topics into the frame, showing how ideas about 'us and them' connect with ideas about civilization, racialization and multiculturalism.

'Shame' has nevertheless been engagedcreatively and inventively by LGBTQ activists and HIV/AIDS activists, to renarrate the nation.[27] With this context in mind, Sedgwick argues that shame also has radical potential.[28] Drawing on the work of Silvan Tomkins, she argues that shame ultimately marks us as engaged with and interested in the world. This is because it 'derives from and aims towards sociability'.[29] Indeed, Elspeth Probyn concurs, and argues that shame can present something more interesting than empathy – where we pretend there are lines of connection with others.[30] Shame invites us to be 'interested in those we see as our enemy', and where the impossibility of sharing commonality may nevertheless produce 'localized action'.[31] This reworking of shame presents an opening that displaces the attention on 'unconscious drives' or 'false consciousness' to consider the 'transmission of force or intensity across bodies, and not only human bodies'.[32] Shame here emerges alongside other affects, including excitement, enjoyment, anger and fear, and invites us to think about how they not only touch and cohere collectivities, but also cut across the identity groups cast through this referendum. Operating between consciousness and unconsciousness, Eve Sedgwick and Elspeth Probyn invite us to address shame as open to change and lively formulations. The next section seeks to further depart from group identities as a framework for reading Brexit, by interrogating the idea that the vote to leave formed a 'perverse politics' and examining feelings of disaffection.

A perverse politics?

One of the news stories that perplexed the cosmopolitan liberal broadsheets in the aftermath of the Brexit vote was how people living in the South Wales Valleys could vote to leave the EU when they had benefitted so much financially from European subsidies.[33] This region lost most of its major industries under Thatcherism, is one of the poorest in the European Union and has for that reason, received significant funding from EU structural funds.[34] Health indices show that women who live in Blaenau Gwent can expect to have a 'healthy life' expectancy of 59.3 years in comparison with 70.7 years in nearby Monmouthsire.[35] Yet Ebbw Vale (a town in Blaenau Gwent) was singled out in the aftermath of this vote as a 'town showered with cash'.[36] There is much to unpack in the question of how some places get singled out as intensely interesting (or responsible) at times of national crisis. But the key point I want to follow here is how this issue of people apparently voting 'against their own interests' brought group identities into view. The narrative invites us to imagine a coherent class or identity that has failed to grasp how much it benefitted from Europe. It also postulates another, more learned group, that is well educated enough to know how important it is to remain part of Europe. This framing reproduces 'us and them' narratives about some people being more enlightened than others. It also ensured that Brexit had transnational resonances, for a similar question – of how people can vote against their own interests – was being asked in the United States, notably in books such as Kathleen Cramer's *The Politics of Resentment* and Arlie Russell Hochschild's *Strangers in Their Own Land*.[37]

In Cramer and Hochschild's books, the authors (self-confessed liberal-minded democrats) go and meet people in other parts of the United States (Wisconsin and Louisiana, respectively) to understand increasing resentment and divisiveness in US politics. In their different ways, both authors try to move beyond 'shame' towards a genuine engagement. Both present rich ethnographic work. Indeed, the everyday views presented in Cramer's study could have been spoken in Swansea: people speak of the sadness of watching people in other cities able to offer much more to their children; of feeling that voting never makes a difference; and of the significant difference it makes to everyday life when one local petrol station, shop, bank or post office closes. But this is also why Cramer's explanation of her participants' feelings, as something that results from a 'rural consciousness', does not convince – because these views are heard in cities too. In her review of Hochschild's book, Raka Ray suggests a way out of the rural–urban distinction by encouraging us to unpack further this presumption that voters act in 'perverse' ways. For example, Ray suggests that it might not seem to the people of Louisiana, which ranks forty-ninth out of the 50 American states for human development, as though the state is on their side.[38] As Ray argues, the problem in Hochschild's book is that the state continues to be presumed as a unifying force for good.[39] The proposed solution is part of the problem, not least for how the state collaborates in thinking about people as coherent and unified groups.

A 'perverse politics' is defined by Ann Shola Orloff, Evren Savci and Raka Ray as involving, firstly, at the level of policies and institutions, unexpected outcomes, and secondly, in civil society as incorporating 'individual and collective contrariness, unruliness and resistance to guidance among political actors'.[40] This description fits Brexit very well, because none of the dominant institutions, media organizations and pollsters expected this result. Orloff, Savci and Ray's analysis is helpful because it goes further than the assumption of 'false consciousness' in what is presumed to be a homogenous group.[41] A post-colonial lens therefore adds much needed richness to the question of why people act in 'perverse' ways, by drawing attention to the importance of context and culture, and querying the universalizing tendencies in critical theories that posit some ways of living and acting as the only ways of being progressive. For example, Orloff, Savci and Ray draw on post-colonial feminist theorists Chandra Mohanty and Saba Mahmood, and their discussions of how women who veil are often postulated as 'perverse'. Mohanty takes Western feminism to task for its portrayal of the 'third world woman' as 'ignorant, poor, uneducated and tradition-bound'.[42] Mahmood builds on that analysis arguing that it presents a monolithic understanding of human agency and inadvertently presumes the 'Western liberal mode of life as infintely desirable'.[43] Understanding the practice of veiling as 'perverse' relies on ignoring questions about different ways of experiencing the world. In the context of populism, Orloff, Savci and Ray argue that presenting a vote as 'perverse' ignores questions about inequality, employment, health, culture and housing. In this way, the Marxist concept of 'false consciousness' is taken out of its relationship to political economy and pinned to a political subject that must desire itself to be free.[44] In contrast, these authors argue for an interpretative framework that can acknowledge questions of geographical context, structural inequalities and plural ways of seeing the world.

In my interview with 'The Populars' director Paul Davies, we talked about this idea that the vote to leave was 'perverse'. While we both took for granted that the fantasy of English nationalism at work in Brexit is perverse,[45] we were troubled by critical theorists and commentators positing places like Swansea as backward, uneducated and as failing to understand what was in their own interests. Paul Davies and I discussed the blue signs with EU flags that are dotted throughout this landscape, and which identify buildings, roads and infrastructure made possible by EU structural funds (payments made because of the extent of this region's poverty). Davies commented on the gap between the promise of a different future made through these impressive building projects, and the experiences of inequality and poverty on the ground:

> prior to [the vote], I'd been up the Valleys, photographing where my family is from ... You just got the feeling that ... it [Europe] just doesn't mean anything ... Yes you see the wee little flag on the side of a road but we are miles away from all that ... So I guess that's a lived feeling ...[46]

As Davies indicates, the idea of 'Europe' as an opportunity and aspiration seemed a long way away for many people, even as 'Europe' was in other ways very close. That is, EU citizens that live in South Wales are neighbours, friends, lovers, school-friends. However the further point here is that political and economic inequalities were not appeased through great buildings projects. Lived feelings of inequality and injustice remained real. What happens when we refuse to translate the collective anger and sense of injustice felt by many into recognizable identity positions, such as 'remain' or 'leave' voter, urban or rural citizen, English or Welsh citizen? The next section suggests that thinking from the perspective of this theatre's position on the High Street offers further resources for undoing narratives of group identities.

Thinking from the street

The High Street in Swansea connects the central train station with its historic castle. Her Majesty's Land Registry show the price paid for a flat here in May 2015 was £71,000, another was bought in July 2017 for £60,000, and in January 2020 for £150,000. This is in comparison to the average cost of a flat or maisonette in the UK which in November 2018 was £202.663 and in January 2022 was £224.186.[47] This street is emblematic of the brutal nature of global capitalism: it looks very different to the pictures of what was in the early twentieth century a buzzing street, with a tram, colourful shop awnings and advertising boards above windows. As several shops today stand empty or boarded up, with many buildings converted into student housing, it is evident that High Street has suffered from the growth of private cars, large out-of-town chain stores, the redistribution of wealth to other UK towns and cities and more lately, the expansion of online shopping. Luckily, this street remains poor enough to be of little interest to the large chain stores and upmarket restaurants. As a result, on this street today are markers of Swansea's ordinary cosmopolitanism: a world food supermarket with a large Polish food section, a Turkish restaurant, an Italian café, and several artist studios. For some, the abandoned shops are a sight for sore eyes; for others they are aesthetically inspiring.[48] Indeed, High Street, Swansea, has made national headlines for the small but innovative initiatives at regeneration that decorate this street.[49] These include painted empty shop fronts and artist designed awnings. In sum, the 'affective urbanism' of this street and its everyday conviviality offers us a different starting point for thinking about Brexit.[50] The affective life of the urban street[51] affirms the plurality of relations, sensorial encounters between bodies and things, and experiences of agency that compose life in this city.

Between 27 March and 8 April 2017, on this street, at Volcano Theatre, 'The Populars' was performed. I watched the 'patient experimentation'[52] of the rehearsal process, which opened a space for thought and discussion. The process allowed the cast and broader crew to talk through what kind of a political crisis this was. In being new to this city at the time, it formed an invaluable space for me to make sense of the times with others. Paul Davies questioned the shock on the part of arts institutions and organizations at the result of the vote, as well as the relationship between the event and creative responses:

> I think it became apparent that within liberal arts constituencies in Wales and beyond, that there was a huge amount of concern as to the prospect of a Leave vote and then after the Leave vote there was a huge amount of concern, and agitation and groups being set up and outrage in terms of media and conferences but then nothing actually being presented in performance. [So I thought], if it was that important and that galvanizing, how come it doesn't generate anything actually creative?[53]

Brexit formed a political event insofar as people departed from the scripts that they were expected to follow. But it was not, at least for a while, accompanied by broader debate and demonstrations. This event was deeply felt yet seemed to unfold more as collective shock than as a movement of people, energies and ideas. However, this street remained a 'theatre of human life',[54] and as such, formed an ideal site for reflecting on the result, and for considering how to interrupt and subvert heavy ideas of 'us and them'.

'The Populars'

'The Populars' began for Paul Davies with how people felt, but the aim was not to give voice to public moods and views that were already vocal. For Brexit had also unfurled in people's homes and among family and friends: a critical response needed to somehow address *that*. In our interview, Davies insisted the play was not only about Brexit. In casting, he had avoided mentioning it as such. This allowed him to engage Brexit through another register – involving music, dancing, and movement. Given the intensity of the political atmosphere, this was both a difficult and a necessary task:

> When I did get four actors in a room for a kind of R&D [Research and Development], around two months after the vote, it was apparent that it kind of,

that it touched on all sorts of weird things like family, lovers, quite human things really, rather than policy or GDP. And then I thought oh there is something that connects back to dramatic realism here. Not that that interests me much. And I was looking at a book called *Human Space* by Otto Fredrich Bollnow (1963). Quite an old book now. I had these actors in a space and they had no idea what I was thinking about. And I was thinking about space, and proximity and I deliberately wanted four people who didn't know each other and put them apart-together, apart-together. It was only on the third day when I played The Clash's 'Safe European Home' ... that they all went, oh right, this sounds like it's about ... BREXIT!'[55]

The performance was built from a series of structured improvisations and fragments of script, including dialogues and anecdotes, stories and quizzes. There was no set design or special lighting: only some fancy-dress costumes for selected routines. It was performed in promenade and the audience mainly stood around the space, with spaces for some to sit. We were invited to listen, attune and eventually join in the dancing. The cast of four actors, two men (Neal McWilliams and Rick Yale) and two women (Elin Phillips and Roanna Lewis) – all white, was not representative of this city's young people, and when the performance returned a year later, the cast was changed to include a Welsh-speaking actor of colour (Mali Ann Rees). The cast worked hard to establish a mood. As such, this was much more demanding on them than a play that presented different viewpoints to an audience of passive receptors. The atmosphere varied with different audiences, but it was often fragile, as we were conscious that the invitation to move together could easily be rejected. But most of all, this performance refused to present a moral story about Brexit, or hold up a mirror to the group identities that were meant to be circulating.

To open the show, the audience moved from the front end of the 'shop' to the theatre space at the back of the building where the supermarket's deep freezers used to be housed, which is partially beneath street level. A temporary bar had been built front of house, which welcomed us from the street to this open, low-cost space. In the dimly lit theatre, two of the actors could be seen dancing to Chet Baker's 'Alone Together'. Against this modest backdrop and jazz music, a mood was created. The actors danced as if they were alone, but in entering, we became aware of ourselves sharing this intimate space together, on leave just for a short while from whatever else awaited us.

The music moved into pop and the lights went up: all four actors were present and began dancing energetically to the hit song, 'Jump Around' by House of Pain then later Fleetwood Mac's 'Everywhere' (a rejoinder to the citizens from

Figure 10. 'The Populars', April 2017. From left to right: Elin Phillips, Rick Yale, Neal McWilliams, Roanna Lewis. Photograph by Volcano Theatre.

somewhere or nowhere debate), as well as a string of 1980s and 1990s feel-good music including Madonna's 'Material Girl', Right Said Fred's 'I'm Too Sexy' and Pulp's 'Common People' (Figure 10). This was a 'happy to be alive' kind of dancing. It was dancing that was hard to watch without finding your toes tingling, eager to move. The two women jumped for the entire song as the two men gyrated on the floor. In my interview with the movement director Catherine Bennett, held following the show's run, she felt it was important that none of the actors were trained dancers: they were strong, but they did not make far-reaching movements look easy through years of repetitive practice. The actors were all young people (under thirty-five), which felt significant given that 75 per cent of those aged eighteen to twenty-four had voted to 'remain' in Europe.[56]

After the slow then fast tempo of the music and dancing, we arrived at the first of a series of improvised fragments. Elin Phillips began by asking audience members about 'being cool'. She took a microphone and gently asked an audience member: 'are you cool?' In the performance I went to see with my undergraduate students, this question was met with quiet laughter and nervousness: who would say something first? What was the right thing to say? One pitched in and said: 'Yes, I'm cool!' Everyone laughed. We relaxed. The actors laughed with us. In another fragment, the actors talked about the similarities and differences between

Figure 11. 'The Populars', April 2017. Photograph by Volcano Theatre.

European people, in a way that mimicked the world of 'alternative facts': 'Did you know that in Italy it's illegal to drink cappuccino after 11am?' 'Did you know that in France it's illegal to name your pet pig Napoleon?' Through their funny, made-up questions, which changed in each performance, we slowly had to leave behind representations of the 'serious views' of the people. This was not an easy task in this political climate, for in the context of populist politics and this most potent symbol of the will of the people – a won referendum – the people, who were of course, not all of the people – appeared as both loud and difficult to challenge. But this performance refused to engage on this terrain. This was not about countering false facts with truth. Rather than seek to return politics to the right people, this performance set the idea of the people in motion (Figure 11).

Movement and modes of being-with-others

Erin Manning's *The Minor Gesture* develops a philosophy of movement concerned with how to foster modes of being with others.[57] Indeed, she defines politics along these lines – as what 'awakens new modes of encounter and creates new forms of life-living'.[58] In order to get there, she attends to the co-composition of bodies and worlds and the interplay of conscious and non-conscious movements. For example, rather than assume a philosophy of still life, from which bodies begin to move, she encourages us to think about bodies and the world as in perpetual movement. She draws on the work of dancers, choreographers and philosophers, as well as work on depression, and on living with autism – all, she is careful to say, very different life experiences. I turn here briefly to the work she develops drawing on writers who write about autism – Ido Kedar, Tito Mukhopadhyay, DJ Savarese and Amelia Baggs. Mindful not to romanticize this condition, nor underplay the serious challenges of living with different forms of bodily disturbance in a world that is not planned around such needs, she uses this work to develop a discussion of the presumed split between body and world, endemic to a 'neurotypical' account of experience. The point is to learn from an account of perception that 'privileges the complexity of experience of category'.[59] For example, drawing on Anne Corwin, who writes about her experience of autism, Manning relays how the 'entry into an environment begins not with a perception of objects (chairs, tables) or of subjects (people) but with an edging into form, a tending of light and shadow and color'.[60] Unlike a neurotypical account of experience, which might notice the objects and subjects first, this is an account that prioritizes the 'active ecologies of experience' as they take shape.[61] The decision made in 'The Populars' to eschew the theatrical conventions of characters, script and identity positions aligns with Manning's sensitive writing here: that is, to begin from a consideration of the affective environment, made in this case, through music, movement, dimmed lights and low-cost building materials, rather than characters, subject positions, viewpoints and argument.

I reproduce these points carefully because I feel they have much to offer the ways we tend to think about politics. They also connect with the focus on vulnerability in the Chapter 4. For example, what brings Manning to these literatures is an interest in thinking against the image of a self-sufficient, self-directing body: a body that 'can consciously make decision based on a strong sense of where the body ends and the world begins'.[62] Instead, it posits the body as already in motion: to point out that bodies 'walk, crawl, gesture, run, stumble, reach, fall and embrace', challenging the presumption of a split between body and mind.[63] Manning's account is interested in the minutiae of bodily experiences, such as a minor gesture 'that often goes by unperceived'.[64] This is close to geographer Patricia Noxolo's account of 'place ballet', which she develops from the work of David Seamon.[65] Place ballet focuses on habit or routine, and the minutiae of 'corporeal decision-making' at work in the repeated journeys we make across cities.[66] As David Bissell discusses in his work on commuting, everyday journeys are achieved through a combination of conscious and subconscious processes, involving the microelements of bodily capacities, lived memories as well as 'forces of enablement and constraint'.[67] This engagement with the micropolitics of barely perceived or seemingly unchanging movements is powerful for thinking about what took place in this theatre production. Much like Ruth Raynor recounts the openings made possible through the repetition of theatre exercises and structured improvisations, the achievements of this performance unfolded at a scale of 'micro-intensities'.[68] That is to say, 'The Populars' did not weigh into the political directly, by reproducing excerpts of political speeches, of people's 'real' opinions about the vote, or by dramatizing two positions in the debate. Rather, it intervened at *this* register, which Manning, together with Noxolo, Bissell and Raynor, describes: by addressing questions about how we are affected and moved by others, and seeking to shift the tone away from the loud, ugly political atmospheres that had accumulated.

The performance challenged the idea of sovereignty as something that can be contained within a body. For example, in the work of inviting the audience to move and play, what arose in this production was the idea that feelings are not contained within bodies but shared between bodies in a space and can be reworked and reenergized accordingly.[69] Of course, we might describe the experience of attending any piece of theatre as one of sharing feelings with others. What was different in this case was that it also invited us to challenge the assumption that '*we* are the absolute directors of our movements'.[70] Through moving, dancing, laughing and a shared humility, the performance encouraged ways of being that are not centred around being in control. Although the Vote Leave campaign's motto, 'Take Back Control' was never mentioned in the play, the performance formed a clear response to the fantasy of control that had contributed in large parts to this vote – the fantasy that a body (or nation) could be the absolute director of its own movement and destiny.

Of course, having some sense of control over space, movements and futures is critical, whether we consider that in relation to people living with disabilities or making streets safe for women, gay or trans people. This performance did not reject the idea of control. Rather, we can read this performance as already intertwined with the precarities of everyday life, suggesting how 'control' is unevenly distributed. As Noxolo describes in relation to the Drum in Birmingham, UK, an arts centre that was pivotal for Black-led arts in that city for twenty-two years, the widespread cuts in public funding make it difficult for any public, innovative and non-permanent arts institutions to survive.[71] Both the focus on control as lost and so needing to be regained is different, as it assumes that we already occupy self-sufficient bodies. It buys into the fantasy that autonomy is what we most desire. This remains a very Western way of imagining freedom, and it is evident in the Brexit fantasy, as well as in some efforts at opposing Brexit. What this performance did instead was embody and act out other ways of understanding what it means to be in common with others, formed through shared vulnerabilities.

The affects put to work in this performance complement Judith Butler's efforts to consider subjectivity through vulnerability, in ways that exceed ideas about sovereign mastery. For example, Butler describes the action of 'parking my body in the middle of another's action' as a way of acting that is neither my act nor yours but 'something that happens by virtue of the relation between us'.[72] This idea of thinking about what is created between us is significantly different to a politics that begins with the presumption of autonomous subjects. As Erin Manning puts it, the between-us is formed of sensory encounters, vibrations and minor movements. As such, Manning gestures towards a reading of politics as something that is less a distinct action and more folded into the affective relations of everyday life. What links Manning and Butler's interventions is that starting with the everyday work of being-with-others displaces some of the focus on 'control'. In this performance, a focus on tonality, gesture and movement, interrupted, albeit very modestly, the nationalist affective atmospheres circulating.

In its attention to the affective politics of movement, this performance encouraged reflection on the categories and standpoints we might rely on in understanding 'Brexit'. It also opened other ways of thinking about being-with-others: through moments of shared laughter, moving together with others and considering how we are already in motion, undoing the assumption of a static, ahistorical 'people', engaging in 'perverse' acts. It also showed the impossibility of distinguishing between 'somewhere' and 'nowhere'. As such, the performance avoided amplifying moods of hostility, suspicion and shame. Instead it generated other affects and potential lines of connection. In opening up a space to move and to dance, the performance activated 'new modes of perception, inventing languages that speak in the interstices of major tongues'.[73] Overall, this performance offered significant insights for social scientists and humanities scholar-activists engaging nationalist populism. By engaging Brexit feelings through conversations between families and loved ones, and the tightly held intense feelings that spilled out in spectacular ways following this referendum, the performance avoided presenting characters with views we already know, and whom we assume to be different from us. For example, in one scene, involving a row between a newly married couple, the performance connected Brexit to the ordinary ways we project feelings of frustration and rage on others. It suggested that 'the micropolitics of barely perceived transitions' are inseparable from the macropolitics of social formations.[74] However, it also investigated other ways of being-with-others. It embraced Erin Manning's idea of the political as 'what awakens new modes of encounter', by making space for new ways of coming together and understanding one another.[75]

Performing the people anew

Brexit is based on a fantasy of establishing the exclusiveness of the English and British people. The problem is that many of the ways through which Brexit was opposed also relied on mobilizing accounts of a separate community of people. This figure of the people is central to the system of nation-states, and serves as an originary, yet elusive, symbol of sovereignty.[76] As Butler puts it: 'The discursive move to establish "the people" in one way or another is a bid to have a certain border recognized, whether we understand that as a border of a nation or as the frontier of that class of people to be considered "recognizable" as a people'.[77] However, the people have always been full of contradictions, and the people are also in motion. In this chapter, I have addressed Brexit through the affective idea of the people and by turning to the micro-register of the everyday affects through which people are drawn together and pulled apart. In addressing this event through the plurality of the urban street, and by suggesting that shame does not only operate as a national affect but can also 'illuminate our intense attachment to the world', I have explored other ways into this moment.[78] By sidestepping a framing of the theoretical and political task as that of revealing, recognizing and representing a singular and unified people, I have looked at the people as a category that is mobile, shifting and plural. This offers us a way out of the focus on identity groups, which had become so heavy in this context, that it no longer allowed any space for debate, and at worst, reproduced the categories of populist nationalism. I have argued that attuning to the micro-intensities of everyday relations can yield new modes of encounter, showing that the 'people' are never unmoving in their standpoints, perspectives, and politics.

    In this invitation to move and dance, this performance generated insights about the initial steps that must be taken if people are to gather and explore new forms of being together. It presents politics as something different to the task of returning power to the 'right' people. Instead, it presents politics as the work of establishing connections. This insight can be expanded by drawing on Costas Douzinas's comments on the massive gathering of people at Syntagma Square, Athens on 25 May 2011.[79] Inspired by the mass protests in Tahrir Square, Egypt in 2011, and the worldwide Occupy movement that followed the 2007–8 financial crisis, a 'multitude of men and women of all ideologies, ages and occupations' occupied Syntagma Square to object to the punitive austerity measures imposed by the International Monetary Fund (IMF) and European Union (EU) on Greece. In this moment, Douzinas argues, politics returned to the street and to the square in the performance of new forms of subjectivity. These gatherings and rallies did not fit with conventional ways of understanding politics: political parties and banners were discouraged and the scenes were described as 'non-political' by many journalists and politicians.[80] But in the many people who took their turn democratically to speak to the crowd for two minutes at a time, Douzinas describes seeing in Athens the formation of new forms of political subjectivity. The Syntagma multitude did not form a united nation or class, the conditions we tend to think of as foundational for becoming political, but 'formed a material coming together of people in public spaces'.[81] The performance of 'The Populars' gestured towards the everyday relations created in gathering together, so that people can 'act like citizens'.[82]

New ideas, stories and understandings of what it means to be European will eventually emerge from the aftermath of the nationalist populist self-sabotaging decision to leave the EU. But these cannot rely on fantasies of control, bounded subjectivities and self-mastery. These are part of something broader than Brexit and populism, and are foundational to ways of thinking made possible by the system of nation-states. Ultimately, 'nationalist populism' still has *no answers*; as Étienne Balibar argues: 'it poses in unreal and discriminatory terms the question of *place*; that is, the question of the spaces in which we live, work, meet and struggle.'[83] A globalized world has to work out questions of work, energy, health and social security at global and local scales, and in relation to environmental urgencies, colonial histories and people's meaningful cultural ties. The struggles against this new, further shift to the right will therefore have to be much more imaginative than a revived British social contract or the promise of national self-determination. What this chapter has shown is that it won't be sufficient to suggest that the right, simply 'duped unsuspecting folk'.[84] In considering people as 'creatures of affect',[85] and as moved by more than calculating reason or their rooted, inherited identities, we can recover other styles and spaces of feeling and being political. These alternative social and political initiatives, meeting places and attachments, between citizens and non-citizens, are already present– in the unlikely alliances and gentle gatherings around us.

6

Affective listening and the politics of change

As I walked to catch the 12.29 train from Swansea to Cardiff, I did not know that it was a rugby match day. I started to sense that something was different from the number of people wearing high-visibility jackets and the barriers put in place at the train station to control the crowds. When I arrived, one man in an official jacket told me I could forget catching the 12.29 train; it was already full. A woman standing beside me was told the same thing. She complained that she had been looking forward to visiting her mother in Cardiff, and that she didn't get to see her mother often. She had no idea that it was a rugby match day either. I wondered whether I was really this oblivious to the calendar of significant social events or whether I had decided somewhere along the way to block all such information from my mind.

The man in charge of the queues told us to come back for the 1.30 pm train, and that he would make sure we'd get on. I went to the coffee shop where I sat down with a book, grateful for a quiet space. A young man came to sit next to me, and started crying, loudly. This was another surprising interruption to my plan of an afternoon of fieldwork in Cardiff.

I was planning to get to Cardiff to join rehearsals for a work called 'Ways of Being Together' by the choreographer and dancer Jo Fong. I had met Jo Fong on a cold day in early January 2017, after she had written to me saying she was putting together a project on this title. She wanted to assemble different people in a room and to ask what being together might mean in the aftermath of Brexit as well as other political events. She had invited artists, writers, dancers, and wondered whether I might have something to contribute, given that I work as a 'human geographer'. Here was an invitation that I could not refuse. And there was something special about meeting new people in a cold rehearsal room at the beginning of a brand-new year. Rehearsals were underway by November, and that is how I came to be waiting at the train station, to go and see how the project was developing.

I asked the man crying next to me whether he was ok. He either failed to hear me or chose to ignore me. I left and went to catch my train. Later in the day I wondered about my decision to leave him: did I think he was not my problem? On the train, people were sat as families, and as groups of women and groups of men. Some were travelling as boyfriend and girlfriend, and this train journey on the day of a rugby match did not present a friendly atmosphere for a same-sex couple. People were dressed in red, signalling their support for Wales I thought about how I don't understand why people would want to dress the same. The atmosphere was jovial, relaxed, but there was no doubt that the crowd in red were in charge. This was the dominant majority, and only a fool would have a go at disturbing their force. I texted Jo explaining why I'd be late.

I arrived at Cardiff train station with bodies pressed beside me as the crowds made their way to the mighty national stadium, initially built for the 1999 Rugby World Cup. I could sense the buzz, the connection, the thrill and pleasures shared. But on this day, I also experience of a sense of what Clare Hemmings calls 'affective dissonance'.[1] For Hemmings, feminism begins from what Elspeth Probyn describes as the dissonance between our own sense of being, and what is made available for us as the conditions of possibility for a liveable life. We find ourselves with feminism because we feel out of place with the dominant expressions of how to enjoy ourselves and build a life. I walked a bit faster, eager to make a path towards another part of the city and the university rehearsal rooms where an eclectic mix of dancers, teachers of taek won do and capoeira, yoga instructors, drummers, as well as members of Hijinx, an inclusive theatre company for actors with learning disabilities, are due to meet. As the atmosphere bubbled across the city, and rose and fell in line with the success of the players on the field, the city also hosted other spaces for coming together.

This chapter continues with Chapter 5's focus on how dance and movement yield other ways of understanding being-with-others. However in this case, I address the challenge through two projects developed by the dancer and choreographer Jo Fong (Figure 12). One is 'Ways of Being Together', initially developed for the final night of the Cardiff Dance Festival, on 19 November 2017, and performed again at the Chinese Arts Now (CAN) festival on 22 February 2020. The second is 'Neither Here Nor There', created by Fong with artist, writer and performer Sonia Hughes (Figure 13). This was performed for

Figure 12. Jo Fong. Photograph by Janire Najera.

Figure 13. Sonia Hughes. Photograph by Lidia Crisafulli.

the first time at the Experimentica Festival, Chapter Arts Centre, Cardiff in 2018, and in 2019 it travelled to Summerhall for the Edinburgh Festival and to Bush Theatre, London. It was also performed by two other artists in a Welsh-language version ('*Heb Fod Fan Hyn na Man Draw*', with Eddie Ladd and Sara McGaughey). I followed these performances because of how they addressed two key questions in the context of a populist political atmosphere: first, what does it mean to listen to others, including those we disagree with? And second, what does political change involve? As Chapter 5 noted, these questions have been asked by many theorists responding to nationalist and populist governments.. However, this chapter discusses how the tone set in both Fong and Fong and Hughes's works offers a different response. They appealed to me because they did not begin from a shared identity or stable ground. Rather, coming together, in these works, presented something of a risk – for example, one of the few shared understandings was that we would meet people that we had not met before. These performances went about addressing the heavy political atmosphere by subverting them 'from within', rather than pointing from outside. In contrast to an adversarial approach that presumes politics is made up of different groups that see the world in different ways, these works asked what, from this messy, uncertain starting point, might we do? They pursued new and minor spaces for coming together, working to the side of, and not in complete rejection of the dominant gatherings – including those represented by the rugby. As Cindi Katz argues, the minor does not represent a stable political form that is opposing something major but is 'relentlessly transformative and inextricably relational'.[2] These works operated beside the forms, languages and affects that they were mobilizing against, while acknowledging how they were also related to them.

Accordingly, this chapter begins with a short discussion of the relationship between dance, movement and belonging, before turning to questions about listening. I ask what might listening mean when we refuse to assume the presence of identity groups? And what does it mean to listen to others using our hands, chests, and feet – not only our ears? Finally, the chapter asks what can we learn from affective listening about the possibilities of political change? 'Ways of Being Together' and 'Neither Here Nor There' provide the intellectual materials for this chapter, advancing the affective understandings of political action and being-with-others developed in Chapters 4 and 5. Working with these performers and artists taught me how other understandings of living together need to be cultivated, rehearsed and practised in space. I conclude with an account of how to cultivate incremental change that shifts toxic atmospheres. This means approaching politics as something other than a struggle against an enemy, which as Michel Foucault argues, leads only to oppression.[3] It does not turn away from the horrors of the world, but seeks a joyful, nonviolent and steadfast politics of response.

Dance and national affects

Dance and music are central to the performance, circulation and commodification of ideas about national identity and for activating national affects. As Elisabeth Militz argues, dance offers 'bodily movements and sensations' that 'activate national categorizations.'[4] Indeed, Allison Abra provides a full analysis of how dance produces cultural meanings and constructs national identities in her study of popular dance forms in Britain from 1918 to 1950. Abra shows how people navigated the significant social questions arising during the two world wars, about the instability of gender relations, class tensions, race relations, and the role and impact of foreign cultures, through the medium of popular dance.[5] The UK television show, *Strictly Come Dancing* (or in the United States, *Dancing with the Stars*), offers a contemporary manifestation of this point. This show articulates ideas about national identity and coheres the sense of a community coming together, not least through its scheduling on a Saturday night on linear television. It normalizes the heterosexual couple and centres whiteness as what belongs on the ballroom dance floor;[6] yet demonstrates the interstitial spaces where different ways of being and moving are also already at work. As Abra's study also shows, dance articulates dominant relationships of class, gender and sexuality, but it has also been a space through which these codes are transgressed and the rules rewritten.[7]

Geographer Tim Cresswell also studies the connections between dance and national belonging through a study of ballroom dancing codes in Britain in the 1920s and 1930s. Cresswell unpacks how all nations have a history of attempts at prescribing 'appropriate' and 'inappropriate' forms of movement.[8] For example, in the context of ballroom dancing in Britain in the 1920s and 1930s, dance teachers regularly met to discuss, then publish 'correct' forms of movement and policed the development of dancing styles that were considered improper, uncivilized or morally dubious. The codification of ballroom dancing styles by the Imperial Society of Teachers of Dancing in England in this period shows how English ballroom dancing style was developed against its 'other' – the dances of African and Latin American cultures, and how 'acceptable' forms of movement were explicitly racialized. As Cresswell discusses, the society established the importance of a 'strict tempo' (against what was deemed the loose and unstructured tempo of more improvised dancing styles, influenced by Jazz),[9] and preferred 'graceful', 'dignified' and 'uniform' dancing styles instead of something 'primitive', 'barbaric' and 'eccentric'.[10] These racist and colonial descriptors were designed to protect 'dancing' from other cultures, and especially the influences of African dance and music. Cresswell's analysis shows how dance and movement were interpreted and situated within a 'moral lexicon' to sustain ideas about Englishness and empire. Yet as he acknowledges, the *experience* of dancing and movement, and the affective relations produced from moving together, also hold the capacity to undermine and subvert the moral codings. Dance not only involves processes of exclusion and othering, but it also forms an experience of pleasure that cannot be fully controlled or manipulated.[11]

As these literatures intimate, dance suggests how power is negotiated in the movement of bodies, and why the state has an interest in bodily capacities, gestures and movements. Indeed dance theorist and sociologist Randy Martin helps us attune to these points, by reminding us of how states coerce bodies as a means of regulating society. We see this most clearly in war when bodies are compelled to be risked or killed in service of the state. But we also see it in the everyday organization of a school or the working day, in how bodies are expected to conform to a certain order, and to demonstrate particular capabilities in terms of performance, energy and perfectibility. Randy Martin describes how we can read processes of coercion through dance techniques, and in what appear to be 'benign' institutional sites, including schools, hospitals and social services.[12] A set of techniques are taught and practised in pursuit of the transformation and regulation of bodies. As Martin argues, dance makes some of these practices legible. But as he points further, dance also allows us to consider how practices of coercion on bodies *fail*. This is especially interesting, for as Martin makes clear, ideas about order, belonging, hierarchy and unity are not only achieved through the regulation of bodies: they can also, through the movement of bodies, be resisted, reworked and overturned. While bodily techniques and movements, practice and discipline are necessary for authority to maintain its authority, in combination, they also supersede the purposes to which they are put.

Martin provides an ethnography of a dance class to explore the connections between movement, discipline, the state and resistance.[13] It is an all-women class, and Martin along with the teacher and accompanist are the only men in the room.[14] He discusses the mimetic relationship between self and other, and in relation to the role of the mirror in a dance class. For Martin, the role of the other is assumed by a perfected view of the self, the very image of what the self is meant to arrive at. Martin describes how the dancer 'progresses through the self-savagery of her own aspirations to attain the perfection in a mirror that recedes as she approaches it'.[15] The mirror signals the 'to-be-looked-at-ness associated with becoming a dancer'.[16] This fits Angela McRobbie's account of ' "the perfect" as a horizon of expectation' for young girls, and a pernicious narrative in terms of what it means to become a woman. McRobbie argues that this myth of perfectibility has been 'made compatible with an individualising project and … with the idea of competition', and that some forms of feminism have been co-opted by these ideals.[17] The myth of freedom through bodily self-transformation therefore extends its reach far beyond dance. As Martin also outlines, the idea that pursuing talent, hard work and applying one's own innate creativity will allow one to overcome all limitations is part of the promise of freedom offered by the American nation.[18] But the myth relies on leaving others behind, and no doubt damages all involved. Nevertheless, what emerges from Martin's discussion is how the dance class itself operates in excess of these ideologies. He describes how the 'authority that was supposedly indifferent to gender here gives rise to it as a social category that can act against what denies it'.[19] What emerges, through the repetitive training of bodies, is also alliances, friendships, and the mobilization of a collective, suggesting the potential of an alternative feminist gathering. These are the remains, the vitalities and relations that 'authority gives rise to but cannot contain'.[20] Dance therefore forms a site through which we can better understand the unifying forces of national affects, and the ways they are redirected, with or without intention, to develop other forms of affective solidarity.

'Ways of Being Together'

Jo Fong's 'Ways of Being Together' (WOBT) was from the outset uninterested in perfectibility. It formed an experiment in practising ways of 'listening, talking, thinking, moving and even swimming together' to consider what is necessary for belonging.[21] It was described as 'An Installation of People, A Gathering, A Show, A Happening, A Listening'.[22] As Fong told me when she invited me to the initial research and development phase in January 2017, the project was in part a conversation, and 'the hope is that the conversation will be around for much longer than the finished piece'.[23] The process of considering the affective energies between-us mattered as much as the final performance. In attending the rehearsals throughout October and November 2017, I learned to consider the politics of being-with-others through a range of corporeal encounters. For example, how do we consider being-with-others when thinking with choreographer Deborah Hay's image, of the 206 bones in the human body, the 26 bones in each foot and the body as 53 trillion cells at once?[24] The cast for this work included both dancers and non-dancers working together. Overall, the work invited me to ask how the atmospheric politics of 'us and them' might be resisted by fostering other forms of togetherness, starting with bodily gestures and movements.

Rehearsals for this work took place at the Drama and Performance spaces of the University of South Wales, as well as the old Canton High School building now owned by Chapter Arts Centre. The structured improvisations developed in the rehearsal process included walking around the space together in pairs, taking turns to lead and be led. The movements experimented with the ways we are attracted to and thrown off balance by others, and all the tiny ways in which we negotiate being-in-common in everyday life. As the cast moved at different speeds, rhythms and in multiple directions, Fong would offer one-word instructions, including: 'breath', 'skin' or 'touch', to provide focus, then, 'find a new partner', so that the cast walked with someone taller or shorter, someone more or less used to dancing in public, or someone more used to leading than being led. They then touched different parts of each other's bodies, according to the timed instructions, including hands, feet, backs and arms. Through these various exercises, the cast had to listen to each other's bodies. The exercises tapped into considerations about the vulnerability of bodies, a subject discussed in Chapter 4. In experimenting with what a body can do when lifted by or held by others, they also investigated collective strengths, through probing the body's capabilities and limits, by way of the ties between us. In contrast to ideas about mastery, the aim was to consider the body as 'a generative source of ideas'.[25] In this space of mixed genders, ages, ethnic backgrounds and different degrees of able bodiedness, the cast engaged in listening, lengthening, stretching, loosening, touching, rubbing, chatting, laughing: they worked on the microdynamics of how we are with others, paying attention to minor movements and different ways of relating.

What was significant about these exercises, and the work more generally, was that it was being developed against the backdrop of a heightened political atmosphere, where narratives, allegiances and positions were noisy and self-certain. My conversations with the cast suggested that everyone had responded to Fong's invitation with enthusiasm to find other ways of being-with-others, and were finding joy in creating something to the side of the political theatre of populism. This was not only a post-Brexit context; it was also the time of the #MeToo movement, as high-profile female actors in Hollywood and later in the media and politics spoke out about their experiences of everyday sexual harassment in their industries and workplaces.[26] Suddenly, it seemed possible to say things that were not possible to say previously, demonstrating exciting as well as unsettling openings. The everyday violence that is normally hidden in advanced liberal democracies was being made explicit. Exacerbating inequalities and racial exclusion were similarly made horrifically clear by the fire in Grenfell Tower on 14 June the same year. The scale and dissemination of suffering drew people towards each other in this assembly, which was much looser and less purposeful than an 'orchestrated collectivity', but nevertheless suggests how things happen 'by virtue of the relation between us'.[27]

Drawing on William Walters and Barbara Lüthi, we can describe the political backdrop as a 'cramped space': the national affects were clamorous, claustrophobic, and generally made debate difficult. A cramped space is not an overarching experience, however. As Walters and Lüthi explain, while there may be pockets of crampedness, there are also spaces where it is also possible to come together otherwise. A cramped space includes 'degrees of deprivation, constriction, and obstruction but always and simultaneously a concern for the ways in which such

Figure 14. 'Ways of Being Together', Cardiff Dance Festival, 2017. Photograph by Heloise Godfrey-Talbot.

limits operate to stimulate and incite movements of becoming and remaking'.[28] The point here is that in cramped and constraining environments, there are pockets of air that can sustain other ways of being. This is what was being developed and practised in 'Ways of Being Together' (Figure 14). By experimenting with the ways bodies are energized, revitalized, strengthened and emboldened by virtue of their relations with others, the work avoided treating people as individuals that were bounded in terms of their emotions and affects, and instead researched and experimented with the conditions necessary for assembling with others. As Judith Butler puts it in her performative theory of assembly: 'it is *this* body, and *these* bodies, that require employment, shelter, health care, and food, as well as a sense of a future that is not the future of unpayable debt; it is *this* body, or *these* bodies, or bodies *like* this body or these bodies, that live the condition of an imperiled livelihood, decimated infrastructure, accelerating precarity'.[29] The political context of fear, anger and pain was being addressed in concrete terms by practising walking and stopping, running to and from others, walking with one person then a new person, singing, listening to sound – to learn 'how you are rather than who you are'.[30]

'Neither Here Nor There'

I arrived at the performance of 'Neither Here Nor There' at Capel y Graig, Ffwrnais (Furnace), late in the afternoon on 6 July 2019 – a day that was not as hot as the ones that had preceded it (Figure 15).[31] Although this tiny village in mid Wales, is only 12 miles north from Aberystwyth, where I was raised, I was unfamiliar with the landscape. It lies at the northern edge of Ceredigion, is tempered by the mountains on one side and the Dyfi estuary on the other. Ffwrnais is the village where poet R. S. Thomas once preached and forms the site of the only Welsh UNESCO Biosphere reserve: the saltmarshes and wet grasslands provide a home for lapwings and redshanks, grasshopper warblers, dragonflies, barnacle geese, ospreys and red kites. It is also home to Capel y Graig, where this performance took place – a chapel converted into an arts space by Avi Allen, curator and custodian of the building.[32] The clean wooden floors, the high ceilings and pared back design allows for a simple, meditative space. Inside had been left largely empty other than for a few pews that can be moved around, some woollen Welsh blankets and the small pulpit – kept from this building's use as a chapel, and with the words 'Sancteiddrwydd' (Welsh for holiness or sacredness) written above it on the

Figure 15. Neither Here Nor There (*Heb Fod Fan Hyn Na Fan Draw*). Capel-y-Graig, Ffwrnais, 6 July 2019. Photograph by the author.

wall. Outside, tall foxgloves clambered up the low stone walls that divided the road from the surrounding fields. The grass was freshly cut and dotted with dozens of symmetrical spherical bales. The good weather had enabled a good harvest.

This performance was put together around a series of six-minute conversations, all prompted by one question written in small delicate font on white cards. As we entered the space and took our seats at the various tables and few pews laid out, we saw the first cards which carried the instruction: 'Small talk'.[33] The audience knew that this was the pretext of the performance – to carry out conversations with strangers – advertised as it was along these lines. After the opening, improvised conversation between Jo Fong and Sonia Hughes, we sat at the makeshift tables and took our turn to speak or listen. New cards were introduced during the performance with new questions and instructions. Importantly, the two people around the table would take turns to listen and to speak, and when one spoke, the other was not allowed to speak themselves until the full six minutes allotted was up. In all the conversations I had with people, everyone commented on how staying silent turned out to be more difficult than we expected.

After six minutes, there was a change in rhythm, and Fong and Hughes would either ask us to move on and talk to someone new, or we would listen to the music, by Nina Simone, Louis Armstrong and Talking Heads. The next person would then ask or answer a different question, meaning that the conversation moved on. At other intervals, Fong and Hughes took turns to speak. At this performance, Sonia talked about accidentally finding out through Facebook that her neighbour had 'liked' the far-right political organization, Britain First. She talked about caring for her father living with Alzheimer's, her effort to keep him in his own home and the impossible costs of social care. But she also spoke about a good year of work, a nice holiday and attending a wedding in Italy. Everyday racism was presented as folded into the strains and the habits of everyday life.

All the questions or prompts were written in a way that encouraged us to tell a different story to the ones that we are used to narrating. For example, one question was: 'Where does your father come from?' This was informed by Sonia Hughes and Jo Fong's own conversations about relationships with their fathers, and it was a deliberate play on the racialized question: 'Where do you come from?' Another question was, 'How does where you live inform how you live?' The performance brought people together but not to a degree that ever got too comfortable. The invitation to talk was generous, warm, supportive: but as they discussed in an interview with me, we were not going to be offered cake.[34] The chairs remained wooden and hard-backed; there were no cushions. This was neither a therapy session nor a conversation with friends. It was an invitation to come together, but also to approach ourselves and each other anew. As we loosened up and got used to the format, the questions shifted to: 'Which battles have you given up on, and which ones do you need to pursue?' They concluded with, 'In these times, what do you hold dear?', referencing John Berger's book, *Hold Everything Dear*. As one participant said in a message posted on twitter following the performance on 6 July 2019: 'thank you for the valuable pause'.

Listening with attention

One of the questions raised by this work was, what does it mean to listen? Listening was made central by way of the six minutes we spent with a partner, paying attention – or at least staying quiet – as they addressed the question on the card. But it was also framed within the realm of ordinary life: we needed no special props or training to participate. What this work included was an effort to bracket a segment of time and organize the space for us to have a go at listening, and in doing so, invite us to think about the act itself. Fong and Hughes's approach complements Leah Bassel's reflections on the politics of listening. Like Bassel, Fong and Hughes began from an understanding that politics involves 'social forces that deflect attention from particular voices, and is necessarily adversarial as well as active and creative'.[35] From this perspective, Bassel argues that the art of listening in *itself* acknowledges inequality and difference, as well as the impossibility of complete understanding. Fong and Hughes approached listening, as Bassel does, through a micropolitical register, by opening spaces to challenge the existing distribution of subject positions and narratives. Appreciating that 'understanding can only be imperfect and outcomes ... fragile and uncertain',[36] they sought possibilities without presuming that there had to be agreement or recognition. They created a space for people to work on making sense together without seeking commonality.

The experience of listening pursued in this work can be further developed through Charles Hirschkind's study of cassette sermons and the ways these circulate as the 'omnipresent background of daily urban life in most Middle Eastern cities'.[37] His reflections on listening are interesting as they are not explicitly political. Hirschkind develops an account of listening as something different from absorbing information, and that involves more than the ears. He unpacks an account of listening that involves the whole body, and describes it as both an affective and a kinaesthetic experience. Firstly, he draws attention to a form of active listening that is about 'listening with attention'.[38] This is something different to what Eurocentred forms of knowledge might articulate as the difference between hearing and listening, or passive as opposed to active listening. We may be used to hearing this distinction from teachers or parents, in the injunction: Are you listening? Although Hirschkind's participants in Cairo recognize this form of distinguishing between *al-insat* – a complex sensory skill of paying attention, and *sam'*, a 'passive and spontaneous receptivity'[39] – these everyday accounts of how people tune in to the cassettes undermines this distinction. For example, one of his participants, Beha, who lives in Imbaba, a poor neighbourhood of Cairo, talks about listening to the cassette sermons as his companion on eighteen-hour working days driving taxis. Another, Ahmad, lights a cigarette as he listens to a sermon at the end of the working day, and laughs in response to Hirschkind's question of whether smoking is compatible with listening to a sermon. For this respondent, Hirschkind's question reveals a presumption that *proper listening must be active*. As Hirschkind points out, most of the people he met in Cairo seldom organized their listening 'in an exact or rigorous manner'.[40] In contrast to a distinction drawn between listening 'with the appropriate gravity',[41] and hearing background noise, Hirschkind draws on his fieldwork to articulate a mode of listening that incorporates both these modes. This performance by Fong and Hughes similarly combined both these understandings of listening, as something requiring attention, but also as involving bodies attuning to their environment. This understanding of listening combines both passive and active elements.

In this account of listening with attention, what matters is the role of attuning to the sermon by establishing an auditory and bodily connection. Hirschkind describes the role of listening as a form of 'pious relaxation' – a 'practice that calmed the mind and body'.[42] This form of listening with attention is something that is practised and cultivated through 'repeated and sensitive listening'.[43] It is not achieved by paying *more* attention, or by listening *harder*. If anything, it is achieved by way of greater relaxation. This aspect of repetition rather than depth of listening, is central. Practice and attuning allows for the potential experience of *inshirah* – 'the Quranic concept referring to the opening of the heart that accompanies drawing near to God'.[44] Regular listening orients the listener towards humility and faith.[45] Muhammad, another participant, describes this as feeling 'lighter, fresh, and relieved', allowing him to adapt to the 'rhythms, movements, and social contexts characteristic of contemporary forms of work and leisure'.[46] This is more about a way of living than a change in particular behaviour. This is instructive for the way 'Neither Here Nor There' also sought to establish connection through attunement.

Although different, there is much in this account of listening that will sound familiar to people who run, swim, practice yoga, make music or walk a dog, and experience these as practices that calm the mind and body, allowing an opening to sensual experience and orienting us towards preferred modes of living. Hirschkind draws on the anthropologist Marcel Jousse's work on traditions of oral recitation to better understand the role of repetitive bodily actions and rhythmic gestures in producing knowledge. These are forms of action that operate 'independently of conscious thought', better understood as part of the body's 'affective involvement with the world'.[47] Hirschkind develops this by arguing that cassette listening intervenes at the affective register.[48] Drawing on the work of Brian Massumi, Michel Foucault and William Connolly, in addition to Jousse and the participants' own words, Hirschkind describes this as a practice of cultivating the body to act as an auditory instrument.[49] This form of affective listening invites 'latent tendencies of ethical response'.[50] But the register runs underneath, or to return to Eve Sedgwick's spatial concept, *beside* more well-established and defined emotions. Put another way, this process of attuning is not defined by particular emotions or coded with ethical principles. It is about orienting, attuning and paying attention.

When in 'Neither Here Nor There', Fong and Hughes invited us to listen, they were doing so in a way that resonated with this account of listening. This experience involved attuning to affective and kinaesthetic experiences. For example, a short walk was staged at the beginning of the show to establish some distance from whatever feelings, strains and struggles we had arrived with, and worked to take us away from ourselves by walking with others. It helped us 'walk off' the feelings of discomfort at being invited to a performance that called for participation: taking a very short walk with others felt manageable. It also suggested a mode of being together that was not about encountering one another face to face, but side by side.[51] Building on Hirschkind's analysis of listening as affective involvement, we can say that the work of listening did not only take place in the explicit tasks of walking with others and the six-minute conversations. Of course, these were the building blocks of the performance. But the setting had also been carefully curated to shape the experience of listening. The space had been arranged in a way designed to calm the body and mind and allow an opening for engaging difference, otherness and the environment. This included the choice of music, the amount of tea and fruit laid out on a side table, the choice of the performance space, the lighting and the organization of the tables and chairs. Of course, these were not necessarily universally appreciated as such: these will have made some uncomfortable. My point is that listening involved more than a task that individuals took on: it was enabled by the environment and it was a shared, not a solitary act. These elements provided the conditions for the possibility of attuning to others.

As we listened to each other, we also heard the murmur of other conversations, and the hum of other groups of people chatting or just sitting. We listened out for the bell announcing that the time for talking was up. We listened to Fong and Hughes's improvised dialogue, their warm and funny exchanges, which appeared spontaneous but was built on years of co-working, understanding and trust. In these myriad ways, this performance bypassed ideas about serious or proper listening, while nevertheless inviting us to ask what it might mean to listen well and to listen without responding with our own ready prepared answers. The demand that the one who listened did not talk was crucial to the performance. This contributed directly to the attempt at developing an aesthetic register that refuses the language of morality. Put another way, they intervened in the present without imposing meaning on it.[52] The method encouraged the audience 'to pause and reflect rather than to adopt a particular moral code'.[53] Overall, Fong and Hughes did not tie the notion of listening to a claim about moral or civic improvement, as we hear in the refrain 'were you listening?' The performance also refused to suggest some transformation that would come about through attending the show. Altogether, the performance was curated in a way that sidestepped ideas about listening as a 'good thing' and instead explored what it means to listen, without suggesting we might reach full understanding or recognition.

Participation and atmospheric shifts

In its contemporary iteration in the UK cultural arts scene, participatory theatre can play out as a familiar and didactic genre. For some theatre companies, it is an area of expertise; but it is often a device put in place to secure funding because of government demands that the arts explicitly demonstrate 'social purpose'. The problem with participatory elements in theatre when it is not done in an interesting or reflective way is that it can either be intimidating or it can divulge a didactic and moralizing tone. People don't want to go to the theatre to learn a lesson. Participation can therefore summon engagement in a dehistoricized and depoliticized way, where what it means to be a 'good citizen' is not open to debate. However, 'Neither Here Nor There' bypassed ideas about securing 'active' participation instead of passive reception. It did not seek to generate transformation on the part of audiences. This work was interesting precisely because it did not follow these conventions, and because it criss-crossed the boundaries between ethics and entertainment in refreshing ways.[54] Here, it did not matter *what* we talked about, *how much* talking went on or whether people *really* listened. The performance worked at another register, less concerned with a qualitative change from one state to another, and more interested in exploring the possibilities of shifting the atmosphere. In order to explore this account of affective change, I turn to Lise Paulsen Galal and Kirsten Hvenegård-Lassen's discussion of organized interfaith walks. Their close study of these walks begins somewhere other than with the idea of different identities coming together. Following an affective approach that understands people as already shaped in relation to others, and not autonomous beings that proceed to mix together, they address these walks through a focus on how they enable an intensification of affect, prompting moments when some things shift. What is relevant for my discussion of 'Neither Here Nor There' is that Galal and Hvenegård-Lassen are also interested in how these walks hold the potential of *shifting the atmosphere*, without rationalizing or interpreting those shifts as 'good' or 'bad'.[55] Indeed, what made 'Neither Here Nor There' especially refreshing was that it cut through the over-determined format of participatory theatre. In this performance, the combination of design, tone and mood cultivated was not designed to activate us, but rather to investigate the fine lines between activity and passivity, mobility and stuckness,[56] listening and talking, asking how can we sustain interest, care and attention to the world around us.

This work engaged the everyday register to host another approach to time, as less a linear experience that follows a story, and more as a circulatory experience, involving repetition, and hosting a multiplicity of time-spaces through memories, reflections, connections, disconnections and synergies. This is interesting when we recall the concept of a 'cramped space'. This concept is used by Walters and Lüthi to describe a much harsher and more treacherous everyday environment than what we as an audience for this theatre work had likely experienced. However, they argue that a cramped space does not only describe a real site involving 'physical cramping and spatial confinement'. Developed from Giles Deleuze and Felix Guattari's work, it describes 'social situations where relations are saturated and passages blocked'.[57] In this regard, it resonates with the heavy atmospheres that followed the Brexit vote in the UK, and the heightened everyday nationalisms of the current moment. At this register, it becomes possible to address all the 'ambiguous affective dimensions' involved in a cramped space. As Walters and Lüthi outline, 'Despite the seemingly "obstructed agency" of cramped spaces and the blocked ways ahead, this does not equal a condition of standstill or of "a-social isolation", but rather one full of social relations.'[58]

This performance addressed ideas about time as involving repetition and difference. It also engaged space in a non-dualistic way. As the title indicates, the work did not promise to take us from *here* to *there*, on a journey towards redemption. Rather, it sought to work on this very terrain of the in-between. This is exemplified in the small walks that were staged to take us out of the building and back in again, shifting whatever expectations we might have arrived with. It can also be exemplified by way of another influence on Fong's work, Frank Bock and Katye Coe's exercises around talking and listening, which were formative for 'Ways of Being Together'. One of the principles that Fong takes from Coe's work is her refusal to think about work in terms of outcome – a current buzzword for arts councils in the UK, as it is for universities too. As Coe elaborates in her article on the work, '[to] Constantly Vent', which involves dancers running a circuit through the theatre and out into the cityscape, she had to begin by detaching running from any sense of *outcome* in terms of distance or time. Instead, Coe wanted to recover how running as a practice led to a 'shift in consciousness'.[59] '[to] Constantly Vent' involves repetitive movements between inside and outside the theatre to explore how movement encourages a shift in consciousness. This is slightly different to an outdoor performance or site-specific work, which is designed to *conjure* an atmosphere or sense of place. In contrast, the point here is about the process of moving between inside and out, here and there, where 'coming into the building you drop away from your usual relationship with the activity and the world, and when you come out of the building it is a little bit like opening your eyes because everything falls back into its usual set of conditions'.[60] In '[to] Constantly Vent', the aim was to attune to how a repeated action can establish the conditions for political change.[61] This is comparable to 'Neither Here Nor There' in its focus on how we might prepare and work on the atmospheric conditions for generating shifts in consciousness, new subjectivities or lines of connection. Critically, that shift does not come about by running further or listening harder, but through cultivating a practice and generating and maintaining spaces where alternative gatherings and collectivities can be grown. I want to suggest that this work experimented with the conditions necessary for bodies to assemble politically, and to deliver 'a bodily demand for a more liveable set of economic, social, and political conditions no longer afflicted by induced forms of precarity'.[62]

This work matters because nationalist ideas about 'us and them' work through and are often experienced as an atmosphere. That is, intolerance, hostility, hatred and xenophobia manifest not only in speech, physical attacks, institutional structures and cultures, but also, in a choice of phrase, a gesture, a way of holding or turning one's body, in a joke, a refrain or unquestioned expectations. William Connolly's work describes these as attitudes, habits, dispositions and affects that work on the nervous system.[63] If these are central to the possibility of nationalist sentiments taking hold, it also suggests that the work of building alternative structures of feeling must pay attention to bodily rhythms, gestures, movements and tone. This is where we can learn from performance works such as this one. For it addresses the political by asking how we build spaces where other forms of being-with-others can emerge, through movement, postures and styles. 'Neither Here Nor There' addresses how we forge spaces that support alternative ways of speaking and listening to one another. It shows us that, while all politics relies on aesthetics, a different aesthetics yields alternative forms, styles and tones for intervening politically.

Yet there is a significant critique of the argument that resistance can involve practising an 'aesthetic micropolitics'. For example, according to the political theorist Jodi Dean, aesthetic micropolitics cannot amount to a revolutionary politics, because it neglects to engage the 'very real challenges of building and maintaining spaces and forms of enduring struggle'.[64] I want to address this argument that thinking politically through the aesthetic and the micro can only amount to maintaining 'a miserable status quo'.[65] The first point to make here is that the arts are never a model for political action. Indeed, most artworks are never intended to form explicitly political interventions. The second point is that the aesthetic register is inseparable from the political. As I discussed in the introduction to this book, they are intertwined in some cases because they reflect subjects, characters, and groups back to us. But they are also intertwined because of the ways they engage in producing sensations, affects and intensities, which in turn suggests the possibility for changing the arrangement of subjects, characters and groups. Any serious engagement with the politics of change has to engage this register of people's affective inclinations and habits, as well as the possibilities for introducing new social and affective experiences. Thinking politically on this register of the micro and aesthetics directly addresses the possibilities for building political communities. Rather than wait for people to arrive at a better or improved moral position, to educate themselves or substantively change from holding one set of views to another, turning to this register reveals how we are all compromised and have our blind spots. It starts from where we are, and what can be done to shift a situation, to move past a blockage or to make things marginally better. Of course, this means something different in each context, and we all face different and incomparable experiences of violence and obstruction. But the focus here is on how to keep supporting the possibility of new subjectivities and new modes of being together. In contrast to an adversarial model of politics that begins from a division of the world into those who are with us and those who are against us, sitting and walking in the presence of Fong and Hughes allows us to consider the forms of power we already have between us – the collective strength, energy, humour, experience, empathy, diplomacy and determination that is already present and bubbling. Aesthetic micropolitics therefore offers substantial possibilities. And yet, it is not enough.

Thinking and practising change

The question of 'what can we do' recurs in my global politics classes, as indeed it should. In feeling a combination of hope and impatience, I borrowed my students' question and asked it at the end of my interview with Fong and Hughes at Capel y Graig. Hughes responded by saying that we had not yet discussed 'hospitality' and that this was an important concept for this work. Hospitality refers to forms of welcome towards guests or people we have just met, and the idea of encountering and sitting with strangers was one of the premises of this work. However, while most critical theorists have pursued this concept in relation to tensions between hosts and guests,[66] Sonia Hughes took the concept beyond a discussion of identity categories to ask what, in those encounters, can we do? To visualize her sense of hospitality, Hughes pointed away from the arts space to the spherical bales that had been collected and ordered in the fields beside us. The bales of hay signalled how there was regular, repeated, hard work to be done:

> Sonia: I suppose there's hospitality in the sense of something to get done …
>
> We'll make it as enjoyable as possible but there's work to be done. I suppose that's why I'm quite insistent that we don't have cakes. Because we could have had cakes.[67]

'Neither Here Nor There' moved beyond a discussion of the identities of the different people who came together by selecting unexpected questions, and refusing to allow us to settle around telling familiar stories. In this way, movement was built into the work, by way of the small atmospheric shifts enabled in going for a walk, the timing of the questions, and the fact that we moved on, and went and met someone new. These mechanisms combined to generate new, albeit provisional forms of togetherness. Hospitality was reframed as the challenge of considering what to do with those socialities and the energies held between us. In some ways then, Hughes posits another answer to the critique of aesthetic micropolitics: what remains is the need to get something done.

'Neither Here nor There' addressed the possibility of change as something that was ongoing, involving multiple capacities and possibilities, and which required spaces to connect with others. It formed a response to the question of how we intervene to shift the atmospheres of a cramped space. As such, it chimed with Jessica Dempsey and Geraldine Pratt's affirmative understanding of radical geographical practice as the work of creating 'wiggle room'. Dempsey and Pratt begin by acknowledging how so many of the spaces where we work, move, live and play are cramped: they are constrained owing to 'material constraints, the structuring logics of patriarchy, racism, the incessant drive to accumulation' and the frustration of not being able to be who we want to be and live in ways that are more equal, democratic and peaceful.[68] In writing about the importance of creating room to wiggle, they say that: 'It's not as much about a space as making space.' Thinking back to my experience of walking through Cardiff on a rugby match day, their image of 'wiggle room' fits with the image of making another path through a city's landscape, by walking in search of other ways of coming together. Dempsey and Pratt emphasize the 'verbiness' of movement and the importance of 'repeated actions'.[69] In contrast to settled identity categories, they place an emphasis on 'the sweaty, laborious, restless, creation (and re-creation) of dominant power relations/norms/codes that are in constant "parasitic" engagement with similarly ceaseless resisting, evading, playing, enduring, inventing, refusing, strategising, and living'.[70] Wiggle room might be absorbed or crafted within current social and economic structures, or built alongside. There is no prescription. However, as with Sonia Hughes's image of the bales in the field, the focus is on the labour of wiggling, listening, moving and acting.

Interlude: Words on a wall

On a brick wall, to the side of the 'Quadrant' Shopping Centre in Swansea, stood a magnificent artwork designed by Jeremy Deller – before the council decided to knock it down to build a car park. The artwork was composed of a brick wall painted in charcoal black, with these words written on it in elegant white font, across two stories: 'More poetry is needed'.

Afterword: Covid-19, the national frame and communities of sense

This book draws to a close in the middle of the Covid-19 pandemic, a global crisis and a national tragedy for the UK – a country where more than 120,000 died within a year of the first national lockdown.[1] The pandemic has disproportionately impacted countries led by populist and nationalist governments, including Brazil, India, the UK and the United States. The crisis demands a coordinated international response, but at this point, there is little sign of countries looking beyond their own self-interest. The national frame dominates. Borders have closed and travel has been restricted as a necessary response to a global health crisis. But national borders have also been reinforced in more everyday ways and have framed many public responses to the crisis. This includes the way the virus is imagined as coming from elsewhere, and as likely to be carried by different or minority populations, and national rhetoric mobilized through wartime analogies to narrate a way through the tragedy of mass death. It has allowed the overwhelming focus to be on improving things *here* and turning away from the virus's effects over *there*. However, this has also been a moment through which other communities of sense have emerged, based less on a common identity 'shaped by some common feeling,'[2] and more around loose assemblages moved to act. Communities of sense name something outside of an identitarian politics.[3] They involve relations of connection and disconnection.[4] And they also invoke the two meanings of sense. That is, they are composed through feeling and they are in search of other ways of making meaning. The pandemic has brought the national frame firmly into view, but this has been accompanied by, and revealed other communities of sense. These have included the energizing large-scale 'Black Lives Matter' protests and grassroots mobilizations dismantling statues of racist figures, mutual-aid groups in urban streets and groups of people in towns and cities finding new and less harmful ways of living together.

On 23 March 2020, the UK went into a national lockdown – far later than scientists had recommended. Prime Minister Boris Johnson's government and cabinet failed to address the warnings, and reportedly, Johnson never turned up to the government's national emergency committee (COBRA) meetings in January and February.[5] In April 2020, one thousand people died every day from Covid-19, for twenty-two consecutive days.[6] People stayed at home and overwhelmingly obeyed the order to care for each other by keeping apart. Black and Asian people in the UK died and continue to die of Covid in disproportionate numbers: a further national atrocity. It is hard to understand what took the government so long to act, a point that will become the subject of a public inquiry. Some scientists wrote that the actions needed were just so unimaginable to us: the demand for wholescale societal change. Was there a sense, as we watched the news of overfilled hospitals in northern Italy, struggling to cope, or mass graves being dug in New York City that we were somehow just by nature, *different?* Was this disbelief, ignorance, or some need to believe that large-scale humanitarian disasters do not happen in advanced liberal societies? Ideas about 'us and them' were at work from the very beginning of this crisis. But they were also imaginatively subverted through new ways people invented for supporting and providing for each other.

This book has argued that a focus on how the nation emerges and circulates as an affective force is critical for understanding how nationalism endures. The lines that establish a distinction between society and enmity, to follow Achille Mbembe's formulation of the problem, forms part of a long-standing way in which we understand ourselves, and they are persistent.[7] What remains urgent to address in this context of the Covid-19 pandemic however, is not only how some self-centred, dangerous people ended up in charge, but how people went along with them, legitimized them and cheered them on. What we have witnessed is the capacity of ideas about 'us and them' to return and assume a new intensity, despite decades of theories, reports, museums, monuments and novels that warn us precisely of the dangers of these ways of thinking. How is it that we continue to find ourselves ready to fear, distrust or hate a social group that we deem to be different from ourselves? How are we no better at recognizing these dangerous frameworks and their power at working affectively? What I hope to have done in this book is contribute approaches and frameworks for identifying these ideas, showing how they emerge in ordinary and extraordinary contexts, so that when we encounter them, we can consider how to diffuse and steer them elsewhere. Part of the influence of theories of everyday life includes showing that dangerous ideas do not belong to some special category of unpleasant people. Rather, dangerous ideas take different forms, and we all find ourselves entangled in them.

For Achille Mbembe, the desire for an enemy, and for a clear line that separates us from them, forms 'the dominant affective tonality of our times'.[8] My argument is that focusing on the affective force of these ideas is significant for understanding how they recur, maintain their force, as well as for asking how they can be undermined, repurposed and mellowed. I have drawn attention to how these ideas are diffuse, how they may appear both clear and vague, predictable and surprising, take on both old and new forms. We cannot therefore fully step outside of such ideas, and it is no good positioning ourselves as immune to them. Ideas about 'us and them' pop up or glow in all sorts of different sites and spaces, from the school yard to the shopping mall, the university to the beach. But this means they can also be challenged, subverted and undermined. Across these different sites and spaces, what we need is to practice, recover and amplify other understandings of being-with-others.

The atmospheres of being political

In pursuing the affective dimensions of these ideas, I have been able to trace how they work beyond instances of exceptional or heightened nationalism. While I have alighted on moments of crisis for the ways they conjure images of the nation at risk, and yield ways into how the nation forms an 'aspect of our historical way of being',[9] crises allow us to consider how we are already part of other communities of sense. There are, necessarily, all sorts of other ways of being-with-others that run beneath, alongside and together with ideas about 'us and them', formed 'through the division and distribution of sensation and signification'.[10] My approach has therefore involved not only attending to the emotional and affective aspects of nationality, but also to the ways affects are excessive, and spill out in ways that cannot be captured in narratives of 'us and them'. My critique of the dominant ways of understanding togetherness as a common identity lies partly with how too many people remain excluded. But it is also about how these dominant frameworks are unable to hear other experiences and alternative structures of affect. Attuning to affect leads us to the force of the dominating ways of understanding being in common, but it also leads to other forms of collective sociality. For example, addressing communities of sense highlights the loose assemblages of people brought together through the Covid-19 pandemic, including bereaved families, survivor groups, those living with long-Covid and new disabilities, women who found their caring responsibilities quadruple, women who found that the men's jobs would take priority, children who spent month after month not being allowed to play with any other child, students, as well as people newly politicized by the Black Lives Matter and #MeToo protests. While we do not yet know what kinds of political assemblages will emerge from these experiences, as of now, they have a history.

Using the framework of affect, I have been especially interested in the sense of an atmosphere taking form, and an energy gathering around certain refrains, narratives, and images. An atmosphere is not a coherent structure, and it lacks one central authority or point of sovereignty responsible for putting it all together and keeping it in place. It emanates from multiple points of origin and resonates across plural spaces, from social media to the street, to an advert on television or a line repeated at school, on a train or at the supermarket. During the first UK-wide lockdown, a national community was affectively mobilized through several different images and refrains, involving both improvised and organized elements. Children drew pictures of rainbows that were placed in house windows, which echoed with rainbow signs placed in closed shop windows and cafés, as well as makeshift signs built on the side of the road thanking 'key workers' and the NHS (National Health Service). Following a social media campaign, people joined to clap NHS workers from their doorsteps every Thursday night at 8.00 pm. This grew to be a widespread event, televised on the news, and we participated and watched the extraordinary echo of clapping bounce across otherwise silent urban streets. NHS workers were filmed clapping outside hospitals, as the blue lights of ambulances flashed across the evening light. The energy that lay in this repeated exercise, could have gone in any direction. For at this early point in the UK's experience of the Covid-19 pandemic, government ministers did not even pretend that they knew what to do. They were visibly lost, slow to respond: they were out of their depth. They had spent weeks ignoring warnings. The people emerged as a force that showed what they were already capable of.

In this period, thousands of people signed up to volunteer to help the national effort. Nightingale hospitals were built in record speed, only to be closed a year later when the government was unable to provide additional healthcare staff to run them. The government gave daily updates that were broadcast live by the

BBC, and people were reminded that linear television had its purpose. Politicians and journalists reached for war-time metaphors, including the 'front line', 'key workers' and later, when vaccines were developed, 'jabs army'. On 5 April 2020, the Queen broadcast a special television message that repurposed the lines, 'we will meet again' – well known to some of the audience watching as a line from a 1939 song that captured the mood of the Second World War, famously sung by Dame Vera Lynn.[11] On 8 May, a bank holiday weekend, Union Jack banners and bunting were hung on streets throughout the UK, on the 'Victory in Europe' (VE) celebration day, held to mark seventy-five years since the end of the Second World War. The BBC broadcast a speech by Prime Minister Winston Churchill at 3.00 pm, and people got together for the first time in many weeks. Forming a well-established mechanism for providing comfort and stability in uncertain times, the nation emerged in this context as a familiar framework. But the narratives of belonging also invoked clear ideas about who did not belong. In this case, verbal, and physical attacks against people of Asian background increased significantly in the UK during the first stage of the pandemic.[12] Data showed Black and other minority ethnic communities were significantly more likely than white people to be fined by the police for gathering, and for breaking Covid safety measures.[13] As ever, some people were more able than others to break the rules. The belief that the virus would come from *outside* the community, carried by rule-breakers, and imposed on otherwise rule-abiding, moral citizens, demonstrated more about the persistence of a national frame than it did about knowledge of infectious diseases. The whole focus on a national effort distracted from how Covid-19 disproportionately impacted and caused death in areas where healthy life expectancy was already lower than in other parts of the country.

The banal and ordinary dimensions of ideas about 'us and them' unfolded on the ground as a 'tangle of trajectories, connections and disjunctures'.[14] I have focused on these ordinary dimensions as my way into 'major events' or crises, but everyday life also formes a register through which I have investigated the possibilities for other modes of being-with-others and for pursuing political change. I have argued that ideas about 'us and them' unfold, impact and co-opt us through a meme on a timeline, a new profile picture, an image repeated on the news, a poster, a song, a refrain, the assumptions that have become part of the culture of institutions, which appear impossible to reduce to a set of policies, rules, persons or the design of buildings, and yet somehow incorporates all these elements. Achille Mbembe describes how this banality is central to racism. He calls it 'nanoracism' for how it unfolds in a thousand tiny elements, decisions, affects, positions, postures and habits. These stay alive and mutate, he says, through 'seemingly anodyne everyday gestures, often apropos of nothing, apparently unconscious remarks, a little banter, some allusion or insinuation, a slip of the tongue, a joke, an innuendo, but also, it must be added, consciously spiteful remarks, like a malicious intention, a deliberate dig or jab, a profound desire to stigmatize and, in particular, to inflict violence, to wound and humiliate, to degrade those not considered to be one of us'.[15] The little stuff matters, then, because it is integral to the possibility of a larger narrative establishing its legitimacy. But it also provides a portal for how these elements and ideas can be challenged, interrupted and diffused.

What I have termed the affective atmospheres of nationalism shape how we think of ourselves, and also how we imagine what is possible politically. As post-colonial writers including Frantz Fanon and Ashis Nandy have argued, the projection of hate against an enemy is also lived 'within oneself'.[16] Projecting all that is problematic on an enemy out there forms a way of securing our own identity, distinctiveness and sovereignty. The effort to persecute another involves the whole body and relies on fantasies about ourselves, as distinct, different, separable: 'the evil object and I can never be entirely separated'.[17] However, Mbembe identifies a positive mode of resistance to this affective fantasy of separation, and that is the presence of doubt and uncertainty.[18] As Chapters 2, 3 and 4 have explored, doubt, uncertainty and ambivalence unfold as modes of contesting the self-certain geographies of 'us and them' heard in ideas about civilization and its enemies, the people and the refugees. I have argued for a politics of resistance that avoids marshalling an opposing geography that is certain in its own righteousness, but rather meets these ideas with doubt, hesitancy and questioning. Mbembe argues that doubt is important because:

> in the concrete struggle opposing us to our enemies, doubt hinders the total freeing of voluntarist, emotional and vital energies necessary for the use of violence and, when required, the shedding of blood.[19]

Doubt is important politically because it hinders and intrudes on the energy needed to carry out violence.

Finally, attending to the ordinary register invites us to study the political in new or unlikely sites and spaces, or at least, in sites and spaces that are not typically covered in academic studies of global politics.[20] The enduring question for me, is what is at stake in calls to unify around a culture or a people, and how do such ideas make themselves felt in everyday encounters? The effort of minimizing or denying the plurality of cultures, peoples, lifeworlds that we inhabit is a legacy of how we think about being together as a political community under the system of nation-states. While the nation is often encountered as something comforting, reassuring, self-affirming, we also already know its capacity for harm. The question that emerges is what other communities of sense are already available, for a politics of 'multidimensional pluralism'?[21] This might include loose assemblages that cut across faith, creed, unions, parties, interests and backgrounds. These are doubtful of claims about a more original or rightful people. They are composed of compromises, differences and various imaginaries of belonging to place and to the earth. Finally, they involve 'multiple sites of potential citizen action, within and above the state'.[22]

Living otherwise

In April 2021, a year following the first period of lockdown in the UK, a huge temporary, improvised memorial to those people lost in the pandemic was built on a wall opposite the Houses of Parliament. The wall stretches for half a mile (Figure 16) and stands adjacent to the river Thames. It is canopied by a long line of trees that are, at this point in the year, full of leaves. On the stone wall, people have come to paint thousands of pink hearts, one to remember all the people who have died to date. The hearts are all different sizes. Some have names and memories written in them; many are just a painted image. Permanent pens have been left on the ground, together with bunches of flowers, and people can pick up the pens to write additional messages. The wall is an evolving work, semi-authorized, built by a community of bereaved families.

The messages include the following statements, which I read when I visited on 30 April 2021: 'Nanny, 1.4.2020', 'Love you Nanny Jean', 'Dada we love you so much x', 'All the NHS workers lost', 'Husband', 'dad', 'Miss you gran. RIP', 'I love you mum', 'Stolen too soon', 'keyworkers', 'please come back', 'Loved', 'Wendy', 'For all humanity', 'Best dad ever', 'Jarek', 'Alan', 'Colin', 'John', 'Annie', 'Jane', 'Keith', 'Sandra', 'Paul', 'Sunil', 'Brenda', 'Eileen', 'Amrit', 'Myrna', 'To all lost to covid-19', 'Love to all the world', 'Papa', 'all FEMALE workers', 'Daddy we miss you so much', 'Dad, Forever in our hearts, Missing you so much, Love your girls.' Reading them, and looking at more and more pink hearts while walking is a disorientating experience. There are so many. The wall forms a visual attempt to capture the numbers of people lost, and the effect simultaneously is that the numbers are hard to visualize or take on board.

Figure 16. The National Covid Memorial Wall, 30 April 2021. Photograph by the author.

Among the messages are ones that pay tribute to people in different parts of the world. There is one for 'Li Wenliang, Wuhan Whistleblower, 1985–2020', the young doctor based in Wuhan, China, who tried to warn medics about the new respiratory disease circulating, and who died from it on 7 February 2020.[23]

Referencing the way the British National Health Service relies on workers from all over the world, messages remember a 'NHS Filipine worker', 'Philippines, NHS Frontliners', 'Love from Ghana', 'LOVE FROM EVERYWHERE', 'Ethiopia', 'Ecuador covid victims'. Although English is predominant, messages are also left in different languages. Messages are left by health practitioners including: 'for my patients, from a Tommy's doctor' (referencing St Thomas' Hospital, which is just nearby). Also, 'For all our patients, their loved ones, our loved ones, Milton Keynes University Hospital'. Seven hearts were painted close together, spelling 'J U S T I C E'.

Distance and proximity are drawn in complex ways, and crises appear near and far at different points. It might take us a long time to know how to make sense and seek justice for those who died. The pandemic also threw a new light on ideas about personhood and 'political action', ideas that I have revisited throughout this book. What is worth remembering about this context is that the idea of striving, to enforce human action on the world around us, was precisely what was not needed. Indeed, this model of acting, for a moment, lost its shine. What was needed in response to this crisis, for most people, was to do less, to reduce the business of their lives drastically: to stop driving to the office and to school, to cut back on how much they shopped, to work less and consider different work that needed doing. I don't want to underestimate how people experienced this moment very differently. Many families experienced this period as one of intensified work, with several members of some families ill or hospitalized. It was, for many, many people, traumatic and devastating. But beyond these situations that demanded immediate action, what many people witnessed was the absolute uselessness of ideas about a self-determining, striving subject. There were a few weeks in March and April 2020 when we watched these ideas wash away, making room for other ideas that were much needed, such as our interdependency. What was needed was care, love, patience, modesty, ingenuity, a capacity to slow down as well as to improvise and to turn up and be present when we had no answers or were unsure about the ways forward. Many of the people in charge, and who had done well out of the old way of doing things, simply went missing. They retreated to private, highly sanitized, uncrowded homes. The virus, if only for a short moment, exposed all the pretence of action as self-motivation and ruthless striving, and the ridiculousness of claiming that 'we' were going to be better at this than 'them'. What came through in this moment was a sense of our common, yet uneven, human vulnerabilities.

Put another way, what emerged in this pandemic was what Judith Butler describes as our interdependency. We needed neighbours, friends, a health infrastructure, green spaces, predictable payments, an informal as well as formal economy of care and social support. Will we remember all this? Butler did not write this account of interdependency in response to the Covid-19 pandemic, but the crisis nevertheless magnified her point of what this means:

> Interdependency, though accounting for differentials of independence and dependence, implies social equality: each is dependent, or formed and sustained in relations of depending upon, and being depended upon. What each depends upon, and what depends upon each one, is varied, since it is not just other human lives, but other sensate creatures, environments, and infrastructures: we depend upon them, and they depend upon us, in turn to sustain a livable world.[24]

The pandemic forms a story not of self-centred individuals all driven to protect their own interests, but of how much people cared for those they had never met and will never know. We also learned how able we are to adapt to large-scale sweeping societal change, almost overnight. We collectively proved this was possible. This is a powerful social memory in the age of increasing climate emergencies.

It is not yet the time for commemoration. Those calls are beginning to formulate, as are the plans for a public inquiry, but we don't know yet what forms they will take and what shape this event will take as part of a global memory. In this space of uncertainty, governments are mobilizing to establish the 'new normal', which includes extended police powers, compulsory ID cards and Covid passports, new restrictions and prohibitions on political protest, privatization of healthcare systems and other public services, cuts to education especially the humanities and the arts, increasing restrictions on protest and the free movement of people. However, this experience of global uncertainty attunes us to other forms of relating to one another and of imagining our collective futures. The affective force of living through this collective event briefly opened new understandings of ourselves and how we want to live in the world. That felt experience remains a shared memory of living otherwise.

Notes

Preface

1 Raymond Williams, 'Wales and England' in *What I Came to Say* (London: Hutchinson Radius, 1990), 72.

2 I'm referring here to the campaigns for a Welsh language television channel in the early 1980s and the early campaigns of the Welsh Language Society, which in 1963 blocked Trefechan bridge in Aberystwyth, and went on to call on the authorities to produce birth certificates, post-office documents, car licenses and road signs in Welsh. See John Davies, *Hanes Cymru* (The History of Wales) (London: Penguin, 1990).

3 Nigel Jenkins, *Real Swansea* (Bridgend: Seren Books, 2008).

Introduction

1 Kathleen Stewart, *Ordinary Affects* (Durham, NC: Duke University Press, 2007).

2 Vanessa May, Bridget Byrne, Helen Holmes and Shaminder Takhar, 'Nationalism's Futures', *Sociology*, 54(6), 2000: 1055–71; Sivamohan Valluvan, *The Clamour of Nationalism: Race and Nation in Twenty-First-Century Britain* (Manchester: Manchester University Press, 2019).

3 Raymond Williams, *Marxism and Literature* (Oxford: Oxford University Press, 1977).

4 Benedict Anderson, *Imagined Communities: Reflections on the Origin and Spread of Nationalism* (London: Verso, 1991); Homi Bhabha, *The Location of Culture* (London: Routledge, 1994); Partha Chatterjee, *Nationalist Thought and the Colonial World: A Derivative Discourse? Third World Books* (London: Zed, 1993); Ernest Gellner, *Nations and Nationalism* (Oxford: Blackwell, 1983).

5 Michel Billig, *Banal Nationalism* (London: Sage, 1997); Tim Edensor, *National Identity, Popular Culture and Everyday Life* (Oxford: Berg, 2002); Paul Gilroy, *After Empire: Melancholia or Convivial Culture* (London: Routledge, 2004); Ghassan Hage, *White Nation: Fantasies of White Supremacy in a Multicultural Society* (New York: Routledge, 2000).

6 Sara Ahmed, 'Collective Feelings: Or, the Impressions Left by Others', *Theory, Culture & Society*, 21(2), 2004a: 28.

7 Ahmed, 'Collective Feelings', 27; see also Sara Ahmed, 'Orientations: Towards a Queer Phenomenology', *GLQ: A Journal of Lesbian and Gay Studies*, 12(4), 2006: 543–74; *The Cultural Politics of Emotion* (Edinburgh: Edinburgh University Press, 2004); and *The Promise of Happiness* (Durham, NC: Duke University Press, 2010).

8 Geraldine Pratt and Victoria Rosner, *The Global and the Intimate* (New York: Columbia University Press, 2012), 6.

9 There is by now an extensive literature on affect. For key collections, see Patricia Clough and Jean Halley (eds), *The Affective Turn: Theorizing the Social* (Durham, NC: Duke University Press, 2007) and Melissa Gregg and Greg Seigworth, *The Affect Theory Reader* (Durham, NC: Duke University Press, 2010). Most of this literature draws either on Eve Sedgwick's work in *Touching Feeling: Affect, Pedagogy, Performativity* (Durham, NC: Duke University Press, 2002) which in turn draws on the work of Silvan Tomkins on affects and drives. For Sedgwick, affects can be 'attached to things, people, ideas, sensations, relations, activities, ambitions, institutions and any number of things, including other affects' (Sedgwick, 2003: 19). Brian Massumi draws a Deleuzian framework, where affect names the intensive quality of life; see Brian Massumi, *Politics of Affect* (Cambridge: Polity Press, 2015) and *Parables for the Virtual* (Durham, NC: Duke University Press, 2002).

10 Gregg and Seigworth, *Affect Theory Reader*, 2.

11 Ben Anderson, *Encountering Affect: Capacities, Apparatuses, Conditions* (Farnham: Ashgate, 2014).

12 Randy Martin, *Critical Moves: Dance Studies in Theory and Politics* (Durham, NC: Duke University Press, 1998), 3.

13 Susanne Gannon, 'Ordinary Atmospheres and Minor Weather Events', *Departures in Critical Qualitative Research*, 5(4), 2016: 79–90.

14 Bhabha, *The Location of Culture*, 200.

15 See, for example, Shanti Sumartojo, *Trafalgar Square and the Narration of Britishness, 1900–2012: Imagining the Nation* (Oxford: Peter Lang, 2013).

16 Jenny Edkins, *Change and the Politics of Certainty* (Manchester: Manchester University Press, 2019), 10.

17 Further to Edkins, ibid., see Les Back, 'Hope's Work', *Antipode*, 53(1), 2021: 3–20.

18 Deborah Dixon, 'Repurposing Feminist Geopolitics: On Estrangement, Exhaustion and the End of the Solar System', *Dialogues in Human Geography*, 8(1), 2018: 88.

19 Helen F. Wilson and Ben Anderson, 'Detachment, Disaffection and Other Ambivalent Affects', *Environment and Planning C: Politics and Space*, 38(4), 2020: 592.

20 Marie Beauchamps, *Governing Affective Citizenship: Denaturalization, Belonging, and Repression* (London: Rowman & Littlefield International, 2018); Jack Holland and Ty Solomon, 'Affect Is What States Make of It: Articulating Everyday Experiences of 9/11', *Critical Studies on Security*, 2(3), 2014: 262–77; Joseph Masco, *The Theatre of Operations: National Security Affect from the Cold War to the War on Terror* (Durham, NC: Duke University Press, 2014).

21 Wilson and Anderson, 'Detachment, Disaffection and Other Ambivalent Affects', 592.

22 Rogers Brubaker, *Ethnicity without Groups* (Cambridge, MA: Harvard University Press, 2004).

23 I borrow this formulation from Jenny Edkins, 'Face', in Roland Bleiker (ed.), *Visual Global Politics* (Oxon: Routledge, 2018), 121–6.

24 Teresa Brennan, *The Transmission of Affect* (New York: Cornell University Press, 2004), 52.

25 Ibid., 165.

26 Émile Durkheim, *The Elementary Forms of Religious Life* (Oxford: Oxford University Press, 2001).

27 Durkheim, *Elementary Forms of Religious Life*, 161.

28 For a fuller discussion of the social sciences as a form of knowledge, rather than *as* knowledge, see Sanjay Seth, *Beyond Reason: Postcolonial Theory and the Social Sciences* (Oxford: Oxford University Press, 2021).

29 Elizabeth Povinelli, *The Cunning of Recognition: Indigenous Alterities and the Making of Australian Multiculturalism* (Durham, NC: Duke University Press, 2002), 86–7.

30 Michael Shapiro, *Methods and Nations: Cultural Governance and the Indigenous Subject* (London: Routledge, 2004), 6–11.

31 Akhil Gupta and James Ferguson, 'Beyond "Culture": Space, Identity and the Politics of Difference', *Cultural Anthropology*, 7(1), 1992: 6–23.

32 Seth, *Beyond Reason*.

33 Sneja Gunew, 'Subaltern Empathy: Beyond European Categories in Affect Theory', *Concentric: Literary and Cultural Studies*, 35(1), 2009: 11–30; Carolyn Pedwell, 'De-colonising Empathy: Thinking Affect Transnationally', *Samyukta: A Journal of Women's Studies*, 16(1), January 2016: 27–49.

34 Ruth Frankenberg and Lata Mani, 'Crosscurrents, Crosstalk: Race, "Postcoloniality" and the Politics of Location', *Cultural Studies*, 7(2), 1993: 296.

35 Ibid.

36 Geraldine Pratt and Victoria Rosner, *The Global and the Intimate* (New York: Columbia University Press, 2012), 1. Sedgwick argues that an affective approach seeks to collapse the gap between everyday theory and academic theory. *Touching Feeling*, 145.

37 Naeem Inayatullah and Elizabeth Dauphinee (eds), *Narrative Global Politics: Theory, History and the Personal in International Relations* (London: Routledge, 2017);

Naeem Inayatullah (ed.), *Autobiographical International Relations, I, IR* (London: Routledge, 2010); see also Roxanne Lynn Doty, 'Writing from the Edge', in Nevat Soguk and Scott G. Nelson (eds), *The Ashgate Research Companion to Modern Theory, Modern Power, World Politics: Critical Investigations* (London: Routledge, 2016).

38 Naeem Inayatullah, 'Falling and Flying: An Introduction', in *Autobiographical International Relations* (London: Routledge, 2011), 7.

39 Lydia Davis, *Essays One* (New York: Farrar, Straus and Giroux, 2019), 205.

40 See, for example, Sam Okoth Opondo, *Diplomatic Para-Citations: Genre, Foreign Bodies, and the Ethics of Co-Habitation* (Rowman and Littlefield, 2022); Claudia Rankine, *Citizen: An American Lyric* (London: Penguin Books, 2015); Christina Sharpe, *In the Wake: On Blackness and Being* (Durham, NC: Duke University Press, 2016).

41 Shanti Sumartojo and Sarah Pink, *Atmospheres and the Experiential World: Theory and Methods* (Oxon: Routledge, 2019).

42 Yasmin Gunaratnam, *Death and the Migrant: Bodies, Borders and Care* (London: Bloomsbury, 2013), 17.

43 Elizabeth Dauphinee, *The Politics of Exile* (London: Routledge, 2013).

44 Sharpe, *In the Wake*, 8.

45 Wendy Brown, 'Wounded Attachments', *Political Theory*, 21(3), 1993: 390–410; see also Linda Alcoff, 'The Problem of Speaking for Others', *Cultural Critique* (winter 1991–2): 5–32.

46 Chandra Mohanty, 'Under Western Eyes: Feminist Scholarship and Colonial Discourses', *Feminist Review*, 30(1), 1988: 61–88. In a more recent example, Alison Phipps critically engages the politics of the #MeToo movement, where survivors publicize experiences of sexual harassment or abuse online. Careful not to discredit survivors' stories, she asks us to consider how 'speaking out' can 'easily become speaking *over* in mainstream and social media publics'. See '"Every Woman Knows a Weinstein": Political Whiteness and White Woundedness in #MeToo and Public Feminisms around Sexual Violence', *Feminist Formations*, 31(2), 2019: 7.

47 Lauren Berlant, 'The Subject of True Feeling: Pain, Privacy, and Politics', in Karyn Ball (ed.), *Traumatizing Theory, The Cultural Politics of Affect in and beyond Psychoanalysis* (New York: Other Press, 2007), 343.

48 On anecdotes as method, see Lisa Baraitser, *Maternal Encounters: The Ethics of Interruption* (London, Routledge, 2009).

49 Ghassan Hage, *Is Racism an Environmental Threat?* (Cambridge: Polity Press, 2017), 8.

50 Ibid., 71.

51 Michael Shapiro, *Violent Cartographies: Mapping Cultures of War* (Minneapolis: University of Minnesota Press, 1997); *Cinematic Political*

Thought: Narrating Race, Nation and Gender (New York: New York University Press, 1999); *For Moral Ambiguity: National Culture and the Politics of the Family* (Minneapolis: University of Minnesota Press, 2001).

52 Étienne Balibar, 'The Nation Form: History and Ideology', in Étienne Balibar and Immanuel Wallerstein (eds), *Race, Nation, Class: Ambiguous Identities* (London: Verso, 1991), 86–106.

53 David Theo Goldberg, *The Threat of Race* (Malden, MA: Blackwell, 2009), 6.

54 Ibid., 2; on the principle of familiality in global politics, see also, see Engin Isin, 'Citizens without Nations', *Environment and Planning D: Society and Space*, 30(3), 2012: 450–67.

55 Ibid.

56 Cynthia Weber, *Queer International Relations* (Oxford: Oxford University Press, 2016), 4.

57 Ibid.

58 Ibid., 7.

59 Anthony W. Marx, *Faith in Nation: Exclusionary Origins of Nationalism* (Oxford: Oxford University Press, 2005), ix); see also, Arjun Appadurai, *Fear of Small Numbers* (Durham, NC: Duke University Press, 2005).

60 Kathleen Stewart, 'Atmospheric Attunements', *Environment and Planning D: Society and Space*, 29, 2011: 445.

61 Shapiro, *Methods and Nations*, 40.

62 Jason Dittmer, *Captain America and the Nationalist Superhero: Metaphors, Narratives and Geopolitics* (Philadelphia, PA: Temple University Press, 2013); Cynthia Weber, *Imagining America at War: Morality, Politics and Film* (New York: Routledge, 2006).

63 Cynthia Enloe, *Bananas, Beaches and Bases: Making Feminist Sense of International Politics*, 2nd edn (Berkeley: University of California Press, 2014); Debbie Lisle, *Holidays in the Danger Zone*; Christine Sylvester, *Art/Museums: International Relations Where We Least Expect It* (London: Routledge, 2015).

64 Lisle, *Holidays in the Danger Zone*, 23.

65 Sedgwick, *Touching Feeling*, 9; for more on how this shapes our understandings of global politics and security, see William Walters, *Governmentality: Critical Encounters* (Abingdon: Routledge, 2012).

66 Ibid., 11.

67 As Eve Sedgwick puts it, critical theory can often make our view of the world appear so settled that it risks making us immune to the surprises of it. *Touching Feeling*, 130.

68 Ben Highmore, 'Bitter after Taste: Affect, Food and Social Aesthetics', in Melissa Gregg and Gregory Seigworth (eds), *The Affect Theory Reader* (Durham, NC: Duke University Press, 2010), 122.

69 Michael Taussig, *Walter Benjamin's Grave* (Chicago: University of Chicago Press, 2006), vii.

70 Andrew Bennett, 'Literary Ignorance', in Matthias Gross and Linsey McGoey, *Routledge International Handbook of Ignorance Studies* (London: Routledge, 2015), 37.

71 Ibid.

72 Elizabeth Grosz, *Chaos, Territory, Art: Deleuze and the Framing of the Earth* (New York: Columbia University Press, 2008), 1; for more on how the arts present other framings of world politics, see Roland Bleiker, *Aesthetics and World Politics* (New York: Palgrave, 2012); Alan Ingram, *Geopolitics and the Event: Rethinking Britain's Iraq War through Art* (Oxford: Wiley, 2019).

73 Ibid., 8.

74 Alex Danchev and Debbie Lisle, 'Introduction: Art, Politics, Purpose', *Review of International Studies*, 35(4), 2009: 777–8.

75 Grosz, *Chaos, Territory, Art* , 2.

76 Ibid.

77 Ibid., 5.

78 Ibid., 9.

79 Ibid., 10.

80 Michel Foucault, 'For an Ethic of Discomfort', in James D. Faubion (ed.), *Power: Essential Works of Foucault, 1954–1984* (London: Penguin, 1994), 448.

81 Jean-Jacques Rousseau, *Discourse on the Origin of Inequality* (Oxford: Oxford World Classics, 1994).

1 The affective atmospheres of nationalism

1 This story was reported in the *Daily Mail* on 9 August 2012, http://www.dailymail.co.uk/news/article-2185951/Olympics-2012-How-Olympic-spirit-Games-fan-sells-bottled-100-atmosphere-day-British-gold-rush-began.html.

2 Sebastian Coe, chair of LOCOG repeatedly referred to the 'extraordinary atmosphere', see, for example, http://www.olympic.org/news/coe-praises-london-2012-s-extraordinary-atmosphere/170292.

3 'London 2012: This Closing Ceremony was a Raucous Pageant of Popular Culture', *The Guardian*, 13 August 2012, http://www.theguardian.com/sport/2012/aug/13/olympic-games-closing-ceremony-culture. This was surprising as opinion polls taken four months before the games began indicated that more than half of respondents were not interested in the Olympics: YouGov poll, 30 March 2012, http://yougov.co.uk/news/2012/03/30/interest-london-olympics/.

4 This was the term used long in advance of the beginning of the games, such as by the Mayor of London Boris Johnson, speaking in 2008 about the 'party atmosphere' that the games would bring to London, http://www.theguardian.com/uk/2008/oct/07/olympics2012.boris.

5 For a critique of these narratives of cosmopolitanism, see Dan Bulley and Debbie Lisle, 'Welcoming the World: Governing Hospitality in London's 2012 Olympic Bid', *International Political Sociology*, 6(2), 2012: 186–204.

6 Arjun Appadurai, *The Future as Cultural Fact* (London: Verso, 2013), 109.

7 Stephen Graham, *Vertical: The City from Satellites to Bunkers* (London: Verso, 2018); Luce Irigaray, *The Forgetting of Air in Martin Heidegger* (Austin: University of Texas Press, 1999); P. Sloterdijk, *Terror from the Air* (Los Angeles: Semiotext(e), 2009).

8 Mark Jackson and Maria Fannin, 'Letting Geography Fall Where It May – Aerographies Address the Elemental', Guest editorial, *Environment and Planning D: Society and Space*, 29, 2011: 435–44.

9 Sara Ahmed, 'On Collective Feelings: Or, the Impressions Left by Others', *Theory, Culture and Society*, 20(1), 2004a: 25–42; Lauren Berlant, *The Queen of America Goes to Washington City: Essays on Sex and Citizenship* (Durham, NC: Duke University Press, 1997); Anne-Marie Fortier, *Multicultural Horizons* (London: Routledge, 2008); Jasbir Puar, *Terrorist Assemblages: Homonationalism in Queer Times* (Durham, NC: Duke University Press, 2007).

10 Martin Coward, 'Between Us in the City: Materiality, Subjectivity and Community in the Era of Global Urbanization', *Environment and Planning D: Society and Space*, 30(3), 2012: 468–81; Rhys Jones and Peter Merriman, 'Hot, Banal and Everyday Nationalism: Bilingual Road Signs in Wales', *Political Geography*, 28(3), 2009: 164–73; Rhys Jones and Peter Merriman, 'Network Nation', *Environment and Planning A*, 44(4), 2012: 937–53.

11 Ben Anderson, 'Affective Atmospheres', *Emotion, Space and Society*, 2(2), 2009: 78.

12 Ash Amin and Nigel Thrift, *Arts of the Political* (Durham, NC: Duke University Press, 2013), 161.

13 Denise Riley, *Impersonal Passion. Language as Affect* (Durham, NC: Duke University Press, 2005), 1.

14 Derek McCormack, 'Engineering Affective Atmospheres', *Cultural Geographies*, 15(4), 2008: 413.

15 431 million visited the Olympics website and 150 million tweets were sent about the Olympics worldwide. See LOCOG (2011–12) Report and Accounts http://www.local.gov.uk/web/guest/2012-local-olympic-legacy/-/journal_content/56/10171/3877079/ARTICLE-TEMPLATE.

16 This point is made by Homi Bhabha when he invokes the English weather as 'the most changeable and immanent signs of national difference' which 'encourages memories of the 'deep' nation crafted in chalk and limestone … [and] revives

memories of its daemonic double: the heat and dust of India; the dark emptiness of Africa; the tropical chaos that was deemed despotic and ungovernable and therefore worthy of the civilizing mission'. Homi Bhabha, *The Location of Culture* (London: Routledge, 2004), 243.

17 David Lunt and Mark Dyreson, 'The 1904 Olympic Games: Triumph or Nadir', in Helen Jefferson Lenskyj and Stephen Wagg (eds), *The Palgrave Handbook of Olympic Studies* (London: Palgrave Macmillan, 2012), 48.

18 For example, Hall describes how Black Canadian sprinter Ben Johnson is presented as both hero and villain, following the 1988 Olympics. Stuart Hall, *Representation: Cultural Representations and Signifying Practices* (London: Open University, 1997), 234.

19 Hall, *Representation*, 226.

20 Gillian Rose and Divya Tolia-Kelly (eds), *Visuality/Materiality: Images, Objects and Practices* (London: Routledge, 2016); Sumartojo and Sarah Pink, *Atmospheres and the Experiential World* (London: Routledge, 2019).

21 Lisa Blackman and Valerie Walkerdine, *Mass Hysteria: Critical Psychology and Media Studies* (London: Palgrave, 2001).

22 Stephen Graham, 'Olympics 2012 Security Welcome to Lockdown London', *City: Analysis of Urban Trends, Culture, Theory, Policy, Action*, 16(4), 2012: 446.

23 For a breakdown of the costs of the games, see http://www.guardian.co.uk/sport/datablog/2012/jul/26/london-2012-olympics-money.

24 'Britain's End-of-Year Olympic Verdict: It Was Worth Every Penny', *The Guardian*, 25 December 2012, http://www.guardian.co.uk/politics/2012/dec/25/britain-end-of-year-olympic-verdict.

25 Benedict Anderson, *Imagined Communities: Reflections on the Origin and Spread of Nationalism* (London: Verso, 1991).

26 Eric Hobsbawm and Terence Ranger (eds), *The Invention of Tradition* (Cambridge: Cambridge University Press, 1983).

27 Jean-Paul Thibaud, 'The Horizon of Urban Ambiances, Séminaire Du 11 Et 12 Juin 2012', *MUSE*, 2012: 96.

28 Michael Billig, *Banal Nationalism* (London: Sage, 1995), 4.

29 Billig, *Banal Nationalism*, 5; see also Tim Edensor, *National Identity, Popular Culture and Everyday Life* (Oxford: Berg, 2002).

30 Jones and Merriman, 'Hot, Banal and Everyday Nationalism', 164–73.

31 Achille Mbembe, *On the Postcolony* (Berkeley: University of California Press, 2001), 102–4.

32 Lauren Berlant, *Cruel Optimism* (Durham, NC: Duke University Press, 2011), 15.

33 Lunt and Dyreson, 'The 1904 Olympic Games: Triumph or Nadir?', 48.

34 Felix Driver and David Gilbert discuss a twentieth century London underground poster campaign inviting people to visit the empire by taking a journey on the tube,

where 'Australia could be reached via Temple or the Strand, India via Aldwych, and much of the rest of empire via South Kensington'. F. Driver and D. Gilbert, 'Imperial Cities: Overlapping Territories, Intertwined Histories', in F. Driver and D. Gilbert (eds), *Imperial Cities: Landscape, Display and Identity* (Manchester: Manchester University Press, 1999), 1. For a critique of the 2012 opening ceremony, see Catherine Baker 'Beyond the Island Story? The Opening Ceremony of the London 2012 Olympic Games as Public History', *Rethinking History: Journal of Theory and Practice*, 19(3), 2015: 409–28.

35 Sara Ahmed, 'On Collective Feelings: Or, the Impressions Left by Others', *Theory, Culture and Society*, 20(1), 2004a: 25–42.

36 Ben Anderson, *Encountering Affect: Capacities, Apparatuses, Conditions* (Farnham: Ashgate, 2014), 26 and 31.

37 'How Was It for You?', The *Sunday Times*, 19 August 2012, http://www.thesundaytimes.co.uk/sto/Magazine/Features/article1104115.ece (Paywall).

38 The raw data included 12 million English language tweets that included sentiment values, sent from around the world. Created by Drew Hemment, Studio NAND. A FutureEverything project with MIT SENSEable City Lab for the Cultural Olympiad programme and London 2012 Festival, Project report available at: http://www.emoto2012.org/downloads/emoto_published.pdf.

39 'London 2012 Olympics: The Wonderful and the Weird', 14 August 2012, http://www.bbc.co.uk/news/uk-19166071.

40 Anne-Marie Fortier, 'Proximity by Design? Affective Citizenship and the Management of Unease', *Citizenship Studies*, 14(1), 2010: 22.

41 David Bissell, Maria Hynes and Scott Sharpe, 'Unveiling Seductions beyond Societies of Control: Affect, Security, and Humour in Spaces of Aeromobility', *Environment and Planning D: Society and Space*, 30(4), 2012: 694–710.

42 Ben Anderson and Peter Adey, 'Affect and Security: Exercising Emergency in UK Civil Contingencies', *Environment and Planning D: Society and Space*, 29, 2011: 1092–109.

43 Patricia T. Clough, 'Introduction', in Patricia T. Clough (ed.), *The Affective Turn: Theorizing the Social* (Durham, NC: Duke University Press, 2007), 2.

44 Nigel Thrift, 'Intensities of Feeling: Towards a Spatial Politics of Affect', *Geografiska Annaler*, 86B(1), 2004: 60.

45 Greg Seigworth and Melissa Gregg, 'An Inventory of Shimmers', in Melissa Gregg and Greg J. Seigworth (eds), *The Affect Theory Reader* (Durham, NC: Duke University Press, 2010), 2.

46 Berlant, *Cruel Optimism*, 53.

47 Amin and Thrift, *Arts of the Political*, 167.

48 Teresa Brennan, *The Transmission of Affect* (New York: Cornell University Press, 2004), 20.

49 Ibid., 2.

50 Ibid., 5.

51 This is Sara Ahmed's phrasing in 'On Collective Feelings'.

52 Thibaud, 'The Horizon of Urban Ambiances'.

53 Engin Isin, 'Theorizing Acts of Citizenship', in Engin F. Isin and Greg Nielsen (eds), *Acts of Citizenship* (London: Zed Books, 2008), 19.

54 Ben Quinn, 'George Osborne booed at Paralympics', 3 September 2012, http://www.guardian.co.uk/sport/2012/sep/03/george-osborne-booed-paralympics.

55 Giles Deleuze and Felix Guattari, *A Thousand Plateaus*, translated by Brian Massumi (London: Continuum, 2008), 238.

56 Derek P. McCormack, *Refrains for Moving Bodies* (Durham, NC: Duke University Press, 2013), 118.

57 Kathleen Stewart, *Ordinary Affects* (Durham, NC: Duke University Press, 2011), 27–8.

58 Ibid., 445; see also Michael Taussig, *The Nervous System* (New York: Routledge,1992), 10 and McCormack, *Refrains for Moving Bodies*, 118.

59 Locog press release, 'LOCOG Publishes 2011–2012 Report and Accounts', 8 February 2013, 33. https://www.paralympic.org/news/locog-publishes-2011-2012-report-and-accounts.

60 BBC News, 'London 2012: Joy of Sport-Mad Torchbearer', 19 March 2012, http://www.bbc.co.uk/news/uk-england-london-17387140.

61 Locog press release.

62 This was on 6 June, Day 19 of the Relay, http://www.bbc.co.uk/torchrelay/day19.

63 Ash Amin, Doreen Massey and Nigel Thrift, 'Regions, Democracy and the Geography of Power', *Soundings*, 25, 2003: 61.

64 Mayor of London press release, ' "London's getting ready for a summer like no other" says Mayor', 8 June 2012, https://www.london.gov.uk/press-releases-4744

65 See for example Peter Sloterdijk, 'Foam City', *Distinktion: Journal of Social Theory*, 16, 2008: 47–59.

66 McCormack, *Refrains for Moving Bodies*, 136.

67 http://www.bbc.co.uk/torchrelay/day10. Webpage no longer available.

68 William E. Connolly, *Capitalism and Christianity, American Style* (Durham, NC: Duke University Press, 2008), 40. This cross-reference is also made by Peter Adey in 'Security Atmospheres or the Crystallisation of Worlds', *Environment and Planning D: Society and Space*, 32(5), 2014: 840.

69 Connolly, *Capitalism and Christianity*, 52.

70 Max Weber in Peter Lassman and Ronald Speirs (eds), *Weber: Political Writings* (Cambridge: Cambridge University, 1994), 429.

71 Stewart, *Ordinary Affects*, 27.

72 Ibid., 63.

73 Deleuze and Guattari, *Thousand Plateaus*, 236.

74 Puar, *Terrorist Assemblages*, 175.

75 See also Stuart Hall's discussion of Ben Johnson and Linford Christie as 'Spectacles of the Other' at the 1992 Olympic Games, in Stuart Hall, *Representation*.

76 Sam Okoth Opondo, 'Cinema – Body – Thought: Race Habits and the Ethics of Encounter', in Arun Saldanha and Jason Michael Adams (eds), *Deleuze and Race* (Edinburgh: Edinburgh University Press, 2013), 248.

77 Opondo, 'Cinema – Body – Thought', 248.

78 Puar, *Terrorist Assemblages*, 185.

79 'Games Makers Win Big Society Award', Prime Minister's Office press release, 29 November 2012, https://www.gov.uk/government/news/games-makers-win-big-society-award. Several thousand more volunteered at the ceremonies and as part of Team London.

80 US president Barack Obama's weekly address, 20 April 2013, http://www.bbc.co.uk/news/world-us-canada-22234291.

81 Jean-François Augoyard and Henry Torgue (eds), *Sonic Experience: A Guide to Everyday Sounds*, translated by Andra McCartney and David Paquette (Montreal: McGill-Queen's University Press, 2011), 25.

82 Produced by Leo Burnett PR company for McDonalds.

83 Augoyard and Torgue, *Sonic Experience*, 21.

84 Sara Ahmed, *The Promise of Happiness*. The lyrics of 'Everybody Wants to Rule the World' invoke the dangers of the hunger for power and domination and was written and first performed against the backdrop of the threat of nuclear war. It featured as one of the songs banned by the BBC during the 1990–1 Gulf War. 'More Dangerous Songs: And the Banned Played On', BBC Four, https://www.bbc.co.uk/programmes/articles/5R152hTbVPQdYjn29q5jt4/16-songs-banned-by-the-bbc.

85 Connolly, *Capitalism and Christianity, American Style*.

86 See for example Chancellor George Osborne's speech to the Conservative Party conference on 8 October 2012 in Birmingham, as well as, at the Conservative Party conference on 6 October 2009 in Manchester, before the Conservatives were elected at the 2010 UK general election.

87 Bhabha, *The Location of Culture*.

88 McDonalds has a long-established relationship with the Olympic Games; in 2012 it was one of the select group of 'Olympic Partners' (one of the 10 key sponsors).

89 Raymond Williams, *Television: Technology and Cultural Form* (London: Routledge, 2003), 66.

90 Dan Swanton, 'Flesh, Metal, Road: Tracing the Machinic Geographies of Race', *Environment and Planning D: Society and Space*, 28(3), 2010: 448.

91 Deleuze and Guattari, *Thousand Plateaus*, 236.

92 Ben Anderson and John Wylie, 'On Geography and Materiality', *Environment and Planning A*, 41, 2009: 318–35.
93 'David Cameron Sets Out "Emotional, Patriotic Case" to Keep Scotland in UK', *The Guardian*, 7 February 2014, http://www.theguardian.com/politics/2014/feb/07/david-cameron-scottish-independence-referendum-olympic-park.
94 Anderson, *Imagined Communities*, 4.
95 http://swandown.info/; 'Swandown: Two Men in a Pedalo', *The Guardian*, 18 July 2012, http://www.guardian.co.uk/film/2012/jul/18/swandown-iain-sinclair-and-rew-kotting; Iain Sinclair's critiques of the Olympics can also be read in *Ghost Milk: Calling Time on the Grand Project* (London: Penguin, 2011) and 'Diary', *London Review of Books*, 34(16), 30 August 2012: 38–9.
96 Deleuze and Guattari, *Thousand Plateaus*, 238.

2 Consensus and resistance at Margaret Thatcher's funeral

1 *The Spectator*, 'Portrait of the Week', 13 April 2013, available at: https://www.spectator.co.uk/article/portrait-of-the-week-11-april-2013.
2 *The Telegraph*, 'Margaret Thatcher Funeral: Military Rehearsal Takes Place at Dawn', 15 April 2013, available at: http://www.telegraph.co.uk/news/politics/margaret-thatcher/9994367/Margaret-Thatcher-funeral-military-rehearsal-takes-place-at-dawn.html.
3 *The Spectator*, 'Portrait of the Week'.
4 Ibid.
5 Lauren Berlant, *Cruel Optimism* (Durham, NC: Duke University Press, 2011), 2.
6 *The Guardian*, 'George Osborne Tells Tory Conference: "We're All in This Together"' (Video) 8 October 2012, available at: https://www.theguardian.com/politics/video/2012/oct/08/george-osborne-tory-conference-video.
7 See Margaret Thatcher's speech to the Conservative Party conference on 14 October 1983, available at: https://www.margaretthatcher.org/document/105454.
8 Ben Anderson, 'Neoliberal Affects', *Progress in Human Geography*, 40(6), 2016: 734–53; Wendy Brown, *Undoing the Demos: Neoliberalism's Stealth Revolution* (New York: Zone Books, 2015); Jeremy Gilbert, 'What Kind of Thing Is "Neoliberalism"?' *New Formations*, 80, winter 2013; Paul Gilroy, '… We Got to Get over Before We Go Under … Fragment for a History of Black Vernacular Neoliberalism', *New Emotions* 80–1, 2013: 23–38.
9 Nick Robinson, 'Are We All Thatcherites Now?', 17 April 2013, *BBC News*, available at: https://www.bbc.com/news/uk-politics-22180611.
10 Jacques Rancière, *Disagreement: Politics and Philosophy* (Minneapolis: University of Minnesota Press, 1999), 110.

11 Ibid.

12 Ibid., 10.

13 Ibid.

14 *The Telegraph*, 'Margaret Thatcher Funeral: Military Rehearsal Takes Place at Dawn'.

15 *The Spectator*, 'Portrait of the Week'.

16 *The Telegraph*'s rolling blog from 17 April 2015 (note from 5.15 p.m.), available at: http://www.telegraph.co.uk/news/politics/margaret-thatcher/9997708/Margaret-Thatcher-funeral-as-it-happened.html.

17 'Ding Dong! The Witch Is Dead Enters Chart at Two', *BBC News*, 14 April 2013, available at: http://www.bbc.co.uk/news/entertainment-arts-22145306.

18 Sarah M. Hughes, 'On Resistance in Human Geography', *Progress in Human Geography*, 44(6), 2020: 1141–60; see also Louise Amoore and Alexandra Hall, 'The Clown at the Gates of the Camp: Sovereignty, Resistance and the Figure of the Fool', *Security Dialogue* 44 (2), 2013, 93–110.

19 Stuart Hall, 'The Great Moving Right Show', Marxism Today, 23 (1), 1979; see also Stuart Hall and Martin Jacques, 'Introduction'. In *The Politics of Thatcherism*, edited by Stuart Hall and Martin Jacques, London: Lawrence and Wishart, 1990.

20 'Doreen Massey on the Kilburn Manifesto', YouTube video, https://www.youtube.com/watch?v=P2DyPUDzXIM.

21 Hughes, 'On Resistance in Human Geography', 1146.

22 Wendy Brown, *Undoing the Demos,* 35–6.

23 Michel Foucault, 'Interview with Michel Foucault', in James D. Faubion (ed.), *Power: Essential Works of Foucault* (London: Penguin, 1994), 297.

24 Leila Dawney, 'Figurationing' in Celia Lury et al. (eds), *Routledge Handbook of Interdisciplinary Research Methods* (London: Routledge, 2018), 112.

25 Ibid.

26 Thatcher's government did of course go to war, against Argentina and the people of the Falklands/Malvinas islands. Klaus J. Dodds. 'War Stories: British Elite Narratives of the 1982 Falklands/Malvinas War', *Environment and Planning D: Society and Space*, 11 (6), 1993: 619–40.

27 Nigel Thrift, 'It's the Little Things', in Klaus Dodds and David Atkinson (eds), *Geopolitical Traditions: A Century of Geopolitical Thought* (London: Routledge, 2000), 380–7; see also Lynn A. Staeheli, Patricia Ehrkamp, Helga Leitner and Caroline R. Nagel, 'Dreaming the Ordinary: Daily Life and the Complex Geographies of Citizenship', *Progress in Human Geography*, 36 (5), 2012: 628–44.

28 State funerals are tied to the need to narrate a 'national past' and form key sites through which states manifest their majesty. They are intimately tied to questions about identity, power and belonging and are central to the process of what Fiona McConnell calls, 'rehearsing the state'. They can also form moments when power is challenged: take for example the response to the death of Princess Diana,

when the Queen of the United Kingdom was deemed to be 'out of touch' with the people's impassioned grief, which almost lead to a constitutional crisis. See Osman Balkan, 'Burial and Belonging', *Studies in Ethnicity and Nationalism*, 15(1), 2015: 120–34; Avner Ben-Amos, *Funerals, Politics and Memory in Modern France 1789-1996* (Oxford: Oxford University Press, 2000); Fiona McConnell, *Rehearsing the State* (Oxford: Wiley Blackwell, 2016); Tony Walter, *The Mourning for Diana* (Oxford: Berg, 1999).

29 Rebecca Bramall, 'Dig for Victory! Anti-Consumerism, Austerity, and New Historical Subjectivities', *Subjectivity*, 4(1), 2011: 68–86.

30 *The Guardian*, 'Margaret Thatcher Tributes: David Cameron Speech', [(Video) 10 April 2013, available at: https://www.theguardian.com/politics/2013/apr/10/margaret-thatcher-tributes-david-cameron-speech.

31 A state funeral in the UK is usually reserved for the sovereign, although a special exception is made for particular individuals, such as former prime minister Winston Churchill when he died in 1965. While there were calls in advance and in anticipation of Thatcher's death that she be accorded 'the ultimate salute' – a state funeral, Thatcher was granted a ceremonial funeral – following the model used for the funerals of Princess Diana (1997), the Queen Mother (2002) and later, Prince Phillip, the Queen's husband (2021). See Stuart Jeffries, 'The Question – Who Gets a State Funeral', *The Guardian*, 15 July 2008, available at: https://www.theguardian.com/politics/2008/jul/15/past.margaretthatcher.

32 Lauren Berlant and Jordan Greenwald, 'Affect in the End Times: A Conversation with Lauren Berlant', *Qui Parle*, 20(2), 2012: 73.

33 Paul Gilroy, *Small Acts* (London: Serpent's Tail, 1994), 23–4. In this chapter, Gilroy notes how Black political allegiances also pluralized under Thatcherism, and departed from automatic support for the Labour Party.

34 Berlant and Greenwald, 'Affect in the End Times'.

35 'The Austerity Generation: The Impact of a Decade of Cuts on Family Incomes and Child Poverty', Child Poverty Action Group, November 2017, https://cpag.org.uk/sites/default/files/files/Austerity%20Generation%20FINAL.pdf. For an approach to austerity as atmospheric, see Esther Hitchen, 'The Affective Life of Austerity: Uncanny Atmospheres and Paranoid Temporalities', *Social & Cultural Geography*, 22 (3), 2021: 295–318. For how narratives about austerity are racialized, see Akwugo Emejulu and Leah Bassel, 'Whose Crisis Counts? Minority Women, Austerity and Activism in France and Britain', in Johanna Kantola, and Emanuela Lombardo (eds), *Gender and the Economic Crisis in Europe* (London: Palgrave, 2017).

36 Phillip Vannini, 'Non-Representational Research Methodologies: An Introduction', in Vannini (ed.), *Non-Representational Methodologies: Re-Envisioning Research* (New York: Routledge, 2015), 1–18.

37 Debbie Lisle, *Holidays in the Danger Zone: Entanglements of War and Tourism* (Minneapolis: University of Minnesota Press, 2016), 4.

38 Debbie Lisle, 'Waiting for International Political Sociology: A Field Guide to Living In-Between', *International Political Sociology*, 10(4), 2016: 418.

39 Ibid., 421.

40 Ibid.

41 Kathleen Stewart, 'Atmospheric Attunements', *Environment and Planning D: Society and Space*, 29(3), 2011: 445.

42 Eve Sedgwick, *Touching Feeling: Affect, Pedagogy, Performativity* (Durham: Duke University Press, 2003), 8.

43 *The Telegraph*, 'Margaret Thatcher Funeral: Military Rehearsal Takes Place at Dawn'.

44 House of Commons, 'Speaker's Statement on Baroness Thatcher's Funeral Arrangements', *UK Parliament*, 2013, available at: http://www.parliament.uk/business/news/2013/april/speakers-statement-on-baroness-thatchers-funeral-arrangements/.

45 Ibid.

46 Kathleen Stewart, *Ordinary Affects* (Durham, NC: Duke University Press, 2011).

47 I borrow this formulation from Yasmin Gunaratnam.

48 Lisle, 'Waiting for International Political Sociology', 418.

49 Ibid., 420.

50 Ben Anderson and James Ash, 'Atmospheric Method', in Phillip Vannini (ed.), *Non-Representational Methodologies* (London: Routledge, 2015), 34–51.

51 John Allen and Allan Cochrane, 'Assemblages of State Power: Topological Shifts in the Organization of Government and Politics', *Antipode*, 42(5), 2010: 1072.

52 Mbembe, *On the Postcolony*, 109.

53 Berlant, *The Female Complaint* (Durham, NC: Duke University Press, 2008), 27.

54 Greg Seigworth and Melissa Gregg, 'An Inventory of Shimmers', in Melissa Gregg and Greg Seigworth (eds), *The Affect Theory Reader* (Durham, NC: Duke University Press, 2010), 2.

55 Stewart, *Ordinary Affects*, 63.

56 Berlant uses an example from the former US president George W. Bush, who spoke about how political leaders have to connect with people emotionally: 'He wants the public to feel the funk, the live intensities, the desires that make messages affectively immediate, seductive, and binding'. Berlant, *Cruel Optimism*, 224.

57 Stewart, *Ordinary Affects*, 29.

58 Lisa Wedeen, *Ambiguities of Domination: Politics, Rhetoric and Symbols in Contemporary Syria* (Chicago: University of Chicago Press, 2015), 5.

59 Tim Etchells, *Vacuum Days* (Brighton: Storythings, 2012).

60 Ibid.

61 Ibid.

62 Brian Massumi, *Politics of Affect* (Cambridge: Polity Press, 2015), 31.

63 Etchells, *Vacuum Days*, 2012.

64 Scott Sharpe, J.-D. Dewsbury and Maria Hynes, 'The Minute Interventions of Stewart Lee', *Performance Research: A Journal of the Performing Arts*, 19(2), 2014: 121.

65 Ghassan Hage, *White Nation: Fantasies of White Supremacy in a Multicultural Society* (New York: Routledge and Pluto Press, 2000), 38–9.

66 William Connolly, *Capitalism and Christianity, American Style* (Durham, NC: Duke University Press, 2008), 44.

67 Gulshan Khan, 'Agency, Nature and Emergent Properties: An Interview with Jane Bennett', *Contemporary Political Theory*, 8, 2009: 93.

68 Massumi, *Politics of Affect*, 31.

69 Michel Foucault, 'So Is It Important to Think?', in James D. Faubion (ed.), *Power: Essential Works of Foucault, 1954–1984* (London: Penguin, 1994), 458.

70 Derek McCormack, *Refrains for Moving Bodies* (Durham, NC: Duke University Press, 2013), 136.

71 Hilary Mantel, *The Assassination of Margaret Thatcher* (London: Fourth Estate, 2014), 299.

72 Ibid., 218.

73 Ibid., 220.

74 Ibid., 217.

75 Michel Foucault 'What Is Enlightenment?', in *The Foucault Reader* (New York: Pantheon Books, 1984), 46.

76 Mantel, *Assassination of Margaret Thatcher*, 219.

77 Berlant, *Female Complaint*, 22.

78 Ibid.

Interlude: A night at the cinema

1 Étienne Balibar, 'Populism in the American Mirror', Verso Books blog, 10 January 2017, available at: https://www.versobooks.com/blogs/3039-etienne-balibar-popul ism-in-the-american-mirror.

2 William Walters and Barbara Lüthi, 'The Politics of Cramped Space: Dilemmas of Action, Containment and Mobility', *International Journal of Politics, Culture and Society*, 29, 2016: 364, my emphasis.

3 Emma McCluskey, *From Righteousness to Far-Right: An Anthropological Rethinking of Critical Security Studies* (McGill-Queen's University Press, 2019), xii.

4 R. B. J. Walker, *Inside/Outside: International Relations as Political Theory* (Cambridge: Cambridge University Press, 1993).

5 Drawn from Sianne Ngai, *Ugly Feelings* (Cambridge, MA: Harvard University Press, 2005), 11–12, cited in Walters and Lüthi, 'The Politics of Cramped Space: Dilemmas of Action, Containment and Mobility', *International Journal of Politics, Culture and Society* 29(4), 2016: 363.

6 Walters and Lüthi, 'The Politics of Cramped Space', 363.

7 Ibid., 364.

8 Rebecca Solnit, *Hope in the Dark: Untold Stories, Wild Possibilities* (Edinburgh: Canongate Books, 2016), 7.

9 Solnit, *Hope in the Dark*, xii.

3 Mourning and the transversal geographies of terror

1 A further two police officers, one caretaker and one visitor to the magazine's weekly editorial meeting were killed. Following the initial attacks, on 8 January 2015, a policewoman was killed on duty in Montrogue, in a reportedly connected incident, and on 9 January 2015, four more people were killed and several taken hostage at a Hyper Cacher supermarket in Porte de Vincennes. 'Charlie Hebdo attack: 3 days of terror', BBC News, 14 January 2015, http://www.bbc.co.uk/news/world-europe-30708237.

2 Alyson Cole and Sumru Atuk, 'What's in a Hashtag? Feminist Terms for Tweeting in Alliance', *philoSOPHIA*, 9(1), 2019: 26–52. The 'Charlie Hebdo' events were one of the first to demonstrate how acts of terrorism are increasingly known, followed and interpreted through digital media, and how digital logics and grammars dictate modes of response. For a different example, see Samuel Merrill, Shanti Sumartojo, Angharad Closs Stephens and Martin Coward, 'Togetherness after Terror: The More or Less Digital Commemorative Public Atmospheres of the Manchester Arena Bombing's First Anniversary', *Environment and Planning D: Society and Space*, 30(6), 2020: 1103–22.

3 Judith Butler, *Precarious Life: The Power of Mourning and Violence* (London: Verso, 2006); Zillah Eisenstein, 'Feminisms in the Aftermath of September 11', *Social Text*, 20(3)(72), 2002: 79–99; Derek Gregory, *The Colonial Present* (Malden, MA: Blackwell, 2004); Mahmood Mamdani, 'Good Muslim, Bad Muslim: A Political Perspective on Culture and Terrorism', *American Anthropologist*, 104(3), 2002: 766–75; Jasbir Puar, *Terrorist Assemblages. Homonationalism in Queer Times* (Durham, NC: Duke University Press, 2007); Leti Volpp, 'The Citizen and the Terrorist', *UCLA Law Review* 49, 2002: 1575–600.

4 Mustafa Dikeç, 'Hate', 21 January 2015, https://mediadiversified.org/2015/01/21/hate/.

5 Tariq Ali, 'It Didn't Need to Be Done', *London Review of Books*, 37(2), 22 January 2015.

6 Butler, *Precarious Life*; Puar, *Terrorist Assemblages*.

7   Robert Wokler, 'The Enlightenment and the French Revolutionary Birth Pangs of Modernity', in Johan Heilbron, Lars Magnusson and Bjorn Wittrock (eds), *The Rise of the Social Sciences and the Formation of Modernity: Conceptual Change in Context, 1750–1850* (Dordrecht: Kluwer Academic, 1998), 35–76.

8   Teju Cole, 'Unmournable Bodies', *The New Yorker*, 9 January 2015, http://www.newyorker.com/culture/cultural-comment/unmournable-bodies.

9   Butler, *Precarious Life*; for critiques of the further violence carried out in the name of the 'War on Terror', see Louise Amoore, 'Biometric Borders: Governing Mobilities in the War on Terror', *Political Geography*, 25(3), 2006: 336–51; Ruth Blakeley and Sam Raphael, 'British Torture in the "War on Terror"', *European Journal of International Relations*, 23(2), 2017: 243–66; Fiona De Londras, *Detention in the 'War on Terror': Can Human Rights Fight Back?* (Cambridge: Cambridge University Press, 2011).

10 Christine Helliwell and Barry Hindess, 'The Temporalizing of Difference', *Ethnicities*, 5(3), 2005: 414–18; Dipesh Chakrabarty, *Provincializing Europe: Postcolonial Thought and Historical Difference* (Princeton: Princeton University Press, 2008).

11 Jef Huysmans, *Security Unbound: Enacting Democratic Limits* (London: Routledge, 2014).

12 Judith Butler refers to transversal connections in a blog written following the 13 November 2015 Bataclan attacks. Judith Butler, ' "Mourning Becomes the Law" – Judith Butler from Paris', which was on the Verso website, but which has since been removed. Compare also Michael Shapiro's concept of a 'transversal eye' in *War Crimes, Atrocity, Justice* (London, Routledge: 2015).

13 Dikeç, 'Hate'.

14 Jenny Edkins, *Trauma and the Memory of Politics* (Cambridge: Cambridge University Press, 2003), 95.

15 Ibid., 54.

16 Ibid., 66.

17 Ibid.

18 Athena Athansiou, *Agonistic Mourning: Political Dissidence and the Women in Black* (Edinburgh: Edinburgh University Press, 2017), 1.

19 Women in Black statement, 1992, cited in Athansiou, *Agonistic Mourning*, 10.

20 Athansiou, *Agonistic Mourning*, 10.

21 Ibid., 11.

22 Ibid., 18.

23 Ibid., 12.

24 Ibid.

25 Nicholas De Genova, 'The Whiteness of Innocence: *Charlie Hebdo* and the Metaphysics of Anti-Terrorism in Europe', in Gavan Titley, Des Freedman, Gholam

Khiabany and Aurélien Mondon (eds), *After Charlie Hebdo. Terror, Racism and Free Speech* (London: Zed Books, 2017), 97–113.

26 'Prophet Mohammed Cartoons Controversy: Timeline', *The Telegraph*, 4 May 2015, https://www.telegraph.co.uk/news/worldnews/europe/france/11341599/Prophet-Muhammad-cartoons-controversy-timeline.html.

27 Saba Mahmood, 'Religious Reason and Secular Affect: An Incommensurable Divide?', *Critical Inquiry*, 35(4), 2009: 841.

28 Mahmood, 'Religious Reason and Secular Affect', 849.

29 This is why Mahmood also introduces some doubt about appealing to, or resolving the hurt, through the institutional and juridical languages of the state.

30 Nicholas De Genova, 'The European Question. Migration, Race and Postcoloniality in Europe', *Social Text*, 34(3) (128), 2016: 75–102.

31 Madeleine Fagan, *Ethics and Politics after Poststructuralism* (Edinburgh: Edinburgh University Press, 2013). See in particular her discussion of Louiza Odysseos's work, 19.

32 Matthew Gandy, 'Urban Atmospheres', *Cultural Geographies*, 24, 2017: 353–74.

33 Ash Amin and Nigel Thrift, *Seeing Like a City* (Cambridge: Polity Press, 2016), 20.

34 Martin Coward. 'Between Us in the City: Materiality, Subjectivity and Community in the Era of Global Urbanization.' *Environment and Planning D: Society and Space* 30(3), 2012: 468–81.

35 Hanif Kureishi, *The Black Album* (London: Faber and Faber, 1995), 1.

36 Ibid., 57.

37 Ibid., 4.

38 Sara Upstone, 'A Question of Black or White: Returning to Hanif Kureishi's *The Black Album*', *Postcolonial Text*, 4(1), 2008: 13.

39 Kureishi, *Black Album*, 57–8.

40 Ibid., 103.

41 Sarah Nuttall, 'Literary City', in S. Nuttall and A. Mbembe (eds), *Johannesburg: The Elusive Metropolis* (Durham, NC: Duke University Press, 2008), 195–220. She borrows this concept from the work of Lauren Berlant.

42 Nuttall, 'Literary City', 195.

43 Kureishi, *Black Album*, 275.

44 Colin McFarlane, *Learning the City: Knowledge and Translocal Assemblages* (Hoboken, NJ: Wiley Blackwell, 2011).

45 Thomas Blom Hansen and Oskar Verkaaik, 'Introduction – Urban Charisma: On Everyday Mythologies in the City', *Critique of Anthropology*, 29(1), 2009: 6.

46 Sarah Nuttall and Achille Mbembe (eds), *Johannesburg: The Elusive Metropolis*, 51.

47 Amin and Thrift, *Seeing Like a City*; Ash Amin and Nigel Thrift, *Cities: Re-Imagining the Urban* (Cambridge: Polity Press, 2002). This point is also made by Michael J. Shapiro in relation to the non-linear temporalities articulated in music, novels, films

as well as in the life of the city – see, *The Time of the City: Politics, Philosophy and Genre* (Oxon: Routledge, 2010).

48 Amin and Thrift, *Seeing Like a City*, 31.

49 Ibid.

50 Kureishi, *Black Album*, 132.

51 Ibid., 110.

52 Ibid.

53 Hanif Kureishi, *The Word and the Bomb* (London: Faber and Faber, 2005), 10.

54 Ibid.

55 Leonard Quart, 'The Politics of Irony: The Frears – Kureishi Films', *Film Criticism*, 16(1/2), 1991: 34.

56 Ibid.

57 Ibid., 35.

58 This book was a finalist for the National Book Critics Circle Award, the Ondaatje Prize of the Royal Society of Literature, and the PEN/Hemingway Award.

59 Clare Messud, 'The Secret Sharer', *New York Review of Books*, 14, July 2011.

60 Teju Cole, *Open City* (London: Faber and Faber, 2011), 7.

61 Ibid.

62 Rebecca Solnit, *A Field Guide to Getting Lost* (London: Penguin, 2005), 6.

63 Ash Amin, *Land of Strangers* (Cambridge: Polity Press, 2012), 16.

64 Ibid.

65 Cole, *Open City*, 55.

66 Ibid., 23.

67 Shapiro, *War Crimes, Atrocity, Justice*, 5.

68 Tugba Basaran, Didier Bigo, Emmanuel-Pierre Guittet and R. B. J. Walker (eds), *International Political Sociology: Transversal Lines* (London: Routledge, 2017).

69 Cole, *Open City*, 29.

70 Ibid., 30.

71 Ibid., 31.

72 Ariela Freedman, 'How to Get to 9/11: Teju Cole's Melancholic Fiction', in Paul Pedrovic (eds), *Representing 9/11: Trauma, Ideology and Nationalism in Literature, Film and Television* (London: Rowman & Littlefield, 2015), 177–86.

73 Freedman, 'How to Get to 9/11', 177. She goes on to describe the novel as a pioneer in a 'new genre of twitter literature' (178).

74 Freedman, 'How to Get to 9/11', 179.

75 Giovanna Borradori (ed.), *Philosophy in a Time of Terror: Dialogues with Jurgen Habermas and Jacques Derrida* (Chicago: University of Chicago Press, 2003), 99.

76 Ibid.

77 Hanif Kureishi, 'The Word and the Bomb', in *The Word and the Bomb* (London: Faber and Faber, 2005), 10.

4 Vulnerability and the politics of action

1 'Penally Military Base: Arrest after Protest over Asylum Seekers', *BBC News*, 23 September 2020, https://www.bbc.co.uk/news/uk-wales-54269189.

2 Nishat Awan, 'Digital Narratives and Witnessing: The Ethics of Engaging with Places at a Distance', *GeoHumanities*, 2(2), 2016: 311–30.

3 Susan Sontag, *Regarding the Pain of Others* (New York: Farrar, Strauss and Giroux, 2003), 79.

4 The original photograph was taken by Nilüfer Demir (2015). Walsh, Bryan and Time Photo, 'Alan Kurdi's Story: Behind the Most Heartbreaking Photo of 2015', TIME, 29 December 2015, https://time.com/4162306/alan-kurdi-syria-drow ned-boy-refugee-crisis/. Last accessed 29 March 2022.

5 Sontag, *Regarding the Pain of Others*, 79.

6 Marta Bausells, 'Calais Migrant Camp Gets Makeshift Library – And It Needs More Books', *The Guardian*, 24 August 2015, available at: https://www.theguardian.com/ books/2015/aug/24/calais-migrant-camp-gets-makeshift-library-and-it-needs-mor e-books (Accessed 3 June 2021).

7 Karen Price, 'Theatr Clwyd to Stage First Professional Play at Calais Migrant Theatre', *Wales Online*, 22 January 2016, available at: https://www.walesonline.co.uk/ whats-on/theatre-news/theatr-clwyd-stage-first-professional-10776606 (Accessed 3 June 2021).

8 Abernethy, Paul. 'Greek Football Match Stopped as Players Protest Refugee Deaths', *Global Citizen*, 1 February 2016, available at: https://www.globalcitizen.org/en/cont ent/greek-football-match-stopped-as-players-protest-re/ (Accessed 3 June 2021).

9 This description of a 'refugee crisis' has been criticized by many scholars of migration for the way it occludes the sustained and enduring histories of people forced to cross international borders; for alternative approaches, see Nicholas De Genova and Martina Tazzioli, *Europe/Crisis: New Keywords on 'the Crisis' in and of 'Europe'*, New Keywords Collective, Near Futures Online, vol. 1 (New York: Zone Books, 2016), available at: http://nearfuturesonline.org/wp-content/uplo ads/2016/01/New-Keywords-Collective_11.pdf (Accessed 9 March 2021). For an example of the horrors that were regularly in the news at this time, as people were not provided safe passage to Europe and so left to drown, see Gayle, Damien, 'Hundreds of migrants believed to have drowned off Libya after boat capsizes', 15 April 2015, https://www.theguardian.com/world/2015/apr/14/400- drowned-libya-italy-migrant-boat-capsizes. Last accessed 29 March 2022.

10 Elizabeth A. Povinelli, *Economies of Abandonment. Social Belonging in Late Liberalism* (Durham, NC: Duke University Press, 2011), 116.

11 For extensive, creative engagements with what it means to act, see Engin F. Isin and Greg Nielsen (eds), *Acts of Citizenship* (London: Zed Books, 2008). The ideas

about the sovereign person that gets to be political have historically only been available for men, owners of property, or those that can attest that they belong to the political community; see Engin F. Isin, *Being Political: Genealogies of Citizenship* (Minneapolis: University of Minnesota Press, 2002); Brenna Bhandar, *Colonial Lives of Property: Law, Land and Racial Regimes of Ownership* (Durham, NC: Duke University Press, 2018).

12 I'm drawing here on Sianne Ngai, *Ugly Feelings* (Cambridge, MA: Harvard University Press, 2007).

13 Ibid., 27.

14 Povinelli, *Economies of Abandonment*, 116.

15 See also:Sage Brice, 'Geographies of Vulnerability: Mapping Transindividual Geometries of Identity and Resistance', *Transactions of the Institute of British Geographers*, 45(3), 2020: 664–77; Judith Butler, Zeynep Gambetti and Leticia Sabsay (eds), *Vulnerability in Resistance* (Durham, NC: Duke University Press, 2016), 21; Victoria Browne, Jason Danely and Doerthe Rosenow (eds), *Vulnerability and the Politics of Care: Transdisciplinary Dialogues* (Oxford: Oxford University Press, 2021); Ritu Vij, Elisa Wynne-Hughes and Tahseen Kazi, *Precarity and International Relations* (Springer Nature Switzerland: Palgrave Macmillan: 2021).

16 Ian A. Morrison, *Moments of Crisis. Religion and National Identity in Québec* (Vancouver: UBC Press, 2019).

17 *BBC News* (Courtesy of ITV News). 'David Cameron: "Swarm" of Migrants Crossing Mediterranean,' (Video) 30 July 2015, available at: https://www.youtube.com/watch?v=bx_f_oE6oFk (Accessed 3 June 2021).

18 Liisa H. Malkki, 'Refugees and Exiles: From "Refugee Studies" to the National Order of Things', *Annual Review of Anthropology*, 24(1), 1995: 495–523; on how migrants are governed as groups, see Martina Tazzioli, *The Making of Migration: The Biopolitics of Mobility at Europe's Borders* (London: Sage, 2019).

19 Anna Carastathis and Myrto Tsilimpounidi, *Reproducing Refugees: Photographia of a Crisis* (London: Rowman & Littlefield International, 2020) and Martina Tazzioli, 'The Politics of Counting and the Scene of Rescue: Border Deaths in the Mediterranean', *Radical Philosophy*, 192 (July/August 2015), 2–9, available at: https://www.radicalphilosophy.com/commentary/the-politics-of-counting-and-the-scene-of-rescue. (Accessed 3 June 2021).

20 Peter Nyers, 'Emergency or Emerging Identities? Refugees and Transformations in World Order', *Millenium*, 28(1), 1999: 9.

21 Malkki, 'Refugees and Exiles', 516. As Giorgio Agamben also puts it: 'The status of the refugee is always considered a temporary condition that should lead either to naturalization or to repatriation. A permanent status of man in himself is inconceivable for the law of the nation-state.' See, Giorgio Agamben, 'We Refugees', *Symposium: A Quarterly Journal in Modern Literature*, 49(2) (1995): 114–19.

22 Carastathis and Tsilimpounidi, *Reproducing Refugees*, viii–ix; see also Roland
    Bleiker, David Campbell, Emma Hutchison and Xzarina Nicholson, 'The Visual
    Dehumanisation of Refugees', *Australian Journal of Political Science*, 48(4),
    2013: 398–416.

23 Lilie Chouliaraki and Tijana Stolic, 'Rethinking Media Responsibility in the Refugee
    "Crisis": A Visual Typology of European News', *Media, Culture & Society*, 39(8),
    2017: 1168 and 1173. For how others get portrayed as risky, see Claudia Aradau,
    'The Perverse Politics of Four-Letter Words: Risk and Pity in the Securitisation of
    Human Trafficking', *Millennium*, 33(2), 2004: 251–77.

24 Kathy Burrell and Kathrin Hörschelman, 'Perilous Journeys: Visualising the
    Racialised "Refugee Crisis"', *Antipode*, 51(1), 2019: 45.

25 Chouliaraki and Stolic, 'Rethinking Media Responsibility in the Refugee "Crisis"',
    1168 and 1173.

26 Vicki Squire, *Post/Humanitarian Border Politics between Mexico and the US: People,
    Places, Things* (Basingstoke: Palgrave Macmillan, 2015), 58; see also Lilie
    Chouliaraki, 'Post-Humanitarianism: Humanitarian Communication beyond a
    Politics of Pity', *International Journal of Cultural Studies*, 13(2), 2010: 107–26.

27 Squire, *Post/Humanitarian Border Politics*, 59.

28 Ibid., 60.

29 Martina Tazzioli, 'Greece's Camps, Europe's Hotspots', *Border Criminologies*, 12
    October 2016, https://www.law.ox.ac.uk/research-subject-groups/centre-criminol
    ogy/centreborder-criminologies/blog/2016/10/greece%E2%80%99s-camps.

30 Ngai, *Ugly Feelings*, 31.

31 Feminist scholars have explored the connections between biological and social
    understandings of depression, among other conditions, in relation to the question
    of what it means to be political. For example, Elizabeth Wilson, in her refreshing
    feminist analysis of the relationship between biology, pharmaceutical data and
    depression argues that feminist politics needs to get better at accepting negativity
    as part of its ideas and language. See Elizabeth A. Wilson, *Gut Feminism* (Durham,
    NC: Duke University Press, 2015). For a new collection in geography that thinks
    through the role of negativity, see David Bissell, Mitch Rose and Paul Harrison
    (eds.) *Negative Geographies: Exploring the Politics of Limits* (Lincoln: University of
    Nebraska Press, 2021).

32 Judith Butler, 'Rethinking Vulnerability and Resistance', in Judith Butler, Zeynep
    Gambetti and Leticia Sabsay, *Vulnerability in Resistance* (Durham, NC: Duke
    University Press, 2016).

33 Butler, Gambetti and Sabsay, *Vulnerability in Resistance*, 21.

34 Jennifer Hyndman and Wenona Giles, *Refugees in Extended Exile: Living on the
    Edge* (London: Routledge, 2018).

35 Hyndman and Giles, *Refugees in Extended Exile*, 5.

36 Robin Wagner-Pacifici, *What Is an Event?* (Chicago: University of Chicago Press, 2017), 1. For another engagement with the politics of this image, see Rebecca Adler-Nissen, Katrine Emilie Andersen and Lene Hansen, 'Images, Emotions, and International Politics: The Death of Alan Kurdi', *Review of International Studies*, 46(1), 2020: 75–95.

37 Debbie Lisle, 'Moving Encounters: The Affective Mobilities of Photography', in David Bissell and Gillian Fuller (eds), *Stillness in a Mobile World* (London: Routledge, 2011), 143.

38 'Artist Ai Weiwei Poses as Alan Kurdi for India Today Magazine', *India Today*, 1 February 2016, photograph by Rohit Chawla, available at: https://www.indiatoday.in/india/story/artist-ai-weiwei-poses-as-aylan-kurdi-for-india-today-magazine-306 593-2016-02-01. For more about the context of this image, see: 'For Photo Opp, Ai Weiwei Poses as Dead Refugee Toddler from Iconic Image', *e-flux Conversations*, Feb 2016, https://conversations.e-flux.com/t/for-photo-op-ai-weiwei-poses-as-dead-refugee-toddler-from-iconic-image/3169.

39 Charlotte Higgins, 'Boat in Which Hundreds of Migrants Died Displayed at Venice Biennale', *The Guardian*, 7 May 2019, available at: https://www.theguardian.com/artanddesign/2019/may/07/boat-in-which-hundreds-of-migrants-died-displa yed-at-venice-biennale.

40 Annick T. R. Wibben, 'On Doing "Something" … as Academics', *Duck of Minerva*, 3 September 2015, available at: https://www.academia.edu/17321872/On_doing_som ething_as_academics (Accessed 3 June 2021).

41 Anne McNevin, 'Ambivalence and Citizenship: Theorising the Political Claims of Irregular Migrants', *Millennium: Journal of International Studies*, 41(2), 2013: 185.

42 Ai Weiwei has been a persistent critic of the Chinese government and is well known for work such as his response to the 12 May 2008 earthquake in Sichuan, when around seventy thousand people were killed, and he initiated an effort to document the names of the 5,000 students killed when their school buildings collapsed. 'Ai Weiwei Remembers the Sichuan Earthquake, Ten Years On', the *Art Magazine*, 16 July 2018, https://www.theartnewspaper.com/news/ai-weiwei-remembers-the-sich uan-earthquake-ten-years-on.

43 'Ai Weiwei Covers Berlin Venue with 14,000 Life Jackets', *Al-Jazeera*, 13 February 2016, https://www.aljazeera.com/news/2016/2/13/ai-weiwei-covers-ber lin-venue-with-14000-life-jackets.

44 Nick Gill, *Nothing Personal. Geographies of Governing and Activism in the British Asylum System* (Malden: John Wiley, 2016).

45 Lara Coleman and Hannah Hughes, 'Distance', in Claudia Aradau, Jeff Huysmans, Nadine Voelkner and Andrew Neal (eds), *Critical Security Methods: New Frameworks and Approaches* (London: Routledge, 2015), 1–12.

46 Coleman and Hughes, 'Distance', 9.

47 I was fortunate to be part of an event discussing these works at Tate Modern, Vicki Squire et al., *Dead Reckoning/Crossing the Med: Thinking and Feeling Migration Differently*, https://warwick.ac.uk/fac/soc/pais/research/researchcentres/irs/crossingthemed/symposium_transcript.pdf.

48 Vicki Squire, 'Crossing the Mediterranean Sea by Boat', ESRC Project, https://crossing-the-med-map.warwick.ac.uk/.

49 Vicki Squire, 'Governing Migration through Death in Europe and the US: Identification, Burial, and the Crisis of Modern Humanism', *European Journal of International Relations*, 23(3), 2017: 526.

50 Anat Pick, *Creaturely Poetics: Animality and Vulnerability in Literature and Film* (New York: Columbia University Press, 2011).

51 Yasmin Gunaratnam, *Death and the Migrant: Bodies, Borders and Care* (London: Bloomsbury Academic, 2013), 2.

52 Ali Smith, *Autumn* (London: Hamish Hamilton, 2016), 12–13.

53 Ibid., 17.

54 Lauren Berlant, *Cruel Optimism* (Durham, NC: Duke University Press, 2011), 54.

55 Ibid.

56 Ibid., 81.

57 Ibid.

58 Ibid.

59 'EU–Turkey Deal Continues Cycle of Containment and Despair', Amnesty International, 18 March 2019, https://www.msf.org/eu-turk.ey-deal-continues-cycle-containment-and-despair-greece-refugees.

60 Smith, *Autumn*, 123.

61 As Emily Horton argues in relation to Ali Smith's other novels, she is attentive to the forces of consumer capitalism and global technology, and the affective states they induce, including depression, worry and care for the self, but she nevertheless refuses to cast these as all-encompassing in their power or reach. Indeed, Smith 'calls up the hidden psychic and affective possibilities latent within urban spaces', to challenge 'the hegemony of critical cynicism'. Emily Horton, ' "Contemporary Space and Affective Ethics" in Contemporary Critical Perspectives', in Monica Germanà and Emily Horton (eds), *Ali Smith: Contemporary Critical Perspectives* (London: Bloomsbury Academic, 2013), 10.

62 Bonnie Honig, *A Feminist Theory of Refusal* (Cambridge, MA, 2021), 47.

63 Ibid., 45.

64 Ibid., 46.

65 David Bissell, 'Comfortable Bodies: Sedentary Affects', *Environment and Planning A: Economy and Space*, 40(7), 2008: 1698.

66 Honig, *A Feminist Theory of Refusal*, 46.

67 See Roland Bleiker, David Campbell, Emma Hutchison and Xzarina Nicholson, 'The Visual Dehumanisation of Refugees', *Australian Journal of Political Science*, 48(4), 2013: 398–416.

68 Smith, *Autumn*, 55.

69 I'm drawing here on Hannah Arendt's comments on what it means to act politically, in *The Human Condition*.

70 Lisa Baraitser, *Maternal Encounter: The Ethics of Interruption* (London: Routledge, 2008), 75.

71 This mural was drawn by artists Oguz Sen and Justus Becker, and later vandalized. 'German Mural of Dead Syrian Boy Vandalised', BBC News, 23 June 2016, https://www.bbc.co.uk/news/world-europe-36609793.

72 Adler-Nissen, Andersen and Hansen, 'Images, Emotions, and International Politics: The Death of Alan Kurdi', 85.

73 'Glynn Vivian Becomes First UK Art Gallery of Sanctuary', Swansea Bay News, 24 November 2021, https://swanseabaynews.com/2021/11/24/glynn-vivian-becomes-first-uk-art-gallery-of-sanctuary%EF%BF%BC/.

74 Maurice Stierl and Deanna Dadusc, 'The "Covid Excuse": EUropean Border Violence in the Mediterranean Sea', *Ethnic and Racial Studies* (2021), doi: 10.1080/01419870.2021.1977367.

75 'The Guardian's View on Europe's Refugee Crisis: A Little Leadership, at Last', *The Guardian*, 1 September 2015, https://www.theguardian.com/commentisfree/2015/sep/01/guardian-view-on-europe-refugee-crisis-leadership-at-last-angela-merkel.

76 Alberto Nardelli, 'Angela Merkel's Stance on Refugees Means She Stands Alone against Catastrophe', *The Guardian*, 8 November 2015, https://www.theguardian.com/commentisfree/2015/nov/08/angela-merkel-refugee-crisis-europe.

Interlude: A hot afternoon

1 Cynthia Weber, 'Flying Planes Can Be Dangerous', *Millennium: Journal of International Studies*, 31(1), 2002: 129–47. For other works on air shows, see Peter Adey, *Aerial Life* (Oxford: Wiley-Blackwell, 2010); Matthew F. Rech, 'A Critical Geopolitics of Observant Practice at British Military Airshows', *Transactions of the Institute of British Geographers*, 40(4), 2015: 538.

2 Derek McCormack, *Refrains for Moving Bodies* (Durham, NC: Duke University Press, 2013), 132.

3 Debbie Lisle, *Holidays in the Danger Zone* (Minneapolis: University of Minnesota Press, 2016).

4 Sara Ahmed, *The Promise of Happiness* (Durham, NC: Duke University Press, 2010).

5 Beth Hinderliter, William Kaizen, Vered Maimon, Jaled Mansoor and Seth McCormick, *Communities of Sense. Rethinking Aesthetics and Politics* (Durham, NC: Duke University Press, 2009).

6 Lisle, *Holidays in the Danger Zone*, 20.

7 Ibid., 22; drawing on Michael Shapiro, *Violent Cartographies: Mapping Cultures of War* (Minneapolis: University of Minnesota Press, 1997).

8 Eve Kosofsky Sedgwick, *Touching Feeling: Affect, Pedagogy, Performativity* (Durham, NC: Duke University Press, 2003), 110.

9 William Walters, *Governmentality* (Abingdon: Routledge, 2012), 76.

5 Feeling 'Brexit'

1 Susie Orbach, 'In Therapy, Everyone Wants to Talk about Brexit', *The Guardian*, 1 July 2016, https://www.theguardian.com/global/2016/jul/01/susie-orbach-in-therapy-everyone-wants-to-talk-about-brexit.

2 Zadie Smith, 'Fences: A Brexit Diary', *New York Review of Books*, 18 August 2016, https://www.nybooks.com/articles/2016/08/18/fences-brexit-diary.

3 Smith, 'Fences: A Brexit Diary'.

4 David Goodhart, *The Road to Somewhere: The Populist Revolt and the Future of Politics* (London: Hurst & Co, 2017).

5 Theresa May, 'Full Text: Theresa May's Conference Speech', *The Spectator*, 5 October 2016, https://www.spectator.co.uk/article/full-text-theresa-may-s-conference-speech; for a critique, see Rahul Rao, 'Citizens of Nowhere', *The Disorder of Things*, 28 November 2016, https://thedisorderofthings.com/2016/11/28/citizens-of-nowhere/.

6 Sara Ahmed, *The Cultural Politics of Emotion* (Edinburgh: Edinburgh University Press, 2004b).

7 Melissa Gregg and Gregory Seigworth, 'An Inventory of Shimmers', in Melissa Gregg and Gregory Seigworth (eds), *The Affect Theory Reader* (Durham, NC: Duke University Press, 2010), 1–28.

8 Nicholas De Genova, 'Rebordering "the People": Notes on Theorizing Populism', *South Atlantic Quarterly*, 117 (2), 2018: 357–74; see also Alain Badiou et al., *What Is a People?* (New York: Columbia University Press, 2016).

9 Randy Martin, *Critical Moves: Dance Studies in Theory and Politics* (Durham, NC: Duke University Press, 1998), 3. For more efforts in Geography to think in relation to moving and dancing bodies that have influenced my argument here, see David Bissell, 'Micropolitics and Mobility: Public Transport Commuting and Everyday Encounters with Forces of Enablement and Constraint', *Annals of the American Association of Geographers*, 106(2), 2016: 394–403; Derek McCormack,

'Geographies for Moving Bodies: Thinking, Dancing, Spaces', *Geography Compass*, 2(6), 2008: 1822–36; Patricia Noxolo, 'Flat Out! Dancing the City at a Time of Austerity', *Environment and Planning D: Society and Space*, 36(5), 2018: 797–811; Geraldine Pratt and Caleb Johnston, 'Staging Testimony in Nanay', *Geographical Review*, 103(2), 2013: 288–303; Ruth Raynor, '(De)composing Habit in Theatre – as – Method', *Geohumanities*, 3(1), 2017: 108–21; Amanda Rogers, 'Advancing the Geographies of the Performing Arts: Intercultural Aesthetics, Migratory Mobility, and Geopolitics', *Progress in Human Geography*, 42(4), 2018: 549–68.

10 Paul Davies (2017), Interview with Paul Davies, director of Volcano Theatre, 7 February.

11 Danny Dorling, 'Brexit: The Decision of a Divided Country', *BMJ*, 354(3697), 2016.

12 See for example: Gurminder Bhambra, 'Brexit, Trump, and "Methodological Whiteness": On the Misrecognition of Race and Class', *British Journal of Sociology*, 68(1), 2017: 214–32; Magne Flemmen and Mike Savage, 'The Politics of Nationalism and White Racism in the UK', *British Journal of Sociology*, 68(1), 2017: 233–64; Fintan O'Toole, *Heroic Failure: Brexit and the Politics of* Pain (London: Apollo, 2018); Robert Shilliam, 'Racism, Multiculturalism and Brexit', *Word Press*, 4 July 2016, https://robbieshilliam.wordpress.com/2016/07/04/racism-multicultural ism-and-brexit/.

13 Ben Anderson and Helen Wilson, 'Everyday Brexits', *Area*, 50(2), 2017: 291–5, https://doi.org/10.1111/area.12385.

14 I borrow the idea of a 'perverse politics' from Ann Orloff, Raka Ray and Evren Savcı, 'Introduction: Perverse Politics? Feminism, Anti-Imperialism, Multiplicity', *Political Power and Social Theory*, 30, 2016: 2.

15 Erin Manning, *The Minor Gesture* (Durham, NC: Duke University Press, 2016), x.

16 Dorling, 'Brexit: The Decision of a Divided Country.'

17 Ibid.

18 Robbie Shilliam, *Race and the Undeserving Poor* (Newcastle: Agenda Publishing, 2018), 163.

19 Ibid.

20 Bhambra, 'Brexit, Trump'.

21 Elizabeth Povinelli, *The Cunning of Recognition. Indigenous Alterities and the Making of Australian Multiculturalism* (Durham, NC: Duke University Press, 2002).

22 Ibid.

23 Ahmed, *Cultural Politics of Emotion*; Sara Ahmed, *The Promise of Happiness* (Durham, NC: Duke University Press, 2010); Anne- Marie Fortier, *Multicultural Horizons* (London: Routledge, 2008); Anne-Marie Fortier, 'Pride Politics and Multiculturalist Citizenship', *Ethnic and Racial Studies*, 28(3), 2005: 559–78; Ghassan Hage, *White Nation: Fantasies of White Supremacy in a Multicultural Society* (New York: Routledge and Pluto Press, 2000); Povinelli, *The Cunning of Recognition*.

24 Fortier, 'Pride Politics'.

25 Ibid., 563–4.

26 Ibid., 561.

27 Elspeth Probyn, 'Sporting Bodies: Dynamics of Shame and Pride', *Body & Society* 6(1), 2000: 13–28.

28 Sedgwick, *Touching Feeling*.

29 Ibid., 37.

30 Elspeth Probyn, *Blush. Faces of Shame* (Minneapolis: University of Minnesota Press, 2005).

31 Ibid., 106.

32 Patricia Clough, 'Afterword: The Future of Affect Studies', *Body & Society*, 16(1), 2010: 224.

33 Carole Cadwalladr, 'View from Wales: Town Showered with Cash Votes to Leave EU', *The Guardian*, 25 June 2016, https://www.theguardian.com/uk-news/2016/jun/25/view-wales-town-showered-eu-cash-votes-leave-ebbw-vale.

34 'European Structural Funds 2014–2020', Welsh Government, https://gov.wales/funding/eu-funds/2014-2020/?lang=en (Accessed 5 June 2018).

35 'Measuring Inequalities, Trends in Mortality and Life Expectancy in Aneurin Bevan UHB', Public Health Wales NHS Trust, http://www.publichealthwalesobservatory.wales.nhs.uk (Accessed 12 February 2019).

36 Cadwalladr, 'View from Wales'. This constituency voted 62 per cent to leave, 38 per cent to remain, on a turnout of 68.1 per cent. BBC website, 'EU Referendum Results', https://www.bbc.com/news/politics/eu_referendum/results.

37 Kathleen Cramer, *The Politics of Resentment* (Chicago: University of Chicago Press, 2016); Arlie Hochschild, *Strangers in their Own Land* (New York: New Press, 2016).

38 Raka Ray, 'A Case of Internal Colonialism? Arlie Hochschild's *Strangers in Their Own Land*', *British Journal of Sociology*, 68(1), 2017: 129–33.

39 Ibid., 131.

40 Ann Orloff, Raka Ray and Evren Savcı, 'Introduction: Perverse Politics? Feminism, Anti-Imperialism, Multiplicity', *Political Power and Social Theory*, 30, 2016: 2.

41 Ibid., 4.

42 Ibid., 5.

43 Ibid., 6.

44 Ibid.

45 O'Toole, *Heroic Failure*.

46 Davies, Interview.

47 'UK House Price Index', Land Registry, 17 April 2019, http://landregistry.data.gov.uk/app/ukhpi 'UK House Price Index for October 2021', https://www.gov.uk/government/news/uk-house-price-index-for-october-2021.

48 Anca Pusca, 'Industrial and Human Ruins of Postcommunist Europe', *Space and Culture*, 13(3), 2010: 239–55.

49 Karl West, 'How Art Restarted the Heart of Swansea's High Street', *The Observer*, 8 October 2016, https://www.theguardian.com/business/2016/oct/08/art-resta rts-heart-swansea-high-street.

50 Ben Anderson and Adam Holden, 'Affective Urbanism and the Event of Hope', *Space and Culture*, 11(2), 2008: 142–59.

51 Phill Hubbard and Dawn Lyon, 'Introduction: Streetlife – The Shifting Sociologies of the Street', *Sociological Review*, 66(5), 2018, 937–51.

52 Manning, *Minor Gesture*, 13.

53 Davies, Interview.

54 Hubbard and Lyon, 'Introduction: Streetlife', 939.

55 Davies, Interview.

56 Hortense Goulard, 'Britain's Youth Vote Remain', *Politico*, 24 June 2016, https://www.politico.eu/article/britains-youth-voted-remain-leave-eu-brexit-referendum-stats/.

57 Manning, *Minor Gesture*.

58 Ibid., 8.

59 Ibid., 112.

60 Ibid.

61 Ibid.

62 Ibid.

63 McCormack, 'Geographies for Moving Bodies', 1823.

64 Manning, *Minor Gesture*, 2.

65 Noxolo, 'Flat Out!', 797–811.

66 Ibid., 801.

67 Bissell, 'Micropolitics and Mobility', 394–403.

68 Raynor, '(De)composing Habit', 112.

69 Teresa Brennan, *The Transmission of Affect* (New York: Cornell University Press, 2004).

70 Manning, *Minor Gesture*, 113.

71 Noxolo, 'Flat Out!', 797–811.

72 Judith Butler, *Notes toward a Performative Theory of Assembly* (Cambridge, MA: Harvard University Press, 2015), 9.

73 Manning, *Minor Gesture*, 2.

74 Bissell, 'Micropolitics and Mobility', 399.

75 Manning, *Minor Gesture*, 8.

76 De Genova, 'Rebordering "the People"'.

77 Butler, *Notes toward a Performative Theory of Assembly*, 5.

78 Probyn, *Blush*, 14.

79 Costas Douzinas, 'Athens Rising', *European Urban and Regional Studies*, 20(1), 2013: 134–8.

80 Ibid., 134.

81 Ibid., 137.

82 Martin, *Critical Moves*.

83 Étienne Balibar, 'Populism in the American Mirror', Verso Books blog, 10 January 2017, https://www.versobooks.com/blogs/3039-etienne-balibar-populism-in-the-american-mirror.

84 Stuart Hall, 'The Great Moving Right Show', *Marxism Today*, January 1979: 20.

85 Ash Amin and Nigel Thrift, *The Arts of the Political* (Durham, NC: Duke University Press, 2013), 15.

6 Affective listening and the politics of change

1 Clare Hemmings, 'Affective Solidarity: Feminist Reflexivity and Political Transformation', *Feminist Theory*, 13(2), 2012: 149.

2 Cindi Katz, 'Towards Minor Theory', *Environment and Planning D: Society and Space*, 14, 1996: 489.

3 Michel Foucault, 'Interview with Michel Foucault', in Michel Foucault, *Power: Essential Works of Foucault 1954–1984*, London: Penguin. Edited by James D. Faubion, 297.

4 Elisabeth Militz, 'On Affect, Dancing and National Bodies', in Michael Skey and Marco Antonsich (eds), *Everyday Nationhood. Theorising Culture, Identity and Belonging after Banal Nationalism* (London: Palgrave, 2017), 179.

5 Allison Abra, *Dancing in the English Style: Consumption, Americanisation and National Identity in Britain, 1918–1950* (Manchester: Manchester University Press, 2017), 7.

6 Richard Carter and Julia McManus, 'The Data Is In: Black Strictly Contestants Are More Likely to Be Voted Off', *The Guardian*, 16 December 2016, available at: https://www.theguardian.com/commentisfree/2016/dec/16/black-strictly-come-dancing. In 2019, Motsi Mabuse, a Black South African professional ballroom dancer replaced white English ballerina Antipode Darcey Bussell as a judge for the seventeenth series. The nineteenth series in Autumn 2021 became known as one of the most diverse ever, with deaf contestant Rose Ayling-Ellis, same-sex couple John Waite and Johannes Radebe and Black TV presenter AJ Odudo, who was raised in Blackburn and whose parents are from Nigeria, making it to the final.

7 Abra, *Dancing in the English Style*, 107.

8 Tim Cresswell, ' "You Cannot Shake that Shimmie Here": Producing Mobility on the Dance Floor', *Cultural Geographies*, 13, 2006: 55–77.

9 Ibid., 60.

10 Ibid., 72.

11 Ibid., 55–77.

12 Randy Martin, *Critical Moves: Dance Studies in Theory and Politics* (Durham, NC: Duke University Press, 1998), 156.

13 Martin, *Critical Moves*, 154.

14 Ibid., 160.

15 Ibid., 163.

16 Ibid., 168

17 See Angela McRobbie, 'Notes on the Perfect: Competitive Femininity in Neoliberal Times', *Australian Feminist Studies*, 30 (83), 2015: 3.

18 Martin, *Critical Moves*, 151.

19 Ibid., 179.

20 Ibid.

21 'Ways of Being Together', programme notes, 2017.

22 Score for 'Ways of Being Together'.

23 Email exchange, 2017.

24 Deborah Hay, *My Body, the Buddhist* (Connecticut: Wesleyan University Press, 2000).

25 Susan Leigh Foster, Foreword to Deborah Hay, *My Body, the Buddhist*.

26 Alison Phipps, '"Every Woman Knows a Weinstein": Political Whiteness and White Woundedness in #MeToo and Public Feminisms around Sexual Violence', *Feminist Formations*, 31(2), 2019: 7.

27 Judith Butler, *Notes toward a Performative Theory of Assembly* (Cambridge, MA: Harvard University Press, 2015), 4–9.

28 William Walters and Barbara Lüthi, 'The Politics of Cramped Space: Dilemmas of Action, Containment and Mobility', *International Journal of Politics, Culture and Society*, 29(4), 2016: 359.

29 Butler, *Notes Toward a Performative Theory of Assembly*, 10.

30 From the Score for 'Ways of Being Together'.

31 I also went to see another performance of 'Neither Here Nor There', at Chapter Arts Centre, Cardiff on 9 June 2019.

32 The website announces its aim to enable 'Critical Dialogue through Rigorous Artistic Research and experiment', available at: https://capelygraig.org/history-2/.

33 The work echoed that of George Brecht, who constructed the Fluxus piece, 'Water Yam', which included a box of differently sized white cards with instructions on them. It also included other influences, including Fong and Hughes's work with Quarantine theatre company, Manchester, well known for working with non-performers and using everyday life as a focus.

34 Interview with Sonia Hughes and Jo Fong, Capel-y-Graig, Ffwrnais, 6 July 2019.

35 Leah Bassel, *The Politics of Listening, Possibilities and Challenges for Democratic Life* (London: Palgrave Pivot, 2017), 7.

36 Ibid., 8.

37 Charles Hirschkind, *The Ethical Soundscape: Cassette Sermons and Islamic Counterpublics* (New York: Columbia University Press, 2006).

38 Ibid., 70.

39 Ibid.

40 Ibid., 68.

41 Ibid., 69.

42 Ibid., 68.

43 Ibid., 73.

44 Ibid., 72.

45 Ibid., 70.

46 Ibid., 73.

47 Ibid., 78.

48 Ibid., 82.

49 Ibid., 79.

50 Ibid., 82.

51 Lise Paulsen Galal and Kirsten Hvenegård-Lassen, *Organised Cultural Encounters* (Cham: Palgrave Macmillan, 2020), 151.

52 This is how Shapiro describes his method of writing, drawing on the work of Walter Benjamin. Michael Shapiro, *For Moral Ambiguity: National Culture and the Politics of the Family* (Minneapolis: University of Minnesota Press, 2001).

53 Shapiro, *For Moral Ambiguity*, 5–6.

54 Hirschkind in *The Ethical Soundscape*, 95, notes that for the Greeks, there was no strict distinction between ethics and entertainment.

55 Galal and Hvenegård-Lassen, *Organised Cultural Encounters*, 151–2.

56 Elizabeth Straughan, David Bissell and Andrew Gorman-Murray, 'The Politics of Stuckness: Waiting Lives in Mobile Worlds', *Environment and Planning C: Politics and Space*, 38(4), 2020: 636–55.

57 Walters and Lüthi, *Politics of Cramped Space*, 364.

58 Ibid., 365.

59 Katye Coe and Hetty Blades, 'Running, Resistance and Recollection: A Conversation with Ourselves through Time', *Performance Philosophy*, 2(2), 2017: 336.

60 Ibid., 337.

61 Ibid., 339.

62 Butler, *Notes toward a Performative Theory of Assembly*, 11.

63 William Connolly, *Aspirational Fascism: The Struggle for Multifaceted Democracy under Trumpism* (Minneapolis: University of Minnesota Press, 2017), xxii.

64 Jodi Dean, 'Communicative Capitalism and Revolutionary Form', *Millennium*, 47(3), 2019: 334.

65 Ibid.

66 See for example, Jacques Derrida, *Of Hospitality: Anne Dufourmantelle Invites Jacques Derrida to Respond*, translated by Bowly, R. (Stanford: Stanford University Press, 2000).

67 Interview with Sonia Hughes and Jo Fong, Capel-y-Graig, Ffwrnais, 6 July 2019.

68 Jessica Dempsey and Geraldine Pratt, 'Wiggle Room', in Antipode Editorial Collective (eds), *Keywords in Radical Geography: Antipode at 50*, 2019: 274–9, available online at: https://doi.org/10.1002/9781119558071.ch51.

69 Ibid., 275.

70 Ibid.

Afterword: Covid-19, the national frame and communities of sense

1 Danny Dorling, 'Why Has the UK's COVID Death Toll Been So High? Inequality May Have Played a Role', 4 March 2021, *The Conversation*, available at: https://theconversation.com/why-has-the-uks-covid-death-toll-been-so-high-inequality-may-have-played-a-role-156331.

2 Jacques Rancière, 'Contemporary Art and the Politics of Aesthetics', in Beth Hinderliter, William Kaizen, Vered Maimon, Jaleh Mansoor and Seth McCormick (eds), *Communities of Sense: Rethinking Aesthetics and Politics* (Durham, NC: Duke University Press, 2009), 31.

3 Ranciere, 'Contemporary Art and the Politics of Aesthetics', 31.

4 Ibid., 39.

5 Jonathan Calvert, George Arbuthnott and Jonathan Leake, 'Coronavirus: 38 days When Britain Sleepwalked into Disaster', 19 April 2020, *The Times*, available at: https://www.thetimes.co.uk/article/coronavirus-38-days-when-britain-sleepwalked-into-disaster-hq3b9tlgh; *Office of National Statistics*. 'Coronavirus: A Year Like No Other', 15 March 2021, available at: https://www.ons.gov.uk/peoplepopulationandcommunity/healthandsocialcare/conditionsanddiseases/articles/coronavirusayearlikenoother/2021-03-15.

6 Robert Booth, '22 days in April: The Darkest Hours of the UK Coronavirus Crisis', 19 June 2020, *The Guardian*, available at: https://www.theguardian.com/world/2020/jun/19/22-days-in-april-uk-darkest-hours-of-coronavirus-crisis (Accessed 22 June 2021).

7 Achille Mbembe, 'The Society of Enmity', *Radical Philosophy*, 200, 2016, available at: https://www.radicalphilosophy.com/article/the-society-of-enmity.

8 Ibid., 26.

9 Ian Morrison, *Moments of Crisis: Religion and National Identity in Québec* (Vancouver: UBC Press, 2019), 21.

10 Hinderliter et al., *Communities of Sense*, 15.

11 Luke Turner, 'We'll Meet Again: How Toxic Nostalgia Twisted Vera Lynn's Pop Masterpiece', 18 June 2020, *The Guardian*, available at: https://www.theguard ian.com/music/2020/jun/18/well-meet-again-vera-lynn-pop-masterpiece-sec ond-world-war (Accessed 22 June 2021).

12 *BBC News*, 'Asian Hate Crime in UK Increases during Pandemic,' (Video) 4 May 2021, available at: https://www.bbc.com/news/av/uk-56937299.

13 Vikram Dodd, 'Met Police Twice as Likely to Fine Black People over Lockdown Breaches – Research', *The Guardian*, 3 June 2020, available at: https://www.theg uardian.com/uk-news/2020/jun/03/met-police-twice-as-likely-to-fine-black-peo ple-over-lockdown-breaches-research.

14 Kathleen Stewart, *Ordinary Affects* (Durham, NC: Duke University Press: 2007), 5.

15 Mbembe, *Society of Enmity*, 31.

16 Ibid., 26.

17 Ibid.

18 Ibid., 27.

19 Ibid., 26.

20 Debbie Lisle, *Holidays in the Danger Zone: Entanglements of War and Tourism* (Minneapolis: University of Minnesota Press, 2016), 286.

21 William Connolly, *Pluralism* (Durham, NC: Duke University Press, 2005), 9.

22 Ibid., 7.

23 People in China have left tributes for Li Wenliang on another wall, his personal Weibo social media page; see *BBC News*, 'Li Wenliang: 'Wuhan Whistleblower' Remembered One Year On', 6 February 2021, available at: https://www.bbc.com/ news/world-asia-55963896.

24 Judith Butler, *The Force of Non-Violence* (London: Verso Books, 2020), 16.

Bibliography

Abernethy, Paul. 'Greek Football Match Stopped as Players Protest Refugee Deaths'. *Global Citizen*. 1 February 2016. Available at: https://www.globalcitizen.org/en/cont ent/greek-football-match-stopped-as-players-protest-re/ (Accessed 3 June 2021).

Abra, Allison. *Dancing in the English Style: Consumption, Americanisation and National Identity in Britain, 1918–1950*. Manchester: Manchester University Press, 2017.

Adey, Peter. *Aerial Life*. Oxford: Wiley-Blackwell, 2010.

Adey, Peter. 'Security Atmospheres or the Crystallisation of Worlds'. *Environment and Planning D: Society and Space* 32, no. 5 (2014): 834–51.

Adler-Nissen, Rebecca, Katrine Emilie Andersen and Lene Hansen. 'Images, Emotions, and International Politics: The Death of Alan Kurdi'. *Review of International Studies* 46, no. 1 (2020): 75–95.

Agamben, Giorgio. 'We Refugees'. *Symposium: A Quarterly Journal in Modern Literature* 49, no. 2 (1995): 114–19.

Ahluwalia, Pal, and Toby Miller. 'Populism – Again, Seemingly without End'. *Social Identities* 24, no. 6 (2018): 685–7.

Ahmed, Sara. 'On Collective Feelings: Or, the Impressions Left by Others'. *Theory, Culture and Society* 21, no. 2 (2004a): 25–42.

Ahmed, Sara. *The Cultural Politics of Emotion*. Edinburgh: Edinburgh University Press, 2004b.

Ahmed, Sara. 'Orientations: Towards a Queer Phenomenology'. *GLQ: A Journal of Lesbian and Gay Studies* 12, no. 4 (2006): 543–74.

Ahmed, Sara. *The Promise of Happiness*. Durham, NC: Duke University Press, 2010.

Akama, Yoko, Sarah Pink and Shanti Sumartojo. 'Approaching Uncertainty'. In *Uncertainty and Possibility: New Approaches to Future Making in Design Anthropology*, 1–19, London: Bloomsbury, 2018.

Al Jazeera. 'Ai Wei Wei Covers Berlin Venue with 14,000 Life Jackets'. 13 February 2016. Available at: https://www.aljazeera.com/news/2016/2/13/ai-weiwei-covers-ber lin-venue-with-14000-life-jackets (Accessed 7 February 2022).

Alcoff, Linda. 'The Problem of Speaking for Others'. *Cultural Critique* (winter 1991–2): 5–32.

Ali, Tariq. 'It Didn't Need to Be Done'. *London Review of Books* 37, no. 2 (2015).

Allen, John. 'Ambient Power: Berlin's Potsdamer Platz and the Seductive Logic of Public Spaces'. *Urban Studies* 43, no. 2 (2006): 441–55.

Allen, John, and Allan Cochrane. 'Assemblages of State Power: Topological Shifts in the Organization of Government and Politics'. *Antipode* 42, no. 5 (2010): 1071–89.

Amin, Ash. 'The Remainders of Race'. *Theory, Culture & Society* 27, no. 1 (2010): 1–23.

Amin, Ash. *Land of Strangers*. Cambridge: Polity Press, 2012.

Amin, Ash, and Nigel Thrift. *Cities: Re-imagining the Urban*. Cambridge: Polity Press, 2002.

Amin, Ash, and Nigel Thrift. *The Arts of the Political*. Durham, NC: Duke University Press, 2013.

Amin, Ash, and Nigel Thrift. *Seeing Like a City*. Cambridge: Polity Press, 2016.

Amin, Ash, Doreen Massey and Nigel Thrift. 'Regions, Democracy and the Geography of Power'. *Soundings* 25 (2003): 57–70.

Amoore, Louise. 'Biometric Borders: Governing Mobilities in the War on Terror'. *Political Geography* 25, no. 3 (2006): 336–51.

Amoore, Louise, and Alexandra Hall. 'The Clown at the Gates of the Camp: Sovereignty, Resistance and the Figure of the Fool'. *Security Dialogue* 44, no. 2 (2013): 93–110.

Anderson, Ben. 'Affective Atmospheres'. *Emotion, Space and Society* 2, no. 2 (2009): 77–81.

Anderson, Ben. *Encountering Affect: Capacities, Apparatuses, Conditions*. Farnham: Ashgate, 2014.

Anderson, Ben. 'Neoliberal Affects'. *Progress in Human Geography* 40, no. 6 (2016): 734–53.

Anderson, Ben, and Adam Holden. 'Affective Urbanism and the Event of Hope'. *Space and Culture* 11, no. 2 (2008): 142–59.

Anderson, Ben, and James Ash. 'Atmospheric Method'. In *Non-Representational Methodologies*, edited by Phillip Vannini, 34–51. London: Routledge, 2015.

Anderson, Ben, and John Wylie. 'On Geography and Materiality'. *Environment and Planning: A* 41 (2009): 318–35.

Anderson, Ben, and Peter Adey. 'Affect and Security: Exercising Emergency in UK Civil Contingencies'. *Environment and Planning D: Society and Space* 29 (2011): 1092–109.

Anderson, Ben, and Helen Wilson. 'Everyday Brexits'. *Area* 50, no. 2 (2017): 291–5.

Anderson, Ben, and Paul Harrison. *Taking-Place: Non-Representational Theories and Geography*. Farnham: Ashgate, 2010.

Anderson, Benedict. *Imagined Communities: Reflections on the Origin and Spread of Nationalism*. London: Verso, 1991.

Appadurai, Arjun. *Fear of Small Numbers*. Durham, NC: Duke University Press, 2005.

Appadurai, Arjun. *The Future as Cultural Fact*. London: Verso, 2013.

Aradau, Claudia. 'The Perverse Politics of Four-Letter Words: Risk and Pity in the Securitisation of Human Trafficking'. *Millennium* 33, no. 2 (2004): 251–77.

Arendt, Hannah. *The Human Condition*. Chicago: University of Chicago Press, 1998.

Arendt, Hannah. 'Introduction'. In *Illuminations*, edited by Hannah Arendt, 1–55. New York: Schoken Books, 1969.

Arendt, Hannah. *Eichmann in Jerusalem: A Report on the Banality of Evil*. London: Penguin Classic, 2006.

Arendt, Hannah. *The Origins of Totalitarianism*. London: Penguin Modern Classics, 2017.

Ash, James. 'Rethinking Affective Atmospheres: Technology, Perturbation and Space Times of the Non-Human'. *Geoforum* 49 (2013): 20–8.

Ashley, Richard Key, and R. B. J. Walker. 'Speaking the Language of Exile: Dissident Thought in International Studies'. *International Studies Quarterly* 34, no. 4 (1990): 259–68.

Athansiou, Athena. *Agonistic Mourning: Political Dissidence and the Women in Black*. Edinburgh: Edinburgh University Press, 2017.

Augoyard, Jean-François, and Henry Torgue. S*onic Experience: A Guide to Everyday Sounds*. Translated by Andra McCartney and David Paquette. Montreal: McGill-Queen's University Press, 2011.

Awan, Nishat. 'Digital Narratives and Witnessing: The Ethics of Engaging with Places at a Distance'. *GeoHumanities* 2, no. 2 (2016): 311–30.

Back, Les. 'Hope's Work', *Antipode*, 53, no. 1 (2021: 3–20.

Badiou, Alain, Pierre Bourdieu, Judith Butler, Georges Didi-Huberman, Sadri Khiari and Jacques Rancière. *What Is a People?* New York: Columbia University Press, 2016.

Bailkin, Jordanna. 'Decolonizing Emotions. The Management of Feeling in the New World Order'. In *Science and Emotions after 1945: A Transatlantic Perspective*, edited by Frank Biess and Daniel M. Gross, 278–99. Chicago: University of Chicago Press, 2014.

Baker, Catherine. 'Beyond the Island Story? The Opening Ceremony of the London 2012 Olympic Games as Public History'. *Rethinking History: The Journal of Theory and Practice* 19, no. 3 (2015): 409–28.

Balibar, Étienne. 'The Nation Form: History and Ideology'. *Review* 13, no. 3 (1990): 329–61.

Balibar, Étienne. 'The Nation Form: History and Ideology'. In *Race, Nation, Class: Ambiguous Identities*, edited by Étienne Balibar and Immanuel Wallerstein, 86–106. London: Verso, 1991.

Balibar, Étienne. 'Populism in the American Mirror'. 10 January 2017. *Verso Books*. Available at: http://www.versobooks.com/blogs/3039-etienne-balibar-populism-in-the-american-mirror (Accessed 9 March 2021).

Balkan, Osman. 'Burial and Belonging'. *Studies in Ethnicity and Nationalism* 15, no. 1 (2015): 120–34.

Baraitser, Lisa. *Maternal Encounter: The Ethics of Interruption*. London: Routledge, 2008.

Basaran, Tugba, Didier Bigo, Emmanuel-Pierre Guittet and R. B. J. Walker (eds). *International Political Sociology: Transversal Lines*. London: Routledge, 2017.

Bassel, Leah. *The Politics of Listening: Possibilities and Challenges for Democratic Life*. London: Palgrave Pivot, 2017.

Bausells, Marta. 'Calais Migrant Camp Gets Makeshift Library – And It Needs More Books'. *The Guardian*. 24 August 2015. Available at: https://www.theg

uardian.com/books/2015/aug/24/calais-migrant-camp-gets-makeshift-libr
ary-and-it-needs-more-books (Accessed 3 June 2021).

BBC News. 'London 2012: Joy of Sport-Mad Torchbearer' 2012. 19 March 2012.
Available at: http://www.bbc.co.uk/news/uk-england-london-17387140 (Accessed 24
February 2021).

BBC News. 'London 2012 Olympics: The Wonderful and Weird'. 14 August 2012.
Available at: http://www.bbc.co.uk/news/uk-19166071 (Accessed 24 February 2021).

BBC News. 'Margaret Thatcher Death Song Goes Ahead in Billy Elliot Musical'. 9
April 2013. Available at: https://www.bbc.com/news/entertainment-arts-22076220
(Accessed 26 April 2021).

BBC News. 'Ding Dong! The Witch Is Dead Enters Chart at Two'. 14 April 2013.
Available at: http://www.bbc.co.uk/news/entertainment-arts-22145306 (Accessed 25
March 2021).

BBC News. 'Boston Attacks: President Obama Says Americans Refuse to Be Terrorised'
(Video) 20 April 2013. Available at: https://www.bbc.com/news/av/world-us-can
ada-22234291 (Accessed 24 February 2021).

BBC News. 'Charlie Hebdo Attack: Three Days of Terror'. 14 January 2015.
Available at: https://www.bbc.com/news/world-europe-30708237 (Accessed 24
February 2021).

BBC News (Courtesy of ITV News). 'David Cameron: "Swarm" of Migrants Crossing
Mediterranean'. (Video) 30 July 2015. Available at: https://www.youtube.com/
watch?v=bx_f_oE6oFk (Accessed 3 June 2021).

BBC News. 'German Mural of Dead Syrian Boy Alan Kurdi Vandalised'. 23 June 2016.
Available at: https://www.bbc.com/news/world-europe-36609793 (Accessed 12
March 2021).

BBC News. 'Windrush Generation: Formal Apology for 18 People'. 21 August 2018,
https://www.bbc.co.uk/news/uk-45258866 (Accessed 22 June 2021).

BBC News. 'Penally Military Base: Arrest after Protest over Asylum Seekers'. 23
September 2020. Available at: https://www.bbc.co.uk/news/uk-wales-54269189
(Accessed 11 March 2021).

BBC News. 'Li Wenliang: "Wuhan Whistleblower" Remembered One Year On'. 6
February 2021. Available at: https://www.bbc.com/news/world-asia-55963896
(Accessed 7 May 2021).

BBC News. 'Asian Hate Crime in UK Increases During Pandemic'. (Video) 4 May 2021.
Available at: https://www.bbc.com/news/av/uk-56937299 (Accessed 7 May 2021).

BBC News. 'EU Referendum Results'. 3 May 2021. Available at: https://www.bbc.com/
news/politics/eu_referendum/results (Accessed 29 April 2021).

Beauchamps, Marie. *Governing Affective Citizenship: Denaturalization, Belonging, and
Repression.* London: Rowman & Littlefield International, 2018.

Ben-Amos, Avner. *Funerals, Politics and Memory in Modern France 1789–1996.*
Oxford: Oxford University Press, 2000.

Bennett, Andrew. 'Literary Ignorance'. In *Routledge International Handbook of Ignorance Studies*, edited by Matthias Gross and Linsey McGoey, 36–43. London: Routledge, 2015.

Berlant, Lauren. *The Queen of America Goes to Washington City: Essays on Sex and Citizenship*. Durham, NC: Duke University Press, 1997.

Berlant, Lauren. 'The Subject of True Feeling: Pain, Privacy, and Politics'. In *Traumatizing Theory, The Cultural Politics of Affect in and beyond Psychoanalysis*, edited by Karyn Ball. New York: Other Press, 2007.

Berlant, Lauren. *The Female Complaint*. Durham, NC: Duke University Press, 2008.

Berlant, Lauren. *Cruel Optimism*. Durham, NC: Duke University Press, 2011.

Berlant, Lauren, and Jordan Greenwald. 'Affect in the End Times: A Conversation with Lauren Berlant'. *Qui Parle* 20, no. 2 (2012): 71–89.

Berman, Marshall. *All That Is Solid Melts into Air: The Experience of Modernity*. London: Verso, 1983.

Bhabha, Homi. *The Location of Culture*. London: Routledge, 2004.

Bhambra, Gurminder. 'Brexit, Trump, and "Methodological Whiteness": On the Misrecognition of Race and Class'. *British Journal of Sociology* 68, no. 1 (2017): 214–32.

Bhandar, Brenna. *Colonial Lives of Property: Law, Land and Racial Regimes of Ownership*. Durham, NC: Duke University Press, 2018.

Billig, Michael. *Banal Nationalism*. London: Sage, 1995.

Bissell, David. 'Comfortable Bodies: Sedentary Affects'. *Environment and Planning A: Economy and Space* 40, no. 7 (2008): 1697–712.

Bissell, David. 'Micropolitics and Mobility: Public Transport Commuting and Everyday Encounters with Forces of Enablement and Constraint'. *Annals of the American Association of Geographers* 106, no. 2 (2016): 394–403.

Bissell, David, Maria Hynes and Scott Sharpe. 'Unveiling Seductions beyond Societies of Control: Affect, Security, and Humour in Spaces of Aeromobility'. *Environment and Planning D: Society and Space* 30, no. 4 (2012): 694–710.

Bissell, David, Mitch Rose and Paul Harrison (eds). *Negative Geographies. Exploring the Politics of Limits*. Lincoln: University of Nebraska Press, 2021.

Blackman, Lisa, and Valerie Walkerdine. *Mass Hysteria. Critical Psychology and Media Studies*. London: Palgrave, 2001.

Blakeley, Ruth, and Sam Raphael. 'British Torture in the "War on Terror"'. *European Journal of International Relations* 23, no. 2 (2017): 243–66.

Bleiker, Roland. *Aesthetics and World Politics*. New York: Palgrave, 2012.

Bleiker, Roland (ed.). *Visual Global Politics*. New York: Routledge, 2018.

Bleiker, Roland, David Campbell, Emma Hutchison and Xzarina Nicholson. 'The Visual Dehumanisation of Refugees'. *Australian Journal of Political Science* 48, no. 4 (2013): 398–416.

Booth, Robert. '22 Days in April: The Darkest Hours of the UK Coronavirus Crisis'. 19 June 2020. *The Guardian*. Available at: https://www.theguardian.com/world/2020/jun/19/22-days-in-april-uk-darkest-hours-of-coronavirus-crisis (Accessed 22 June 2021).

Borradori, Giovanna. *Philosophy in a Time of Terror: Dialogues with Jurgen Habermas and Jacques Derrida*. Chicago: University of Chicago Press, 2003.

Boym, Svetlana. *The Future of Nostalgia*. New York: Basic Books, 2001.

Bramall, Rebecca. 'Dig for Victory! Anti-consumerism, Austerity, and New Historical Subjectivities'. *Subjectivity* 4, no. 1 (2011): 68–86.

Brennan, Teresa. *The Transmission of Affect*. New York: Cornell University Press, 2004.

Brice, Sage. 'Geographies of Vulnerability: Mapping Transindividual Geometries of Identity and Resistance', *Transactions of the Institute of British Geographers* 45, no. 3 (2020): 664–77.

Brown, Wendy. 'Wounded Attachments'. *Political Theory* 21, no. 3 (1993): 390–410.

Brown, Wendy. *Undoing the Demos: Neoliberalism's Stealth Revolution*. New York: Zone Books, 2015.

Browne, Victoria, Jason Danely and Doerthe Rosenow (eds). *Vulnerability and the Politics of Care: Transdisciplinary Dialogues*. Oxford: Oxford University Press, 2021.

Brubaker, Rogers. *Ethnicity without Groups*. Cambridge, MA: Harvard University Press, 2004.

Bulley, Dan. *Migration, Ethics & Power*. London: Sage, 2017.

Bulley, Dan, and Debbie Lisle. 'Welcoming the World. Governing Hospitality in London's 2012 Olympic Bid'. *International Political Sociology* 6, no. 2 (2012): 186–204.

Bulley, Dan, Jenny Edkins and Nadina El-Enany. 'Introduction'. In *After Grenfell: Violence, Resistance and Response*, edited by Dan Bulley, Jenny Edkins and Nadina El-Enany, xxi–xxii. London: Pluto Press, 2019.

Burrell, Kathy, and Kathrin Hörschelman. 'Perilous Journeys: Visualising the Racialised "Refugee Crisis"'. *Antipode* 51, no. 1 (2019): 45–65.

Butler, Judith. *Precarious Life: The Power of Mourning and Violence*. London: Verso, 2006.

Butler, Judith. *Notes Toward a Performative Theory of Assembly*. Cambridge, MA: Harvard University Press, 2015.

Butler, Judith. 'Rethinking Vulnerability and Resistance'. In *Vulnerability in Resistance*, edited by Judith Butler, Zeynep Gambetti and Leticia Sabsay. Durham, NC: Duke University Press, 2016.

Butler, Judith. *The Force of Non-Violence*. London: Verso Books, 2020.

Butler, Judith, Zeynep Gambetti and Leticia Sabsay. *Vulnerability in Resistance*. Durham, NC: Duke University Press, 2016.

Cadwalladr, Carole. 'View from Wales: Town Showered with Cash Votes to Leave EU'. *The Guardian*. 25 June 2016. Available at: https://www.theguardian.com/uk-news/2016/jun/25/view-wales-town-showered-eu-cash-votes-leave-ebbw-vale (Accessed 22 February 2021).

Calvert, Jonathan, George Arbuthnott and Jonathan Leake. 'Coronavirus: 38 Days When Britain Sleepwalked Into Disaster'. *The Times*, 19 April 2020. Available at: https://www.thetimes.co.uk/article/coronavirus-38-days-when-britain-sleepwalked-into-disaster-hq3b9tlgh (Accessed 7 May 2021).

Carastathis, Anna, and Myrto Tsilimpounidi. *Reproducing Refugees: Photographia of a Crisis*. London: Rowman & Littlefield International, 2020.

Carter, Richard, and Julius McManus. 'The Data Is in Black Strictly Contestants Are More Likely to Be Voted Off'. 16 December 2016. *The Guardian*. Available at: https://www.theguardian.com/commentisfree/2016/dec/16/black-strictly-come-dancing (Accessed 23 February 2021).

Chakrabarty, Dipesh. *Provincializing Europe: Postcolonial Thought and Historical Difference*. Princeton, NJ: Princeton University Press, 2008.

Channel 4 News. 'George Osborne Booed at Paralympics' (Video) 3 September 2012. Available at: https://www.youtube.com/watch?v=qqM0Ube0oLs (Accessed 24 February 2021).

Chatterjee, Partha. *Nationalist Thought and the Colonial World: A Derivative Discourse? Third World Books*. London: Zed, 1993.

Child Poverty Action Group. 'The Austerity Generation: The Impact of a Decade of Cuts on Family Incomes and Child Poverty'. November 2017. Available at: https://cpag.org.uk/sites/default/files/files/Austerity%20Generation%20FINAL.pdf (Accessed 10 January 2022).

Chouliaraki, Lilie. 'Post-Humanitarianism: Humanitarian Communication beyond a Politics of Pity'. *International Journal of Cultural Studies* 13, no. 2 (2010): 107–26.

Chouliaraki, Lilie, and Tijana Stolic. 'Rethinking Media Responsibility in the Refugee "Crisis": A Visual Typology of European News'. *Media, Culture & Society* 39, no. 8 (2017): 1162–77.

Clark, Tom. 'Britain's End-of-Year Olympic Verdict: It Was Worth Every Penny'. *The Guardian*. 25 December 2012. Available at: https://www.theguardian.com/politics/2012/dec/25/britain-end-of-year-olympic-verdict (Accessed 14 February 2021).

Clarke, John. 'Living with/in and without Neo-Liberalism'. *Focaal* 51, no. 1 (2008): 135–47.

Clifford, James. 'Introduction: Partial Truths'. In *Writing Culture*, edited by James Clifford and George E. Marcus, 1–26. London: University of California Press, 1986.

Closs Stephens, Angharad. *The Persistence of Nationalism: From Imagined Communities to Urban Encounters*. London: Routledge, 2013.

Closs Stephens, Angharad. 'National Atmospheres and the "Brexit" Revolt'. *Society and Space Open Site* (2016).

Clough, Patricia. 'Introduction'. In *The Affective Turn. Theorizing the Social*, edited by Patricia Clough and Jean Halley, 1–35. Durham, NC: Duke University Press, 2007.

Clough, Patricia. 'Afterword: The Future of Affect Studies'. *Body & Society* 16, no. 1 (2010): 222–30.

Coe, Katye, and Hetty Blades. 'Running, Resistance and Recollection: A Conversation with Ourselves through Time'. *Performance Philosophy* 2, no. 2 (2017): 331–41.

Cole, Alyson, and Sumru Atuk. 'What's in a Hashtag? Feminist Terms for Tweeting in Alliance'. *philoSOPHIA* 9, no. 1 (2019): 26–52.

Cole, Teju. *Open City*. London: Faber and Faber, 2011.

Cole, Teju. 'Unmournable Bodies'. *The New Yorker*, 9 January 2015. Available at: http://www.newyorker.com/culture/cultural-comment/unmournable-bodies (Accessed 14 February 2021).

Coleman, Lara, and Hannah Hughes. 'Distance'. In *Critical Security Methods: New Frameworks and Approaches*, edited by Claudia Aradau, Jeff Huysmans, Nadine Voelkner and Andrew Neal, 1–12. London: Routledge, 2015.

Connolly, William. *Pluralism*. Durham, NC: Duke University Press, 2005.

Connolly, William. *Capitalism and Christianity, American Style*. Durham, NC: Duke University Press, 2008.

Connolly, William. *Aspirational Fascism: The Struggle for Multifaceted Democracy under Trumpism*. Minneapolis: University of Minnesota Press, 2017.

Coward, Martin. 'Between Us in the City: Materiality, Subjectivity and Community in the Era of Global Urbanization'. *Environment and Planning D: Society and Space* 30, no. 3 (2012): 468–81.

Cramer, Katherine J. *The Politics of Resentment*. Chicago: University of Chicago Press, 2016.

Crang, Mike, and Divya Tolia-Kelly. 'Nation, Race, and Affect: Senses and Sensibilities at National Heritage Sites'. *Environment and Planning A: Economy and Space* 42, no. 10 (2010): 2315–31.

Cresswell, Tim. 'You Cannot Shake That Shimmie Here: Producing Mobility on the Dance Floor'. *Cultural Geographies* 13, no. 1 (2006): 55–77.

Cresswell, Tim. 'Black Moves: Moments in the History of African-American Masculine Mobilities'. *Transfers* 6, no. 1 (2016): 12–25.

Cull Ó Maoilearca, Laura, Kelina Gotman, Eve Katsouraki and Theron Schmidt. 'Editorial'. *Performance Philosophy* 2, no. 2 (2017): 162–71.

Danchev, Alex, and Debbie Lisle. 'Introduction: Art, Politics, Purpose'. *Review of International Studies* 35, no. 4 (2009): 777–8.

Davies, John. *Hanes Cymru*. London: Penguin, 1990.

Davies, Paul. Angharad Closs Stephens interview with Paul Davies, Volcano Theatre, 7 February 2017. Unpublished.

Davis, Lydia. *Essays One*. New York: Farrar, Straus and Giroux, 2019.

Dawney, Leila. 'Figurationing' in Celia Lury, Rachel Fensham, Alexander Heller-Nicholas, Sybille Lammes, Angela Last, Mike Michael and Emma Uprichard (eds), *Routledge Handbook of Interdisciplinary Research Methods*, 112–15. London: Routledge, 2018.

De Genova, Nicholas. 'The European Question. Migration, Race and Postcoloniality in Europe'. *Social Text* 34, no. 3 (128) (2016): 75–102.

De Genova, Nicholas. 'The Whiteness of Innocence: *Charlie Hebdo* and the Metaphysics of Anti-Terrorism in Europe', in Gavan Titley, Des Freedman, Gholam Khiabany and Aurélien Mondon (eds), *After Charlie Hebdo. Terror, Racism and Free Speech*, 97–113. London: Zed Books, 2017.

De Genova, Nicholas. 'Rebordering "the People": Notes on Theorizing Populism'. *South Atlantic Quarterly* 117, no. 2 (2018): 357–74.

De Genova, Nicholas, and Martina Tazzioli. *Europe/Crisis: New Keywords on 'the Crisis' in and of 'Europe'*. New Keywords Collective, Near Futures Online, Vol. 1. New York: Zone Books, 2016. Available at: http://nearfuturesonline.org/wp-cont ent/uploads/2016/01/New-Keywords-Collective_11.pdf (Accessed 9 March 2021).

De Londras, Fiona. *Detention in the 'War on Terror': Can Human Rights Fight Back?* Cambridge: Cambridge University Press, 2011.

Dean, Jodi. 'Communicative Capitalism and Revolutionary Form'. *Millennium* 47, no. 3 (2019): 326–40.

Deleuze, Giles, and Felix Guattari. *A Thousand Plateaus*. London: Continuum, 2008.

Dempsey, Jessica, and Geraldine Pratt. 'Wiggle Room'. In *Keywords in Radical Geography: Antipode at 50*, edited by Antipode Editorial Collective, 274–9. 2019. Available online at: https://doi.org/10.1002/9781119558071.ch51 (Accessed 17 June 2021).

Derrida, Jacques. *Of Hospitality: Anne Dufourmantelle Invites Jacques Derrida to Respond*. Translated by Bowly, R. Stanford: Stanford University Press, 2000.

Dikeç, Mustafa. 'Hate', 21 January 2015, https://mediadiversified.org/2015/01/21/hate/ (Accessed 24 March 2022).

Dittmer, Jason. *Captain America and the Nationalist Superhero: Metaphors, Narratives and Geopolitics*. Philadelphia, PA: Temple University Press, 2013.

Dixon, Deborah. 'Repurposing Feminist Geopolitics: On Estrangement, Exhaustion and the End of the Solar System'. *Dialogues in Human Geography* 8, no. 1 (2018): 88–90.

Dodd, Vikram. 'Met Police Twice as Likely to Fine Black People over Lockdown Breaches – Research'. *The Guardian*. 3 June 2020. Available at: https://www.theg uardian.com/uk-news/2020/jun/03/met-police-twice-as-likely-to-fine-black-peo ple-over-lockdown-breaches-research (Accessed 7 May 2021).

Dodds, K. J. 'War Stories: British Elite Narratives of the 1982 Falklands/Malvinas War'. *Environment and Planning D: Society and Space* 11, no. 6 (1993): 619–40.

Dorling, Danny. 'Brexit: The Decision of a Divided Country'. *BMJ* 354, no. 3697 (2016): 354.

Dorling, Danny. 'Why Has the UK's COVID Death Toll Been So High? Inequality May Have Played a Role'. 4 March 2021. *The Conversation*. Available at: https://theconve rsation.com/why-has-the-uks-covid-death-toll-been-so-high-inequality-may-have-played-a-role-156331 (Accessed 7 May 2021).

Doty, Roxanne. *Anti-Immigrantism in Western Democracies: Statecraft, Desire and the Politics of Exclusion*. London: Routledge, 2006.

Doty, Roxanne. 'Writing from the Edge'. In *The Ashgate Research Companion to Modern Theory, Modern Power, World Politics: Critical Investigations*, edited by Nevat Soguk and Scott G. Nelson, 149–60. London: Routledge, 2016.

Douzinas, Costas. 'Athens Rising'. *European Urban and Regional Studies* 20, no. 1 (2013): 134–8.

Driver, Felix, and David Gilbert. 'Imperial Cities: Overlapping Territories, Intertwined Histories'. In *Imperial Cities: Landscape, Display and Identity*, edited by Felix Driver and David Gilbert, 1–21. Manchester: Manchester University Press, 1999.

Durkheim, Émile. *The Elementary Forms of Religious Life*. Oxford: Oxford University Press, 2001.

Edensor, Tim. *National Identity, Popular Culture and Everyday Life*. Oxford: Berg, 2002.

Edensor, Tim. 'Sensing National Spaces: Representing the Mundane in English Film and Television'. In *European Film and Television: Cultural Policy and Everyday Life*, edited by IB Bondebjerg, Andrew Higson and Eva Novdrup, 58–80. London: Palgrave, 2015.

Edensor, Tim, and Shanti Sumartojo. 'Geographies of Everyday Nationhood: Experiencing Multiculturalism in Melbourne'. *Nations and Nationalism* 24, no. 3 (2018): 553–78.

Editorial. 'The Guardian's View on Europe's Refugee Crisis: A Little Leadership, at Last', *The Guardian*, 1 September 2015. Available at: https://www.theguardian.com/commentisfree/2015/sep/01/guardian-view-on-europe-refugee-crisis-leadership-at-last-angela-merkel.

Edkins, Jenny. *Trauma and the Memory of Politics*. Cambridge: Cambridge University Press, 2003.

Edkins, Jenny. 'Novel Writing in International Relations: Openings for a Creative Practice'. *Security Dialogue* 44, no. 4 (2013): 281–97.

Edkins, Jenny. 'Face'. In *Visual Global Politics*, edited by Roland Bleiker, 121–6. Oxon: Routledge, 2018.

Edkins, Jenny. *Change and the Politics of Certainty*. Manchester: Manchester University Press, 2019.

Eisenstein, Zillah. 'Feminisms in the Aftermath of September 11'. *Social Text* 20, no. 3 (72) (2002): 79–99.

El-Enany, Nadine. *(B)ordering Britain. Law, Race and Empire*. Manchester: Manchester University Press, 2020.

Emejulu, Akwugo, and Leah Bassel. 'Whose Crisis Counts? Minority Women, Austerity and Activism in France and Britain', in Johanna Kantola and Emanuela Lombardo (eds), *Gender and the Economic Crisis in Europe*, 185–208. London: Palgrave, 2017.

Emoto. 'Visualising the Online Response to 2012'. Available at: http://www.emoto2012.org/downloads/emoto_published.pdf (Accessed 24 March 2022).

Enloe, Cynthia. *Bananas, Beaches and Bases: Making Feminist Sense of International Politics*. Berkeley: University of California Press, 2014.

Etchells, Tim. *Vacuum Days*. Brighton: Storythings, 2012.

Fagan, Madeleine. *Ethics and Politics after Poststructuralism*. Edinburgh: Edinburgh University Press, 2013.

Flemmen, Magne, and Mike Savage. 'The Politics of Nationalism and White Racism in the UK'. *British Journal of Sociology* 68, no. 1 (2017): 233–64.

Fong, Jo, and Sonia Hughes. Angharad Closs Stephens interview with Jo Fong and Sonia Hughes, Capel-y-Graig, Ffwrnais, 6 July 2019. Unpublished.

Fortier, Anne-Marie. 'Pride Politics and Multiculturalist Citizenship'. *Ethnic and Racial Studies* 28, no. 3 (2005): 559–78.

Fortier, Anne-Marie. *Multicultural Horizons*. London: Routledge, 2008.

Fortier, Anne-Marie. 'Proximity by Design? Affective Citizenship and the Management of Unease'. *Citizenship Studies* 14, no. 1 (2010): 17–30.

Foucault, Michel. 'Truth and Power'. In *The Foucault Reader*, edited by Paul Rabinow, 51–75. New York: Pantheon Books, 1984.

Foucault, Michel. 'What Is Enlightenment?' In *The Foucault Reader*, edited by Paul Rabinow, 32–51. New York: Pantheon Books, 1984.

Foucault, Michel. 'For an Ethic of Discomfort'. In *Power: Essential Works of Foucault, 1954–1984*, edited by James D. Faubion, 443–8. London: Penguin, 1994.

Foucault, Michel. 'Interview with Michel Foucault'. In *Power: Essential Works of Foucault 1954–1984*, edited by James D. Faubion, 239–98. London: Penguin, 1994.

Foucault, Michel. 'So Is It Important to Think?' In *Power: Essential Works of Foucault, 1954–1984*, edited by James D. Faubion, 454–8. London: Penguin, 1994.

Frankenberg, Ruth, and Lata Mani. 'Crosscurrents, Crosstalk: Race, "Postcoloniality" and the Politics of Location'. *Cultural Studies* 7, no. 2 (1993): 292–310.

Freedman, Ariela. 'How to Get to 9/11: Teju Cole's Melancholic Fiction'. In *Representing 9/11: Trauma, Ideology and Nationalism in Literature, Film and Television*, edited by Paul Pedrovic, 177–86. London: Rowman & Littlefield, 2015.

Galal, Lisa Paulsen, and Kirsten Hvenegård-Lassen. 'Walking, Dancing, and Listening: Affect and Encounters'. In *Organised Cultural Encounters: Global Diversities*, edited by Lise Paulsen Galal and Kirsten Hvenegård-Lassen, 149–88. Cham: Palgrave Macmillan, 2020.

Gandy, Matthew. 'Urban Atmospheres'. *Cultural Geographies* 24, no. 3 (2017): 353–74.

Gannon, Susan. 'Ordinary Atmospheres and Minor Weather Events'. *Departures in Critical Qualitative Research* 5, no. 4 (2016): 79–90.

Gardiner, Bonnie. 'Interest in the London Olympics'. *YouGov*. 30 March 2012. Available at: http://yougov.co.uk/news/2012/03/30/interest-london-olympics/ (Accessed 24 February 2021).

Gayle, Damien. 'Hundreds of migrants believed to have drowned off Libya after boat capsizes', 15 April 2015, https://www.theguardian.com/world/2015/apr/14/400-drowned-libya-italy-migrant-boat-capsizes. Last accessed 29 March 2022.

Geertz, Clifford. 'Centers, Kings and Charisma: Reflections on the Symbolics of Power'. In *Local Knowledge: Further Essays in Interpretative Anthropology*, edited by Clifford Geertz, 121–46. New York: Basic Books, 1983.

Gellner, Ernest. *Nations and Nationalism*. Oxford: Blackwell, 1983.

Germanà, Monica, and Emily Horton. 'Introduction'. In *Ali Smith: Contemporary Critical Perspectives*, edited by Monica Germanà and Emily Horton, 1–8. London: Bloomsbury Academic, 2013.

Gilbert, Jeremy. 'What Kind of Thing Is "Neoliberalism"?', *New Formations* 80–1 (2013): 7–22.

Gill, Nick. *Nothing Personal. Geographies of Governing and Activism in the British Asylum System*. Malden, MA: John Wiley, 2016.

Gilroy, Paul. *Small Acts*. London: Serpent's Tail, 1994.

Gilroy Paul. *After Empire: Melancholia or Convivial Culture*. London: Routledge, 2004.

Gilroy, Paul. '…We Got to Get over Before We Go Under … Fragment for a History of Black Vernacular Neoliberalism'. *New Emotions* 80–1 (2013): 23–38.

Glissant, Édouard. *Poetics of Relation*. Ann Arbor: University of Michigan Press, 2010.

'Glynn Vivian Becomes First UK Art Gallery of Sanctuary'. Swansea Bay News. 24 November 2021, https://swanseabaynews.com/2021/11/24/glynn-vivian-becomes-first-uk-art-gallery-of-sanctuary%EF%BF%BC/

Goldberg, David. *The Racial State*. Malden, MA: Blackwell, 2002.

Goldberg, David. *The Threat of Race*. Malden, MA: Blackwell, 2009.

Goodhart, David. *The Road to Somewhere: The Populist Revolt and the Future of Politics*. London: Hurst, 2017.

Goulard, Hortense. 'Britain's Youth Vote Remain'. *Politico*. 24 June 2016. Available at: https://www.politico.eu/article/britains-youth-voted-remain-leave-eu-brexit-ref erendum-stats/ (Accessed 22 February 2021).

Graham, Stephen. 'Olympics 2012 Security Welcome to Lockdown London'. *City: Analysis of Urban Trends, Culture, Theory, Policy, Action* 16, no. 4 (2012): 446–51.

Graham, Stephen. *Vertical: The City from Satellites to Bunkers*. London: Verso, 2018.

Gregory, Derek. *The Colonial Present*. Malden, MA: Blackwell, 2004.

Grewal, Inderpal. *Transnational America: Feminisms, Diasporas, Neoliberalisms*. Durham, NC: Duke University Press, 2005.

Grosz, Elizabeth. *Chaos, Territory, Art: Deleuze and the Framing of the Earth*. New York: Columbia University Press, 2008.

Gunaratnam, Yasmin. *Death and the Migrant: Bodies, Borders and Care*. London: Bloomsbury Academic, 2013.

Gunaratnam, Yasmin, and Carrie Hamilton. 'Introduction: The Wherewithal of Feminist Methods'. *Feminist Review* 115, no. 1 (2017): 1–12.

Gunew, Sneja. 'Subaltern Empathy: Beyond European Categories in Affect Theory', *Concentric: Literary and Cultural Studies* 35, no. 1 (2009): 11–30.

Gupta, Akhil, and James Ferguson. 'Beyond "Culture": Space, Identity and the Politics of Difference'. *Cultural Anthropology* 7, no. 1 (1992): 6–23.

Hage, Ghassan. *White Nation: Fantasies of White Supremacy in a Multicultural Society*. New York: Routledge and Pluto Press, 2000.

Hage, Ghassan. *Is Racism an Environmental Threat?* Cambridge: Polity Press, 2017.

Hall, Stuart. 'The Great Moving Right Show'. *Marxism Today* 23, no. 1 (January 1979): 14–20.

Hall, Stuart. *Representation. Cultural Representations and Signifying Practices*. London: Open University, 1997.

Hall, Stuart, and Martin Jacques. 'Introduction'. In *The Politics of Thatcherism*, edited by Stuart Hall and Martin Jacques, 9–18. London: Lawrence and Wishart, 1990.

Hallam, Elizabeth, and Tim Ingold. *Creativity and Cultural Improvisation*. London: Routledge, 2007.

Hansen, Thomas Blom, and Oskar Verkaaik. 'Introduction – Urban Charisma: On Everyday Mythologies in the City'. *Critique of Anthropology* 29, no. 1 (2009): 5–26.

Hay, Deborah. *My Body, the Buddhist*. Connecticut: Wesleyan University Press, 2000.

Helliwell, Christine, and Barry Hindess. 'The Temporalizing of Difference'. *Ethnicities* 5, no. 3 (2005): 414–18.

Helms, Gesa, Marina Vishmidt and Lauren Berlant. 'Notes on Affect & the Politics of Austerity. An Interview Exchange with Lauren Berlant'. *Variant*, no. 39/40 (2010): 3–6.

Hemmings, Clare. 'Affective Solidarity: Feminist Reflexivity and Political Transformation', *Feminist Theory* 13, no. 2 (2012): 149.

Henley, Jon. 'Boris Johnson Wins Huge Majority on Promise to 'Get Brexit Done''. *The Guardian*. 13 December 2019. Available at: https://www.theguardian.com/polit ics/2019/dec/13/bombastic-boris-johnson-wins-huge-majority-on-promise-to-get-brexit-done (Accessed 7 May 2021).

Hess, Sabine, Bernd Kasparek, Stefanie Kron, Mathias Rodatz, Maria Schwertl and Simon Sontowski (Hgs). *Der Lange Sommer Der Migration: Grenzregime III*. Berlin: Assoziation A, 2017.

Higgins, Charlotte. 'Boat in Which Hundreds of Migrants Died Displayed at Venice Biennale'. *The Guardian*. 7 May 2019. Available at: https://www.theguardian.com/artanddesign/2019/may/07/boat-in-which-hundreds-of-ismigrants-died-displa yed-at-venice-biennale (Accessed 3 June 2021).

Highmore, Ben. 'Bitter after Taste: Affect, Food and Social Aesthetics'. In *The Affect Theory Reader*, edited by Melissa Gregg and Gregory Seigworth, 118–37. Durham, NC: Duke University Press, 2010.

Hinderliter, Ben, William Kaizen, Vered Maimon, Jaled Mansoor and Seth McCormick. *Communities of Sense. Rethinking Aesthetics and Politics*. Durham, NC: Duke University Press, 2009.

Hirschkind, Charles. *The Ethical Soundscape: Cassette Sermons and Islamic Counterpublics*. Columbia: Columbia University Press, 2006.

Hitchen, Esther. 'The Affective Life of Austerity: Uncanny Atmospheres and Paranoid Temporalities'. *Social & Cultural Geography* 22, no. 3 (2021): 295–318.

Hobsbawm, Eric, and Terence Ranger. *The Invention of Tradition*. Cambridge: Cambridge University Press, 1983.

Hochschild, Arlie. *Strangers in Their Own Land.* New York: New Press, 2016.

Holland, Jack, and Ty Solomon. 'Affect Is What States Make of It: Articulating Everyday Experiences of 9/11', *Critical Studies on Security* 2, no. 3 (2014): 262–77.

Horton, Emily. ' "Contemporary Space and Affective Ethics" in Contemporary Critical Perspectives'. In *Ali Smith: Contemporary Critical Perspectives*, edited by Monica Germanà and Emily Horton, 9–22. London: Bloomsbury Academic, 2013.

House of Commons. 'Speaker's Statement on Baroness Thatcher's Funeral Arrangements'. *UK Parliament.* 2013. Available at: http://www.parliament.uk/busin ess/news/2013/april/speakers-statement-on-baroness-thatchers-funeral-arrangeme nts/ (Accessed 7 September 2017).

Hubbard, Phill, and Dawn Lyon. 'Introduction: Streetlife – The Shifting Sociologies of the Street'. *Sociological Review* 66, no. 5 (2018): 937–51.

Hughes, Sarah M. 'On Resistance in Human Geography'. *Progress in Human Geography* 44, no. 6 (2020): 1141–60.

Huysmans, Jef. *Security Unbound: Enacting Democratic Limits.* London: Routledge, 2014.

Hyndman, Jennifer, and Wenona Giles. *Refugees in Extended Exile: Living on the Edge.* London: Routledge, 2018.

Inayatullah, Naeem. *Autobiographical International Relations, I, IR.* London: Routledge, 2010.

Inayatullah, Naeem, and Elizabeth Dauphinee (eds). *Narrative Global Politics: Theory, History and the Personal in International Relations.* London: Routledge, 2017.

Independent. 'Theresa May's Keynote Speech at Tory Conference in Full'. 5 October 2016. Available at: https://www.independent.co.uk/news/uk/politics/theresa-may-speech-tory-conference-2016-in-full-transcript-a7346171.html (Accessed 24 February 2021).

India Today. 'Artist Ai Weiwei Poses as Aylan Kurdi for *India Today* Magazine'. 1 February 2016. Available at: https://www.indiatoday.in/india/story/artist-ai-wei wei-poses-as-aylan-kurdi-for-india-today-magazine-306593-2016-02-01 (Accessed 12 March 2021).

Ingram, Alan. 'Making Geopolitics Otherwise: Artistic Interventions in Global Political Space'. *Geographical Journal* 177, no. 3 (2011): 218–22.

Ingram, Alan. *Geopolitics and the Event: Rethinking Britain's Iraq War through Art.* Oxford: Wiley, 2019.

Irigaray, Luce. *The Forgetting of Air in Martin Heidegger.* Austin: University of Texas Press, 1999.

Isin, Engin F. *Being Political: Genealogies of Citizenship.* Minneapolis: University of Minnesota Press, 2002.

Isin, Engin F. 'The Neurotic Citizen'. *Citizenship Studies* 8, no. 3 (2004): 217–35.

Isin, Engin F. 'Theorizing Acts of Citizenship'. In *Acts of Citizenship*, edited by Engin Isin and Greg Nielsen, 15–43. London: Zed Books, 2008.

Isin, Engin F. 'Citizenship in Flux: The Figure of the Activist Citizen'. *Subjectivity* 29 (2009): 367–88.

Isin, Engin F. 'Citizens without Nations'. *Environment and Planning D: Society and Space* 30, no. 3 (2012): 450–67.

Isin, Engin F. and Greg Nielsen (eds). *Acts of Citizenship*. London: Zed Books, 2008.

Jackson, Mark, and Maria Fannin. 'Letting Geography Fall Where It May – Aerographies Address the Elemental'. *Environment and Planning D: Society and Space* 29, no. 3 (2011): 435–44.

Jeffries, Stuart. 'The Question: Who Gets a State Funeral?' *The Guardian*. 15 July 2008. Available at: https://www.theguardian.com/politics/2008/jul/15/past.margaretthatcher (Accessed 26 April 2021).

Jenkins, Nigel. *Real Swansea*. Bridgend: Seren Books, 2008.

Jessop, Bob, Kevin Bonnett, Simon Bromley and Tom Ling. *Thatcherism: A Tale of Two Nations*. Cambridge: Polity Press, 1988.

Jones, Rhys, and Peter Merriman. 'Hot, Banal and Everyday Nationalism: Bilingual Road Signs in Wales'. *Political Geography* 28, no. 3 (2009): 164–73.

Jones, Rhys, and Peter Merriman. 'Network Nation'. *Environment and Planning A* 44, no. 4 (2012): 937–53.

Karatsogianni, Athina, and Adi Kuntsman. *Digital Cultures and the Politics of Emotion*. New York: Palgrave Macmillan, 2012.

Katz, Cindi. 'Towards Minor Theory'. *Environment and Planning D: Society and Space* 14, no. 4 (1996): 487–99.

Khan, Gulshan. 'Agency, Nature and Emergent Properties: An Interview with Jane Bennett'. *Contemporary Political Theory* 8 (2009): 90–105.

Kosofsky Sedgwick, Eve. *Touching Feeling: Affect, Pedagogy, Performativity*. Durham, NC: Duke University Press, 2003.

Kureishi, Hanif. *The Black Album*. London: Faber and Faber, 1995.

Kureishi, Hanif. *The Word and the Bomb*. London: Faber and Faber, 2005.

Labelle, Brandon. *Acoustic Territories/Sound Culture*. New York: Continuum, 2010.

Land Registry 2018 and 2022. UK house price index. http://landregistry.data.gov.uk/app/ukhpi.

Lentin, Alana. 'Charlie Hebdo: White Context and Black Analytics'. *Public Culture* 31, no. 1 (2018): 45–67.

Lentin, Alana, and Gavan Titley. *The Crises of Multiculturalism: Racism in a Neoliberal Age*. London: Zed Books, 2011.

Liberty. 'A Guide to the Hostile Environment'. May 2019. https://www.libertyhumanrights.org.uk/wp-content/uploads/2020/02/Hostile-Environment-Guide-%E2%80%93-update-May-2019_0.pdf (Accessed 22 June 2021).

Lisle, Debbie. 'Moving Encounters: The Affective Mobilities of Photography'. In *Stillness in a Mobile World*, edited by David Bissell and Gillian Fullner, 139–54. London: Routledge, 2011.

Lisle, Debbie. *Holidays in the Danger Zone: Entanglements of War and Tourism*. Minneapolis: University of Minnesota Press, 2016.

Lisle, Debbie. 'Waiting for International Political Sociology: A Field Guide to Living In-Between'. *International Political Sociology* 10, no. 4 (2016): 417–33.

Locog press release. 'LOCOG Publishes 2011–2012 Report and Accounts', 8 February 2013, https://www.paralympic.org/news/locog-publishes-2011-2012-report-and-accounts. Accessed 24 March 2022.

Lunt, David, and Mark Dyreson. 'The 1904 Olympic Games: Triumph or Nadir'. In *The Palgrave Handbook of Olympic Studies*, edited by Helen Jefferson Lenskyj and Stephen Wagg, 43–59. London: Palgrave Macmillan, 2012.

Mahmood, Saba. 'Religious Reason and Secular Affect: An Incommensurable Divide?' *Critical Inquiry* 35, no. 4 (2009): 836–62.

Malkki, Liisa H. 'Refugees and Exile: From "Refugee Studies" to the National Order of Things'. *Annual Review of Anthropology* 24, no. 1 (1995): 495–523.

Malm, Andreas. *Corona, Climate, Chronic Emergency: War Communism in the Twenty-First Century*. London: Verso Books, 2020.

Mamdani, Mahmood. 'Good Muslim, Bad Muslim: A Political Perspective on Culture and Terrorism'. *American Anthropologist* 104, no. 3 (2002): 766–75.

Manning, Erin. *The Minor Gesture*. Durham, NC: Duke University Press, 2016.

Mayor of London press release. ' "London's getting ready for a summer like no other" says Mayor', 8 June 2012, https://www.london.gov.uk/press-releases-4744 (Accessed 24 March 2022).

Mantel, Hilary. *The Assassination of Margaret Thatcher*. London: Fourth Estate, 2014.

Martin, Randy. *Critical Moves: Dance Studies in Theory and Politics*. Durham, NC: Duke University Press, 1998.

Marx, Anthony W. *Faith in Nation: Exclusionary Origins of Nationalism*. Oxford: Oxford University Press, 2005.

Masco, Joseph. *The Theater of Operations: National Security Affect from the Cold War to the War on Terror*. Durham, NC: Duke University Press, 2014.

Massey, Doreen. *For Space*. London: Sage, 2005.

Massey, Doreen. 'Doreen Massey on the Kilburn Manifesto'. Available at: https://www.youtube.com/watch?v=P2DyPUDzXIM (Accessed 24 March 2022).

Massumi, Brian. *Parables for the Virtual*. Durham, NC: Duke University Press, 2002.

Massumi, Brian. *Politics of Affect*. Cambridge: Polity Press, 2015.

May, Theresa. 'Full Text: Theresa May's Conference Speech'. *The Spectator*. 5 October 2016. Available at: https://www.spectator.co.uk/article/full-text-theresa-may-s-conference-speech (Accessed 30 March 2022).

May, Vanessa, Bridget Byrne, Helen Holmes and Shaminder Takhar. 'Nationalism's Futures'. *Sociology* 54, no. 6 (2000): 1055–71.

Mbembe, Achille. *On the Postcolony*. Berkeley: University of California Press, 2001.

Mbembe, Achille. 'The Society of Enmity'. *Radical Philosophy* 200 (2016). Available at: https://www.radicalphilosophy.com/article/the-society-of-enmity (Accessed 7 May 2021).

McCluskey, Emma. *From Righteousness to Far-Right: An Anthropological Rethinking of Critical Security Studies*. McGill-Queen's University Press, 2019.

McConnell, Fiona. *Rehearsing the State*. Oxford: Wiley Blackwell, 2016.

McCormack, Derek. 'Engineering Affective Atmospheres'. *Cultural Geographies* 15, no. 4 (2008): 413–30.

McCormack, Derek. 'Geographies for Moving Bodies: Thinking, Dancing, Spaces'. *Geography Compass* 2, no. 6 (2008): 1822–36.

McCormack, Derek. *Refrains for Moving Bodies*. Durham, NC: Duke University Press, 2013.

McCormack, Derek. *Atmospheric Things*. Durham, NC: Duke University Press, 2018.

McFarlane, Colin. *Learning the City: Knowledge and Translocal Assemblages*. Hoboken, NJ: Wiley Blackwell, 2011.

McNevin, Anne. 'Ambivalence and Citizenship: Theorising the Political Claims of Irregular Migrants'. *Millennium: Journal of International Studies* 41, no. 2 (2013): 182–200.

McRobbie, Angela. 'Notes on the Perfect: Competitive Femininity in Neoliberal Times'. *Australian Feminist Studies* 30, no. 83 (2015): 3–20.

Merrill, Samuel, Shanti Sumartojo, Angharad Closs Stephens and Martin Coward. 'Togetherness After Terror: The More or Less Digital Commemorative Public Atmospheres of the Manchester Arena Bombing's First Anniversary'. *Environment and Planning D: Society and Space* 30, no. 6 (2020): 1103–22.

Merriman, Peter, and Rhys Jones. 'Nations, Materialities and Affects'. *Progress in Human Geography* 41, no. 5 (2016): 600–17.

Messud, Clare. 'The Secret Sharer'. *New York Review of Books* 14, July 2011.

Mezzadro, Sandro. 'The Right to Escape'. *Ephemera: Theory of the Multitude* 4, no. 3 (2004): 267–75.

Mignolo, Walter. *The Darker Side of Western Modernity: Global Futures, Decolonial Options*. Durham, NC: Duke University Press, 2011.

Militz, Elisabeth. 'On Affect, Dancing and National Bodies'. In *Everyday Nationhood: Theorising Culture, Identity and Belonging after Banal Nationalism*, edited by Martin Skey and Marco Antonsich, 177–95. London: Palgrave Macmillan, 2017.

Militiz, Elisabeth, and Carolin Schurr. 'Affective Nationalism: Banalities of Belonging in Azerbaijan'. *Political Geography* 54 (2016): 54–63.

Mohanty, Chandra. 'Under Western Eyes: Feminist Scholarship and Colonial Discourses'. *Feminist Review* 30, no. 1 (1988): 61–88.

Morrison, Ian A. *Moments of Crisis: Religion and National Identity in Québec*. Vancouver: UBC Press, 2019.

Moscoso, Javier. *Pain: A Cultural History*. London: Palgrave Macmillan, 2012.

Mouffe, Chantal. *For a Left Populism*. London: Verso, 2018.

Mounk, Yascha. 'What Boris Johnson Did to the World's Most Stable Democracy'. *The Atlantic*. 28 August 2019. Available at: https://www.theatlantic.com/ideas/arch ive/2019/08/boris-johnsons-radically-undemocratic-maneuver/596983/ (Accessed 7 May 2021).

Nayak, Anoop. 'Purging the Nation: Race, Conviviality and Embodied Encounters in the Lives of British Bangladeshi Muslim Young Women'. *Transactions of the Institute of British Geographers* 42, no. 2 (2017): 289–302.

Nardelli, Alberto. 'Angela Merkel's Stance on Refugees Means She Stands Alone against Catastrophe', *The Guardian*. 8 November 2015. Available at: https://www.theg uardian.com/commentisfree/2015/nov/08/angela-merkel-refugee-crisis-europe (Accessed 12 January 2022).

Ngai, Sianne. *Ugly Feelings*. Cambridge, MA: Harvard University Press, 2007.

Noxolo, Patricia. 'Flat Out! Dancing the City at a Time of Austerity'. *Environment and Planning D: Society and Space* 36, no. 5 (2018): 797–811.

Nuttall, Sarah. 'Literary City'. In *Johannesburg. The Elusive Metropolis*, edited by Sarah Nuttall and Achille Mbembe, 195–221. Durham, NC: Duke University Press, 2008.

Nuttall, Sarah, and Achille Mbembe. *Johannesburg. The Elusive Metropolis*. Durham, NC: Duke University Press, 2008.

Nyers, Peter. 'Emergency or Emerging Identities? Refugees and Transformations in World Order'. *Millennium* 28, no. 1 (1999): 1–26.

Olympic Games. 'Coe Praises London 2012's "extraordinary atmosphere" '. 1 August 2012. Available at:https://olympics.com/en/news/coe-praises-london-2012-s-extrao rdinary-atmosphere (Accessed 24 March 2022).

O'Toole, Fintan. *Heroic Failure: Brexit and the Politics of Pain*. London: Apollo, 2018.

Office of National Statistics. 'Coronavirus: A Year Like No Other'. 15 March 2021. Available at: https://www.ons.gov.uk/peoplepopulationandcommunity/healthandsoc ialcare/conditionsanddiseases/articles/coronavirusayearlikenoother/2021-03-15 (Accessed 7 May 2021).

Opondo, Sam Okoth. 'Cinema – Body – Thought: Race Habits and the Ethics of Encounter'. In *Deleuze and Race*, edited by Arun Saldanha and Jason Michael Adams, 247–68. Edinburgh: Edinburgh University Press, 2013.

Opondo, Sam Okoth. *Diplomatic Para-Citations: Genre, Foreign Bodies, and the Ethics of Co-Habitation*. Rowman and Littlefield, 2022.

Orbach, Susie. 'In Therapy, Everyone Wants to Talk about Brexit'. *The Guardian*. 1 July 2016. Available at: https://www.theguardian.com/global/2016/jul/01/ susie-orbach-in-therapy-everyone-wants-to-talk-about-brexit (Accessed 22 February 2021).

Orloff, Ann, Raka Ray and Evren Savcı. 'Introduction: Perverse Politics? Feminism, Anti-Imperialism, Multiplicity'. *Political Power and Social Theory* 30 (2016): 1–17.

Pain, Rachel. 'Globalized Fear? Towards an Emotional Geopolitics'. *Progress in Human Geography* 33, no. 4 (2009): 466–86.

Painter, Joe. 'Prosaic Geographies of Stateness'. *Political Geography* 25, no. 7 (2006): 752–74.

Painter, Joe. 'Rethinking Territory'. *Antipode* 42, no. 5 (2010): 1090–118.

Panagia, David. *The Poetics of Political Thinking*. Durham, NC: Duke University Press, 2006.

Pedwell, Carolyn. 'Affect at the Margins: Alternative Empathies in a Small Place'. *Emotion, Space and Society* 8 (2013): 18–26.

Pedwell, Carolyn. *Affective Relations: The Transnational Politics of Empathy*. Houndmills: Palgrave Macmillan, 2014.

Pedwell, Carolyn. 'De-Colonising Empathy: Thinking Affect Transnationally'. *Samyukta: A Journal of Women's Studies* 16, no. 1 (January 2016): 27–49.

Phipps, Alison. ' "Every Woman Knows a Weinstein": Political Whiteness and White Woundedness in #MeToo and Public Feminisms around Sexual Violence'. *Feminist Formations* 31, no. 2 (2019): 1–25.

Pick, Anat. *Creaturely Poetics: Animality and Vulnerability in Literature and Film*. New York: Columbia University Press, 2011.

Pink, Sarah. *Doing Sensory Ethnography*. London: Sage Publications, 2015.

Povinelli, Elizabeth. *The Cunning of Recognition. Indigenous Alterities and the Making of Australian Multiculturalism*. Durham, NC: Duke University Press, 2002.

Povinelli Elizabeth. *Economies of Abandonment. Social Belonging in Late Liberalism*. Durham, NC: Duke University Press, 2011.

Pratt, Geraldine, and Caleb Johnston. 'Staging Testimony in Nanay'. *Geographical Review* 103, no. 2 (2013): 288–303.

Pratt, Geraldine, and Victoria Rosner. *The Global and the Intimate*. New York: Columbia University Press, 2012.

Price, Karen. 'Theatr Clwyd to Stage First Professional Play at Calais Migrant Theatre'. *Wales Online*. 22 January 2016. Available at: https://www.walesonline.co.uk/whats-on/theatre-news/theatr-clwyd-stage-first-professional-10776606 (Accessed 3 June 2021).

Prime Minister's Office. 'Game Makers Win Big Society Award'. *GOV.UK*. 29 November 2012. Available at: https://www.gov.uk/government/news/games-makers-win-big-society-award (Accessed 24 February 2021).

Probyn, Elspeth. 'Sporting Bodies: Dynamics of Shame and Pride'. *Body & Society* 6, no. 1 (2000): 13–28.

Probyn, Elspeth. *Blush. Faces of Shame*. Minneapolis: University of Minnesota Press, 2005.

Puar, Jasbir. *Terrorist Assemblages: Homonationalism in Queer Times*. Durham, NC: Duke University Press, 2007.

Pusca, Anca 'Industrial and Human Ruins of Postcommunist Europe'. *Space and Culture* 13, no. 3 (2010): 239–55.

Quart, Leonard. 'The Politics of Irony: The Frears – Kureishi Films'. *Film Criticism* 16, no. 1/2 (1991): 33–41

Quinn, Ben. 'George Osborne Booed at Paralympics'. *The Guardian*. 3 September 2012. Available at: http://www.guardian.co.uk/sport/2012/sep/03/george-osborne-booed-paralympics (Accessed 14 February 2021).

Rancière, Jacques. *Disagreement: Politics and Philosophy*. Minneapolis: University of Minnesota Press, 1999.

Rancière, Jacques. 'Contemporary Art and the Politics of Aesthetics'. In *Communities of Sense: Rethinking Aesthetics and Politics*, edited by Beth Hinderliter, William Kaizen, Vered Maimon, Jaleh Mansoor and Seth McCormick, 31–50. Durham, NC: Duke University Press, 2009.

Rankine, Claudia. *Citizen: An American Lyric*. London: Penguin Books, 2015.

Rao, Rahul. 'Citizens of Nowhere'. *The Disorder of Things*. 28 November 2016. Available at: https://thedisorderofthings.com/2016/11/28/citizens-of-nowhere/ (Accessed 22 February 2021).

Ray, Raka. 'A Case of Internal Colonialism? Arlie Hochschild's *Strangers in Their Own Land*'. *British Journal of Sociology* 68, no. 1 (2017): 129–33.

Raynor, Ruth. '(De)composing Habit in Theatre – as – Method'. *Geohumanities* 3, no. 1 (2017): 108–21.

Raynor, Ruth. 'Dramatising Austerity: Holding a Story Together (and Why It Falls Apart …)'. *Cultural Geographies* 24, no. 2 (2017): 193–212.

Rech, Matthew. 'A Critical Geopolitics of Observant Practice at British Military Airshows'. *Transactions of the Institute of British Geographers* 40, no. 4 (2015): 536–48.

Riley, Denise. *Impersonal Passion. Language as Affect*. Durham, NC: Duke University Press, 2005.

Robinson, Nick. 'Are We All Thatcherites Now?' 17 April 2013. *BBC News*. Available at: https://www.bbc.com/news/uk-politics-22180611 (Accessed 30 March 2021).

Rogers, Amanda. 'Advancing the Geographies of the Performing Arts: Intercultural Aesthetics, Migratory Mobility, and Geopolitics'. *Progress in Human Geography* 42, no. 4 (2017): 549–68.

Rose, Gillian, and Divya Tolia-Kelly (eds). *Visuality/Materiality: Images, Objects and Practices*. London: Routledge, 2016).

Rose, Nikolas, Rasmus Birk and Nick Manning. 'Towards Neuroecosociality: Mental Health in Adversity'. *Theory, Culture & Society* 0, no. 0 (2021): 1–24.

Rose, Steve. 'Swandown: Two Men in a Pedalo'. *The Guardian*. 18 July 2012. Available at: http://www.guardian.co.uk/film/2012/jul/18/swandown-iain-sinclair-andrew-kotting (Accessed 14 February 2021).

Rousseau, Jean-Jacques. *Discourse on the Origin of Inequality*. Oxford: Oxford World Classics, 1994.

Seigworth, Greg, and Melissa Gregg. 'An Inventory of Shimmers'. In *The Affect Theory Reader*, edited by Melissa Gregg and Greg Seigworth, 1–29. Durham, NC: Duke University Press, 2010.

Seth, Sanjay. *Beyond Reason: Postcolonial Theory and the Social Sciences*. Oxford: Oxford University Press, 2021.

Shapiro, Michael. *Violent Cartographies: Mapping Cultures of War*. Minneapolis: University of Minnesota Press, 1997.

Shapiro, Michael. *Cinematic Political Thought: Narrating Race, Nation and Gender*. New York: New York University Press, 1999.

Shapiro, Michael. *For Moral Ambiguity: National Culture and the Politics of the Family*. Minneapolis: University of Minnesota Press, 2001.

Shapiro, Michael. *Methods and Nations. Cultural Governance and the Indigenous Subject*. New York: Routledge, 2004.

Shapiro, Michael. *The Time of the City: Politics, Philosophy and Genre*. Oxon: Routledge, 2010.

Shapiro, Michael. *War Crimes, Atrocity and Justice*. Cambridge: Polity Press, 2015.

Sharpe, Christina. *In the Wake: On Blackness and Being*. Durham, NC: Duke University Press, 2016.

Sharpe, Scott, J-D. Dewsbury and Maria Hynes. 'The Minute Interventions of Stewart Lee'. *Performance Research: A Journal of the Performing Arts* 19, no. 2 (2014): 116–25.

Sherigold, Adam. 'How to Get in the Olympic Spirit: Games Fan Sells Bottled "100% atmosphere" from the Day British Gold Rush Began'. *Daily Mail Online*. 9 August 2012. Available at: http://www.dailymail.co.uk/news/article-2185951/Olymp ics-2012-How-Olympic-spirit-Games-fan-sells-bottled-100-atmosphere-day-Brit ish-gold-rush-began.html (Accessed 13 February 2021).

Shilliam, Robbie. *Race and the Undeserving Poor*. Newcastle: Agenda, 2018.

Shilliam, Robert. 'Racism, Multiculturalism and Brexit', personal blog. 4 July 2016. Available at: https://robbieshilliam.wordpress.com/2016/07/04/racism-multicultural ism-and-brexit/ (Accessed 22 February 2021).

Simmel, Georg. 'The Metropolis and Mental Life'. In *Georg Simmel. On Individuality and Social Forms*, edited and with an Introduction by Donald N. Levine, 324–40, Chicago: University of Chicago Press, 1971.

Sinclair, Iain. *Ghost Milk: Calling Time on the Grand Project*. London: Penguin, 2011.

Sinclair, Iain. 'Diary'. *London Review of Books* 38, no. 13 (2012): 38–9.

Sloterdijk, Peter. *Terror from the Air*. Los Angeles: Semiotext(e), 2009.

Smith, Ali. *Autumn*. London: Hamish Hamilton, 2016.

Smith, Neil. 'Ten Years After'. *Geographical Journal* 177, no. 3 (2011): 203–7.

Smith, Zadie. 'Fences: A Brexit Diary'. *New York Review of Books*. 18 August 2016. Available at: https://www.nybooks.com/articles/2016/08/18/fences-brexit-diary (Accessed 22 February 2021).

Solnit, Rebecca. *A Field Guide to Getting Lost*. London: Penguin, 2005.

Solnit, Rebecca. *Hope in the Dark: Untold Stories, Wild Possibilities*. Edinburgh: Canongate Books, 2016.

Sontag, Susan. *Regarding the Pain of Others*. New York: Farrar, Strauss and Giroux, 2003.

Sparrow, Andrew. '2012 London Olympics Will Have "Party Atmosphere" Says Boris Johnson'. *The Guardian*. 7 October 2008. Available at: http://www.theguardian.com/uk/2008/oct/07/olympics2012.boris (Accessed 13 February 2021).

Squire, Vicki. *Post/Humanitarian Border Politics between Mexico and the US: People, Places, Things*. Basingstoke: Palgrave Macmillan, 2015.

Squire, Vicki. Governing Migration through Death in Europe and the US: Identification, Burial, and the Crisis of Modern Humanism', *European Journal of International Relations* 23, no. 3(2017): 513–32.

Squire, Vicki. 'Crossing the Mediterranean Sea by Boat', ESRC project, 2015–19. Available at: https://crossing-the-med-map.warwick.ac.uk/ (Accessed 24 March 2022).

Squire, Vicki, Jen Bagelman, Inderjit Bhogal, Angharad Closs Stephens, Giovanna Del Sarto, Usifu Jalloh, Alex Ntung and Nira Yuval-Davis, 'Dead Reckoning/Crossing the Med: Thinking and Feeling Migration Differently', Tate Modern. 15 March 2017. Available at: https://warwick.ac.uk/fac/soc/pais/research/projects/crossingthemed/symposium_transcript.pdf (Accessed 24 March 2022).

Staeheli, Lynn A., Patricia Ehrkamp, Helga Leitner and Caroline R. Nagel. 'Dreaming the Ordinary: Daily Life and the Complex Geographies of Citizenship'. *Progress in Human Geography* 36, no. 5 (2012): 628–44.

Stewart, Heather, and Rowena Mason. 'Nigel Farage's Anti-migrant Poster Reported to Police'. *The Guardian*. 16 June 2016. Available at: https://www.theguardian.com/politics/2016/jun/16/nigel-farage-defends-ukip-breaking-point-poster-queue-of-migrants (Accessed 21 April 2021).

Stewart, Kathleen. *A Space on the Side of the Road: Cultural Poetics in an 'Other' America*. Princeton: Princeton University Press, 1996.

Stewart, Kathleen. *Ordinary Affects*. Durham, NC: Duke University Press, 2007.

Stewart, Kathleen. 'Atmospheric Attunements'. *Environment and Planning D: Society and Space* 29, no. 3 (2011), 445–53.

Stierl, Maurice, and Deanna Dadusc. 'The "Covid Excuse": EUropean Border Violence in the Mediterranean Sea'. *Ethnic and Racial Studies* (2021), doi: 10.1080/01419870.2021.1977367.

Stoler, Ann Laura. *Carnal Knowledge and Imperial Power*. Berkeley: University of California Press, 2010.

Straughan, Elizabeth, David Bissell and Andrew Gorman-Murray. 'The Politics of Stuckness: Waiting Lives in Mobile Worlds'. *Environment and Planning C: Politics and Space* 38, no. 4 (2020): 636–55.

Sumartojo, Shanti. *Trafalgar Square and the Narration of Britishness, 1900–2012: Imagining the Nation*. Oxford: Peter Lang, 2013.

Sumartojo, Shanti. 'On Atmosphere and Darkness at Australia's Anzac Day Dawn Service'. *Visual Communication* 14, no. 3 (2015): 267–88.

Sumartojo, Shanti. 'Commemorative Atmospheres: Memorial Sites, Collective Events and the Experience of National Identity'. *Transactions of the Institute of British Geographers* 41, no. 4 (2016): 541–53.

Sumartojo, Shanti, and Sarah Pink. *Atmospheres and the Experiential World: Theory and Methods*. Oxon: Routledge, 2019.

Swanton, Dan. 'Flesh, Metal, Road: Tracing the Machinic Geographies of Race'. *Environment and Planning D: Society and Space* 28, no. 3 (2010): 447–66.

Sylvester, Christine. *Art/Museums: International Relations Where We Least Expect It.* London: Routledge, 2015.

Taussig, Michael. *The Nervous System*. New York: Routledge, 1992.

Taussig, Michael. *Walter Benjamin's Grave*. Chicago: University of Chicago Press, 2006.

Tazzioli, Martina. 'The Politics of Counting and the Scene of Rescue: Border Deaths in the Mediterranean'. *Radical Philosophy* 192 (July/August 2015): 1–6. Available at: https://www.radicalphilosophy.com/commentary/the-politics-of-counting-and-the-scene-of-rescue (Accessed 3 June 2021).

Tazzioli, Martina. 'Greece's Camps, Europe's Hotspots'. *Border Criminologies* (12 October 2016). Available at: https://www.law.ox.ac.uk/research-subject-groups/centre-criminology/centreborder-criminologies/blog/2016/10/gre ece%E2%80%99s-camps (Accessed 11 March 2021).

Tazzioli, Martina. *The Making of Migration. The Biopolitics of Mobility at Europe's Borders*, London: Sage, 2019.

Thatcher, Margaret. 'Speech to Conservative Party Conference'. 14 October 1983, Blackpool. Available at:https://www.margaretthatcher.org/document/105454 (Accessed 24 March 2022).

The Guardian. 'George Osborne Tells Tory Conference: "We're All in This Together"'. (Video) 8 October 2012. Available at: https://www.theguardian.com/politics/video/2012/oct/08/george-osborne-tory-conference-video (Accessed 30 March 2021).

The Guardian. 'Margaret Thatcher Tributes: David Cameron Speech'. (Video) 10 April 2013. Available at: https://www.theguardian.com/politics/2013/apr/10/margaret-thatcher-tributes-david-cameron-speech (Accessed 31 March 2021).

The Spectator. 'Portrait of the Week'. 13 April 2013. Available at: https://www.spectator.co.uk/article/portrait-of-the-week-11-april-2013 (Accessed 26 Mach 2021).

The Sunday Times. 'How Was It for You?' 19 August 2012. Available at: http://www.the sundaytimes.co.uk/sto/Magazine/Features/article1104115.ece (Accessed 24 February 2021).

The Telegraph. 'Margaret Thatcher Funeral: Military Rehearsal Takes Place at Dawn'. 15 April 2013. Available at: http://www.telegraph.co.uk/news/politics/margaret-thatc her/9994367/Margaret-Thatcher-funeral-military-rehearsal-takes-place-at-dawn. html (Accessed 7 September 2017).

The Telegraph. 'Prophet Mohammed Cartoons Controversy: Timeline'. 4 May 2015. Available at: https://www.telegraph.co.uk/news/worldnews/europe/france/11341 599/Prophet-Muhammad-cartoons-controversy-timeline.html (Accessed 24 February 2021).

The Welsh Government. 'Wellbeing of Wales: 2020'. 3 December 2020. Available at: https://gov.wales/wellbeing-wales-2020-html#section-56842 (Accessed 22 June 2021).

Thibaud, Jean-Paul. 'The Horizon of Urban Ambiances, Séminaire Du 11 Et 12 Juin 2012'. *MUSE* (2012): 96.

Thrift, Nigel. 'It's the Little Things'. In *Geopolitical Traditions: A Century of Geopolitical Thought*, edited by Klaus Dodds and David Atkinson, 380–7. London: Routledge, 2000.

Thrift, Nigel. 'Intensities of Feeling: Towards a Spatial Politics of Affect'. *Geografiska annaler* 86, no. 1 (2004): 57–78.

Titley, Gavan. *Is Free Speech Racist?* Cambridge: Polity Press, 2020.

Tolia-Kelly, Divya. 'Race and Affect at the Museum: The Museum as a *Theatre of Pain*'. In *Heritage, Affect and Emotion*, edited by Divya Tolia-Kelly; Emma Waterton and Steve Watson, 33–47. London: Routledge, 2017.

Turner, Luke. 'We'll Meet Again: How Toxic Nostalgia Twisted Vera Lynn's Pop Masterpiece'. 18 June 2020. *The Guardian*. Available at: https://www.theguard ian.com/music/2020/jun/18/well-meet-again-vera-lynn-pop-masterpiece-sec ond-world-war (Accessed 22 June 2021).

UCL. 'Adults Remain at Home Despite Lockdown Easing'. *UCL News*. 18 June 2020. Available at: https://www.ucl.ac.uk/news/2020/jun/adults-remain-home-despite-lockdown-easing (Accessed 7 May 2021).

Upstone, Sara. 'A Question of Black or White: Returning to Hanif Kureishi's *The Black Album*'. *Postcolonial Text* 4, no. 1 (2008): 13.

Valluvan, Siyamohan. *The Clamour of Nationalism: Race and Nation in Twenty-First Century Britain*. Manchester: Manchester University Press, 2019.

Vannini, Phillip. 'Non-Representational Research Methodologies'. In *Non-Representational Methodologies*, edited by Phillip Vannini, 1–18, London: Routledge, 2015.

Vij, Ritu, Elisa Wynne-Hughes and Tahseen Kazi (eds). *Precarity and International Relations*. London: Palgrave Macmillan, 2021.

Volpp, Leti. 'The Citizen and the Terrorist'. *UCLA Law Review* 49 (2002): 1575–600.

Wagner-Pacifici, Robin. *What Is an Event?* Chicago: University of Chicago Press, 2017.

Walker, R. B. J. *Inside/Outside: International Relations as Political Theory*. Cambridge: Cambridge University Press, 1993.

Walsh, Bryan, and Time Photo, 'Alan Kurdi's Story: Behind the Most Heartbreaking Photo of 2015', TIME, 29 December 2015, https://time.com/4162306/ alan-kurdi-syria-drowned-boy-refugee-crisis/ (Accessed 29 March 2022).

Walter, Tony. *The Mourning for Diana*. Oxford: Berg, 1999.

Walters, William. *Governmentality: Critical Encounters*. Abingdon: Routledge, 2012.

Walters, William, and Barbara Lüthi. 'The Politics of Cramped Space: Dilemmas of Action, Containment and Mobility'. *International Journal of Politics, Culture and Society* 29, no. 4 (2016): 359–66.

Watt, Nicholas. 'Boris Johnson to Campaign for Brexit in EU Referendum'. *The Guardian*. 21 February 2016. Available at: https://www.theguardian.com/polit ics/2016/feb/21/boris-johnson-eu-referendum-campaign-for-brexit-david-cameron (Accessed 7 May 2021).

Weber, Cynthia. 'Flying Planes Can Be Dangerous'. *Millennium: Journal of International Studies* 31, no. 1 (2002): 129–47.

Weber, Cynthia. *Imagining America at War: Morality, Politics and Film*. New York: Routledge, 2006.

Weber, Cynthia. *Queer International Relations*. Oxford: Oxford University Press, 2016.

Weber, Cynthia. 'Right-Wing Populism, Anti-genderism, and Real US Americans in the Age of Trump'. *The Disorder of Things*. 6 July 2017. Available at: https://thedisordero fthings.com/2017/07/06/right-wing-populism-anti-genderism-and-real-us-americ ans-in-the-age-of-trump/ (Accessed 22 April 2021).

Weber, Max. 'Weber: Political Writings'. In *Weber: Political Writings*, edited by Peter Lassman and Ronald Speirs, 429. Cambridge: Cambridge University Press, 1994.

Wedeen, Lisa. *Ambiguities of Domination: Politics, Rhetoric and Symbols in Contemporary Syria*. Chicago: University of Chicago Press, 2015.

Wei Wei, Ai. 'Ai Wei Wei Remembers the Sichuan Earthquake, Ten Years On'. *Art Magazine*. 16 July 2018. Available at: https://www.theartnewspaper.com/news/ai-wei wei-remembers-the-sichuan-earthquake-ten-years-on (Accessed 3 June 2021).

West, Karl. 'How Art Restarted the Heart of Swansea's High Street'. *The Observer*. 8 October 2016. Available at: https://www.theguardian.com/business/2016/oct/08/art-restarts-heart-swansea-high-street (Accessed 22 February 2021).

Wetherell, Margaret. 'Feeling Rules, Atmospheres and Affective Practice: Some Reflections on the Analysis of Emotional Episodes'. In *Privilege, Agency and Affect*, edited by Claire Maxwell and Peter Aggleton, 221–39. Basingstoke: Palgrave Macmillan, 2013.

Wetherell, Margaret. 'Affect and Banal Nationalism. A Practical Dialogic Approach to Emotion'. In *Rhetoric, Ideology, and Social Psychology: Essays in Honour of Michael Billig*, edited by Charles Antaki and Susan Condor, 137–50. London: Routledge, 2014.

Wibben, Annick T. R. 'On Doing "Something" ... As Academics'. *Duck of Minerva*. 3 September 2015. Available at: https://www.academia.edu/17321872/On_doing_som ething_as_academics (Accessed 3 June 2021).

Williams, Raymond. *Marxism and Literature*. Oxford: Oxford University Press, 1977.

Williams, Raymond. 'Wales and England' in *What I Came to Say*. London: Hutchinson Radius, 1990.

Williams, Raymond. *Television: Technology and Cultural Form*. London: Routledge, 2003.

Williams, Richard. 'London 2012: This Closing Ceremony Was a Raucous Pageant of Popular Culture'. *The Guardian*, 13 August 2012. Available at: http://www.theguard ian.com/sport/2012/aug/13/olympic-games-closing-ceremony-culture (Accessed 13 February 2021).

Wilson, Elizabeth A. *Gut Feminism*. Durham, NC: Duke University Press, 2015.

Wilson, Helen F., and Ben Anderson. 'Detachment, Disaffection and Other Ambivalent Affects', *Environment and Planning C: Politics and Space* 38, no. 4 (2020): 591–8.

Wintour, Patrick. 'David Cameron Sets Out "Emotional, Patriotic" Case to Keep Scotland in UK'. *The Guardian*. 7 February 2014. Available at: https://www.theguard ian.com/politics/2014/feb/07/david-cameron-scottish-independence-referendum-olympic-park (Accessed 14 February 2021).

Wokler, Robert. 'The Enlightenment and the French Revolutionary Birth Pangs of Modernity'. In *The Rose of the Social Sciences and the Formation of Modernity: Conceptual Change in Context, 1750–1850*, edited by Johan Heilbron, Lars Magnusson and Bjorn Wittrock, 35–76. Dordrecht: Kluwer Academic, 1998.

Woodward, Keith. 'Affect, State Theory and the Politics of Confusion'. *Political Geography* 41 (2014): 21–31.

Yiftachel, Oren. *Ethnocracy: Land and Identity Politics in Israel/Palestine*. Philadelphia: University of Pennsylvania Press, 2006.

Younge, Gary. 'Brexit: A Disaster Decades in the Making'. *The Guardian*. 30 June 2016. Available at: https://www.theguardian.com/politics/2016/jun/30/brexit-disaster-decades-in-the-making (Accessed 22 February 2021).

Index

Note: Figures are indicated by page number followed by "f". Endnotes are indicated by the page number followed by "n" and the endnote number e.g., 20 n.1 refers to endnote 1 on page 20.

www.ingramcontent.com/pod-product-compliance
Lightning Source LLC
Chambersburg PA
CBHW050431280326
41932CB00013BA/2072